OXFORD

UNIVERSITY PRESS

Oxford University Press, Inc., publishes works that further Oxford University's objective of excellence in research, scholarship, and education.

Copyright © 2009 by Oxford University Press, Inc.
Published by Oxford University Press, Inc.
198 Madison Avenue, New York, New York 10016

Library of Congress Cataloging-in-Publication Data

Jasper, Margaret C.
    Veterans' rights and benefits / by Margaret C. Jasper.
        p. cm. — (Oceana's legal almanac series. Law for the layperson)
    Includes bibliographical references.
    ISBN 978-0-19-537652-4 ((hardback) : alk. paper) 1. Military pensions—
Law and legislation—United States. 2. Veterans—Medical care—Law and
legislation—United States. 3. Veterans—Education—Law and legislation—
United States. 4. United States. Dept. of Veterans Affairs. I. Title. II. Series.
    KF7745.J37 2008
    343.73'011—dc22

2008036806

Note to Readers:

This publication is designed to provide accurate and authoritative information in regard to the subject matter covered. It is based upon sources believed to be accurate and reliable and is intended to be current as of the time it was written. It is sold with the understanding that the publisher is not engaged in rendering legal, accounting, or other professional services. If legal advice or other expert assistance is required, the services of a competent professional person should be sought. Also, to confirm that the information has not been affected or changed by recent developments, traditional legal research techniques should be used, including checking primary sources where appropriate.

(Based on the Declaration of Principles jointly adopted by a Committee of the American Bar Association and a Committee of Publishers and Associations.)

To My Husband Chris

Your love and support

are my motivation and inspiration

To My Sons, Michael, Nick and Chris

-and-

In memory of my son, Jimmy

Table of Contents

ABOUT THE AUTHOR xi
INTRODUCTION xv

CHAPTER 1:
THE DEPARTMENT OF VETERANS AFFAIRS
HISTORY AND BACKGROUND 1
BENEFITS 2
EMPLOYMENT 2
Veterans Administration 2
Military Installations 2
Veterans Preference 3
Expert System 3
Complaint Process Under The Veterans Employment Opportunity Act . . . 3
VETERAN STATISTICS 4
Age 5
Ethnicity 5
Branch of Service 5
Operation Enduring Freedom/Operation Iraqi Freedom (OEF/OIF) 5
VA SPECIAL PROGRAMS AND INITIATIVES 5
Health Care Programs 5
Agent Orange Health Effects and Vietnam Veterans 5
Blind Rehabilitation Service 6
Cancer Program 6
Cold Injury Prevention Program 6
Diabetes Prevention Program 6
Flu Program 7
Gulf War Veterans' Health Program 7
Health Care Programs for Elderly and Chronically Ill Veterans 7
HIV/AIDS/Hepatitis Program 7
Kidney Disease Program 7
Mental Health Strategic Healthcare Group 8

Mental Illness Research, Education and Clinical Centers 8
National Center for Post-Traumatic Stress Disorder 8
National Center for Patient Safety 8
Office of Nursing Services 8
Polytrauma System of Care 9
Prosthetics and Sensory Aids Service 9
Recreation/Creative Arts Therapy Service 9
Social Work Program 9
War-Related Illness and Injury Study Center 10
Advisory Committees 10
Center for Faith-Based and Community Initiatives 10
Center for Women Veterans: Programs & Initiatives for Women
Veterans 10
Debt Management Center 10
Homeless Assistance Programs & Initiatives 10
VA Medical Training Program 11
Records Center & Vault 11
VA Franchise Fund 11
VA Vets Center Program 11
Veterans Industries 11
VA ORGANIZATIONS 12
Veterans Benefits Administration 12
Veterans Health Administration 12
National Cemetery Administration 12
Board of Contract Appeals 12
Board of Veterans' Appeals 12
Center for Women Veterans 12
Office of Acquisition & Material Management 13
Office of Alternative Dispute Resolution and Mediation 13
Office of Budget 13
Office of Public Affairs & Intergovernmental Affairs 13
Office of Congressional Affairs 13
Office of Employment Discrimination Complaint Adjudication 13
Office of Financial Management 14
Office of General Counsel 14
Office of Human Resources & Administration 14
Office of Information & Technology 14
Office of the Inspector General 14
Office of Occupational Safety & Health 14
Office of Policy, Planning and Preparedness 14
Office of Regulation Policy and Management 15
Office of Small & Disadvantaged Business Utilization 15
VA RESEARCH 15

CHAPTER 2:
DISABILITY COMPENSATION AND PENSION BENEFITS

IN GENERAL 17
DISABILITY COMPENSATION 17
  Eligibility. 17
  Amount of Benefits. 17
  Application Process 18
VETERANS PENSION 18
  Eligibility. 18
    Countable Income 19
    Exclusions and Deductions. 19
    Veteran's Pension Calculation 20
    Application Process. 20
AID AND ATTENDANCE AND HOUSEBOUND BENEFITS 20
  Aid and Attendance Benefits. 20
  Housebound Benefits. 21
  Applying for Aid and Attendance or Housebound Benefits 21
PERIODS OF WARTIME SERVICE FOR VA BENEFITS ELIGIBILITY. 21
  World War I 21
  World War II 22
  Korean Conflict 22
  Vietnam Era. 22
  Persian Gulf War 22
  Future Dates 22

CHAPTER 3:
HEALTH CARE BENEFITS

IN GENERAL 23
MEDICAL BENEFITS PACKAGE 24
  Preventive Care Services 24
  Ambulatory Diagnostic and Treatment Services 24
  Hospital Diagnostic and Treatment Services 25
  Medications and Supplies 25
ELIGIBILITY 25
THE ENROLLMENT SYSTEM 25
APPLYING FOR BENEFITS 26
  Required Evidence. 27
  Duty to Assist—The Veterans Claims Act of 2000 and Duty to Assist . . . 27
HEALTH CARE APPOINTMENTS. 27
  Priority Scheduling for Veterans with Service-Connected Disabilities . . 27
LONG TERM CARE. 28
SPECIAL AND LIMITED HEALTH CARE BENEFITS 28
  Agent Orange Health Effects and Vietnam Veterans 28

Automobile Assistance 29
Beneficiary Travel 30
Bereavement Counseling 30
Blind Veterans Services 31
Dental Care 31
Domiciliary Care 32
Emergency Care in Non-VA Facilities 33
Extended Care 33
Eyeglasses and Hearing Aids 33
Gulf War Illnesses 33
Home Health Services 33
Home Improvement and Structural Alterations (HISA) 33
Homeless Programs 34
Ionizing Radiation Exposure Treatment and Registry Examination 34
Maternity Care 34
Military Sexual Trauma Counseling 34
Non-VA Health Care Services 34
Nose/Throat Radium Treatment 34
Nursing Home Care 34
Project 112/SHAD Participants 35
Prosthetic Aids 35
Readjustment Counseling 36
Women Veterans Services 36
CO-PAYS AND CHARGES 36
Means Test 36
Income Verification 37
Private Health Care Insurance 37
Exempt Services 37
Co-Pay Waivers and Alternatives 38
VETERANS IDENTIFICATION CARD 38
MY HEALTHEVET PROGRAM 39
The Personal Health Journal 39
Personal Information 39
Wallet ID Card 39
Military Health History 39
Medications 39
Allergies 40
Tests 40
Medical Events 40
Health eLogs 40
MEDICAL BENEFITS FOR FAMILY MEMBERS 40
Civilian Health and Medical Program of VA (CHAMPVA) 40
Eligibility 40

Benefits 41
General Exclusions 41
Medicare Impact 41
New and Expectant Parents 42
Remarried Widows/Widowers 42
Spina Bifida Program 42
Children of Women Vietnam Veterans Program 43
TRICARE 43
Eligible Persons 43
Persons Not Eligible 44

CHAPTER 4:
VETERANS GROUP LIFE INSURANCE

IN GENERAL 45
SERVICEMEMBERS' GROUP LIFE INSURANCE 45
ELIGIBILITY FOR VETERANS GROUP LIFE INSURANCE 46
AMOUNT OF COVERAGE 46
PERIOD OF COVERAGE 46
PREMIUM PAYMENTS 47
CONVERTING SGLI COVERAGE TO VGLI COVERAGE 47
Application Within 120 Days Following Separation 48
Application Between 120 Days and 1 Year and 120 Days
Following Separation 48
ACCELERATED BENEFITS OPTION 48
POLICY BENEFICIARY 49
Designating a Beneficiary 49
Death Claims 49
Alliance Accounts 49
Beneficiary Financial Counseling Services 49
CONVERTING VGLI COVERAGE TO COMMERCIAL LIFE
INSURANCE 50
THE OFFICE OF SERVICEMEMBERS' GROUP LIFE INSURANCE 50

CHAPTER 5:
EDUCATION AND VOCATIONAL REHABILITATION BENEFITS

IN GENERAL 53
MONTGOMERY GI BILL—ACTIVE DUTY 53
Eligibility 54
Category I—Requirements 54
Category II—Requirements 54
Category III—Requirements 54
Category IV—Requirements 55
Amount of Benefits 55

Buy-up Program 55
Application Process 55
MONTGOMERY GI BILL—SELECTED RESERVE 56
Eligibility 56
Application Process 57
VA WORK-STUDY ALLOWANCE PROGRAM 58
Eligibility 58
Amount of Benefits 59
Type of Work 59
Application Process 59
SURVIVORS' AND DEPENDENTS' EDUCATION ASSISTANCE
PROGRAM (DEA) 60
Eligibility 60
Period of Eligibility 60
Son or Daughter 60
Spouse 61
Application Process 61
Eastern Region 61
Central Region 61
Western Region 62
Southern Region 62
VOCATIONAL REHABILITATION 62
Vocational Rehabilitation and Employment Service 62
Eligibility and Entitlement 63
Vocational and Educational Counseling 64
Services for Disabled Children of Vietnam and Korean Veterans 65

CHAPTER 6:
HOME FINANCING BENEFITS

IN GENERAL 67
FEATURES OF THE VA HOME LOAN 67
APPLYING FOR A VA HOME LOAN 68
Requirements for VA Loan Approval 68
Application Process 69
Amount of the Loan 69
Eligible Loan Purposes 69
Refinancing Loans 70
Loan Repayment Terms 70
Traditional Fixed-Payment Mortgage 71
Graduated Payment Mortgage (GPM) 71
Buydowns 71
Growing Equity Mortgage (GEM) 71
Adjustable Rate Mortgages (ARM) 71

Down Payment Requirements 72
Interest Rates 72
Closing Costs 72
Funding Fee 73
THE VA LOAN GUARANTY 73
SERVICE ELIGIBILITY 73
Wartime Service 73
Peacetime Service 74
Service Between September 7, 1980 or October 16, 1981 and
August 1, 1990 74
Active Duty Service Personnel 75
Members of the Selected Reserve 75
Other Types of Service 75
CERTIFICATE OF ELIGIBILITY 76
ENTITLEMENT 76

CHAPTER 7:
DEPENDENT AND SURVIVOR BENEFITS

IN GENERAL 79
DEPENDENCY AND INDEMNITY COMPENSATION 79
Eligibility 80
Surviving Spouse 80
Surviving Child 80
Surviving Parent 80
Application Process 80
Amount of Benefit 81
DEATH PENSION 81
Eligibility 81
Age Restriction 81
Countable Income 82
Exclusions and Deductions 82
Death Pension Calculation 83
Application Process 83
AID AND ATTENDANCE AND HOUSEBOUND BENEFITS 83
SURVIVORS' AND DEPENDENTS' EDUCATIONAL ASSISTANCE (DEA) 84
HOME LOAN GUARANTY PROGRAM 84
BURIAL BENEFITS 85
LIFE INSURANCE BENEFITS AND FINANCIAL COUNSELING 85
BEREAVEMENT COUNSELING 85
VOCATIONAL REHABILITATION & EMPLOYMENT SERVICES (VR&E) 85
MEDICAL BENEFITS FOR FAMILY MEMBERS 86
Children of Vietnam Veterans 86

CHAPTER 8:
BURIAL RIGHTS AND MEMORIAL BENEFITS

HISTORY AND BACKGROUND 87
STATISTICS. 88
BURIAL BENEFITS. 89
  Burial in a VA National Cemetery 89
  Burial in a Private Cemetery 89
ELIGIBILITY 90
  Persons Eligible for Burial in a VA National Cemetery 90
    Veterans and Members of the Armed Forces 90
    Members of Reserve Components and Reserve Officers'
    Training Corps 90
    Commissioned Officers, National Oceanic and Atmospheric
    Administration 91
    Public Health Service 91
    World War II Merchant Mariners 92
    The Philippine Armed Forces 92
    Spouses and Dependents. 92
  Persons Who are Not Eligible for Burial in a VA National Cemetery. . . . 93
    Disqualifying Discharge 93
    Discharge from Draft 93
    Person Found Guilty of a Capital Crime. 93
    Subversive Activities 93
    Active or Inactive Duty for Training. 93
    Former Spouses 94
    Other Family Members 94
VERIFYING VETERAN STATUS 94
ARRANGING FOR BURIAL IN A VA NATIONAL CEMETERY. 95
THE BURIAL FLAG. 95
HEADSTONES AND MARKERS 96
PRESIDENTIAL MEMORIAL CERTIFICATES 96
MILITARY FUNERAL HONORS 97
BURIAL ALLOWANCE. 97
  Eligibility. 97
  Amount of Benefit 98
    Service-Related Death. 98
    Nonservice-Related Death. 98
  Applying for a Burial Allowance. 98

CHAPTER 9:
THE BOARD OF VETERANS APPEALS

IN GENERAL 99
THE APPEALS PROCESS 99

Notice of Disagreement 100
Statement of the Case. 100
THE PERSONAL HEARING 100
THE DECISION 101
Remand 101
Denial 101
THE U.S. COURT OF APPEALS FOR VETERANS CLAIMS 102
Filing the Appeal 102
Filing By Mail 103
Filing By Fax 103
The Appeal Process 103
Finding a Representative 104
Veterans Consortium Pro Bono Program. 104

CHAPTER 10:
THE SERVICEMEMBERS CIVIL RELIEF ACT
IN GENERAL 107
PROVISIONS. 107
INTEREST RATE CAPS 108
STAY OF JUDICIAL PROCEEDINGS. 109
PROTECTION AGAINST DEFAULT JUDGMENTS 109
PROTECTION FROM EVICTION. 110
TERMINATION OF RESIDENTIAL LEASE 110
Prior to Military Service 110
During Military Service 110
MORTGAGE PAYMENT RELIEF. 110
TERMINATION OF AUTOMOBILE LEASE 111
PROTECTION FROM DOUBLE-TAXATION. 111
ADDITIONAL PROTECTIONS. 111

APPENDICES
1: VA BENEFIT CENTERS 113
2: DIRECTORY OF U.S. ARMY MILITARY INSTALLATIONS. 121
3: DIRECTORY OF U.S. NAVY MILITARY INSTALLATIONS 125
4: DIRECTORY OF U.S. AIR FORCE MILITARY INSTALLATIONS. 129
5: DIRECTORY OF U.S. MARINE CORPS MILITARY INSTALLATIONS 135
6: DIRECTORY OF U.S. COAST GUARD MILITARY INSTALLATIONS 137
7: THE VETERANS EMPLOYMENT OPPORTUNITIES
   ACT (PUB. L. NO. 105-339, 10/31/98) 139
8: VETERANS CENTERS 151
9: VETERAN'S APPLICATION FOR COMPENSATION AND/OR PENSION
   (FORM 21-526). 175

10: DIRECTORY OF VA MEDICAL CENTERS 193
11: APPLICATION FOR HEALTH BENEFITS (FORM 10-10EZ) 211
12: APPLICATION FOR VETERANS' GROUP LIFE INSURANCE
     (FORM SGL 8714) 215
13: LIST OF VGLI PARTICIPATING INSURANCE COMPANIES 219
14: APPLICATION FOR VA EDUCATION BENEFITS
     (FORM 22-1990) 221
15: APPLICATION FOR WORK-STUDY ALLOWANCE
     (FORM 22-8691) 229
16: APPLICATION FOR SURVIVORS' AND DEPENDENTS'
     EDUCATIONAL ASSISTANCE (FORM 22-5490) 231
17: APPLICATION FOR VOCATIONAL-EDUCATIONAL COUNSELING
     (FORM 28-8832) 235
18: REQUEST FOR A CERTIFICATE OF ELIGIBILITY
     (FORM 26-1880) 239
19: APPLICATION FOR DEPENDENCY AND INDEMNITY
     COMPENSATION, DEATH PENSION AND ACCRUED
     BENEFITS BY SURVIVING SPOUSE OR CHILD (FORM 21-534) 241
20: DIRECTORY OF VA NATIONAL CEMETERIES 251
21: APPLICATION FOR STANDARD GOVERNMENT HEADSTONE
     OR MARKER (FORM 40-1330) 267
22: APPLICATION FOR U.S. FLAG FOR BURIAL PURPOSES
     (FORM 21-2008) 269
23: PRESIDENTIAL MEMORIAL CERTIFICATE REQUEST
     (FORM 40-0247) 271
24: APPLICATION FOR BURIAL BENEFITS (FORM 21-530) 273
25: SELECTED PROVISIONS OF THE SERVICEMEMBERS
     CIVIL RELIEF ACT (PUB. L. NO. 108-189, 12/19/03) 277

GLOSSARY 293
BIBLIOGRAPHY AND ADDITIONAL RESOURCES 305

ABOUT THE AUTHOR

MARGARET C. JASPER is an attorney engaged in the general practice of law in South Salem, New York, concentrating in the areas of personal injury and entertainment law. Ms. Jasper holds a Juris Doctor degree from Pace University School of Law, White Plains, New York, is a member of the New York and Connecticut bars, and is certified to practice before the United States District Courts for the Southern and Eastern Districts of New York, the United States Court of Appeals for the Second Circuit, and the United States Supreme Court.

Ms. Jasper has been appointed to the law guardian panel for the Family Court of the State of New York, is a member of a number of professional organizations and associations, and is a New York State licensed real estate broker operating as Jasper Real Estate, in South Salem, New York.

Margaret Jasper maintains a website at http://www.JasperLawOffice.com.

In 2004, Ms. Jasper successfully argued a case before the New York Court of Appeals, which gives mothers of babies who are stillborn due to medical negligence the right to bring a legal action and recover emotional distress damages. This successful appeal overturned a 26-year old New York case precedent, which previously prevented mothers of stillborn babies from suing their negligent medical providers.

Ms. Jasper is the author and general editor of the following legal Almanacs:

AIDS and the Law

The Americans with Disabilities Act

Animal Rights Law

Auto Leasing

Bankruptcy Law for the Individual Debtor

Banks and their Customers

Becoming a Citizen

Buying and Selling Your Home

Commercial Law

Consumer Rights and the Law

Co-ops and Condominiums: Your Rights and Obligations As Owner

Copyright Law

Credit Cards and the Law

Custodial Rights

Dealing with Debt

Dictionary of Selected Legal Terms

Drunk Driving Law

DWI, DUI and the Law

Education Law

Elder Law

Employee Rights in the Workplace

Employment Discrimination Under Title VII

Environmental Law

Estate Planning

Everyday Legal Forms

Executors and Personal Representatives: Rights and Responsibilities

Guardianship and the Law

Harassment in the Workplace

Health Care and Your Rights

Health Care Directives

Hiring Household Help and Contractors: Your Rights and Obligations Under the Law

Home Mortgage Law Primer

Hospital Liability Law

How To Change Your Name

How To Form an LLC

How To Protect Your Challenged Child

How To Start Your Own Business

Identity Theft and How To Protect Yourself

Individual Bankruptcy and Restructuring

Injured on the Job: Employee Rights, Worker's Compensation and Disability Insurance Law

International Adoption

Juvenile Justice and Children's Law

Labor Law

Landlord-Tenant Law

Law for the Small Business Owner

The Law of Adoption

The Law of Attachment and Garnishment

The Law of Buying and Selling

The Law of Capital Punishment

The Law of Child Custody

The Law of Contracts

The Law of Debt Collection

The Law of Dispute Resolution

The Law of Immigration

The Law of Libel and Slander

The Law of Medical Malpractice

The Law of No-Fault Insurance

The Law of Obscenity and Pornography

The Law of Personal Injury

The Law of Premises Liability

The Law of Product Liability

The Law of Speech and the First Amendment

Lemon Laws

Living Together: Practical Legal Issues

Marriage and Divorce

Missing and Exploited Children: How to Protect Your Child

Motor Vehicle Law

Nursing Home Negligence

Patent Law

Pet Law

Planes, Trains and Buses: Your Rights as a Passenger

Prescription Drugs

Privacy and the Internet: Your Rights and Expectations Under the Law

Probate Law

Protecting Your Business: Disaster Preparation and the Law

Real Estate Law for the Homeowner and Broker

Religion and the Law

Retirement Planning

The Right to Die

Rights of Single Parents

Small Claims Court

Social Security Law

Special Education Law

Teenagers and Substance Abuse

Trademark Law

Trouble Next Door: What to do With Your Neighbor

Veterans Rights and Benefits

Victim's Rights Law

Violence Against Women

Welfare: Your Rights and the Law

What if It Happened to You: Violent Crimes and Victims' Rights

What if the Product Doesn't Work: Warranties & Guarantees

Workers' Compensation Law

Your Child's Legal Rights: An Overview

Your Rights in a Class Action Suit

Your Rights as a Tenant

Your Rights Under the Family and Medical Leave Act

You've Been Fired: Your Rights and Remedies

INTRODUCTION

"To care for him who shall have borne the battle, and for his widow, and his orphan" - Abraham Lincoln.

This is the mission of the U.S. Department of Veterans Affairs, and today applies to this nation's 24 million veterans, both male and female, who have served this country.

Veterans of the United States armed forces are eligible for a broad range of programs and services provided by the U.S. Department of Veterans Affairs. This Almanac sets forth those rights and benefits afforded the nation's military veterans, including health care, education and vocational rehabilitation, compensation and pension benefits, home financing, life insurance, and burial and survivor benefits. The benefits available to the dependents and survivors of military veterans is also discussed. The role of the U.S. Department of Veterans Affairs in coordinating and administering these benefits is also explored. In addition, protections afforded a member of the armed forces under the Servicemember's Civil Relief Act (SCRA) are also examined.

The Appendix provides resource directories, statutes, sample forms, and other pertinent information and data. The Glossary contains definitions of many of the terms used throughout the Almanac.

CHAPTER 1:
THE DEPARTMENT OF VETERANS AFFAIRS

HISTORY AND BACKGROUND

The Veterans Administration was established as an independent agency on July 21, 1930 pursuant to Executive Order No. 5398 signed by President Herbert Hoover. At that time, there were 54 hospitals, 4.7 million living veterans, and 31,600 employees. In 1933, the Board of Veterans Appeals was established.

On June 22, 1944, President Franklin Roosevelt signed the Servicemen's Readjustment Act of 1944 (Public Law 346), which was unanimously passed by the Congress. The Act, commonly referred to as "The GI Bill of Rights," provided home loan and education benefits to veterans.

In 1946, the Department of Medicine & Surgery was established, which, in 1989, became the Veterans Health Services and Research Administration. In 1991, it was renamed the Veterans Health Administration (VHA), which it is still known as today.

In 1953, the Department of Veterans Benefits was established, which, in 1989, became the Veterans Benefits Administration.

In 1973, the National Cemetery System was established when Congress transferred 82 national cemeteries from the Army to the Veterans Administration. The U.S. Army kept Arlington National Cemetery and the U.S. Soldiers' and Airmens' Home National Cemetery in Washington, D.C. In 1998, the National Cemetery System was renamed the National Cemetery Administration.

On March 15, 1989, the U.S. Department of Veterans Affairs (VA) replaced the agency when President Reagan signed legislation to elevate the VA to Cabinet status. The newly established VA became the fourteenth department in the President's Cabinet. Presently, the VA is the second largest of the fifteen Cabinet departments.

BENEFITS

As further discussed in this Almanac, the VA operates programs to benefit veterans and their family members. These benefits include:

1. Disability compensation and pension;
2. Health care;
3. Educational assistance;
4. Vocational rehabilitation;
5. Home loan assistance;
6. Dependent and survivor compensation; and
7. Burial rights and memorial benefits.

In 2007, more than half of the VA's yearly budget was paid directly to veterans in the form of statutory benefits.

A Directory of VA Benefit Centers can be found in Appendix 1 of this Almanac.

EMPLOYMENT

Veterans Administration

The VA is also one of the nation's largest employers. As of April 30, 2007, the VA had 244,032 employees. Of the total number of VA employees, 216,658 were in the Veterans Health Administration; 12,684 in the Veterans Benefits Administration; 1,562 in the National Cemetery System; 3,254 in the Veterans Canteen Service; and 426 in the Revolving Supply Fund. The remaining 9,448 employees work in various staff and facilities offices.

Further, the VA is a leader in hiring veterans. Approximately 60% of all male employees are veterans. As of April 30, 2007, the VA employed 17,346 women who served in the U.S. armed forces. More than 24% of all veterans employed with the VA are disabled veterans and three hold the Medal of Honor.

Military Installations

There are approximately 440 military installations in the continental United States that serve the employment and educational needs of military veterans and their dependents. Veterans are advised to contact their local military base and request information about available employment opportunities.

Directories of Army, Navy, Air Force, Marine and Coast Guard military installations can be found in Appendices 2 through 6, respectively, of this Almanac.

Veterans Preference

Since the time of the Civil War, veterans of the U.S. Armed Forces have been given some degree of preference in appointments to Federal jobs to prevent them from being penalized because of the time spent in the military service.

By law, veterans who are disabled or who serve on active duty in the Armed Forces during certain specified time periods or in military campaigns are entitled to preference over non-veterans both in Federal hiring practices and in retention during reductions in the workforce.

In addition, the National Defense Authorization Act of 2006 (Public Law 109-163) extends Veterans' Preference to those individuals who served on active duty for a period of more than 180 consecutive days, any part of which occurred during the period beginning on September 11, 2001, and ending on a future date prescribed by Presidential proclamation or by law as the last date of Operation Iraqi Freedom; and, who were discharged or released from active duty in the armed forces under honorable conditions.

Expert System

The Department of Labor's Office of the Assistant Secretary for Policy (OASP) and Veterans' Employment and Training Service (VETS) developed an "expert system" to help veterans receive the preferences to which they are entitled. This system is designed to help veterans determine the type of preference to which they are entitled, the benefits associated with the preference and the steps necessary to file a complaint due to the failure of a Federal agency to provide those benefits.

Complaint Process Under The Veterans Employment Opportunity Act

The Veterans Employment Opportunity Act of 1998 (VEOA) made changes to the veterans' preference and sets forth the process a veteran must follow to make a complaint if a violation of the preference has taken place, as follows:

1. Veterans eligible for preference ("Preference Eligibles") who allege that an agency has violated such individual's rights under any statute or regulation relating to veterans' preference may file a complaint

with the Secretary of Labor, The Veterans Employment and Training Service Agency (VETS). Contact information for VETS is as follows:

Office of the Assistant Secretary for Veterans' Employment and Training

U.S. Department of Labor
200 Constitution Avenue, N.W., Room S-1325
Washington, D.C. 20210
Tel: 202-693-4700
Fax: 202-693-4754

2. Complaints must be filed within 60 days after the date of the alleged violation.

3. Not earlier than 61 days after filing a complaint with VETS, complainants may appeal their case to the Merit Systems Protection Board (MSPB).

4. If the MSPB has not issued a decision within 120 days, claimants may seek judicial redress in the U.S. District Courts. Details of these procedures are identified in section 3 of the VEOA, PL 105-339.

5. Veterans' preference is extended to now apply to employee positions in the Government Accounting Office, Office of the President, certain legislative and judicial positions, and in Reduction In Force (RIF) situations, and the Federal Aviation Agency (FAA).

6. Failure to comply with veterans' preference requirements will be treated as a Prohibited Personnel Practice (PPP) for certain purposes. To knowingly take, recommend, or approve any personnel action if the failure to take such action would violate veterans preference requirements or to fail to take, recommend or approve any personnel action if the failure to take such action would violate veterans' preference requirements is a PPP.

The Veterans Employment Opportunities Act can be found in Appendix 7 of this Almanac.

VETERAN STATISTICS

There are approximately 23.8 million living veterans, including 1.7 million women, and 2.9 million World War II veterans. In addition, there are about 37 million dependents of living veterans and survivors of deceased veterans. This number represents about 20% of the U.S. population.

Sixty percent of veterans live in urban areas. The six states with the largest number of veterans include California, Florida, Texas, Pennsylvania,

New York, and Ohio, and account for about 36% of the total veteran population.

Age

In 2007, the median age of all living veterans was 60 years old, and 39.1% of all living veterans are over the age of 65. The median age for men was 61, and 47 for women. Most living veterans served during wartime. Median ages by period of service include 37 for the Gulf War; 60 for the Vietnam War; 76 for the Korean War; and 84 for World War II. Vietnam era veterans total approximately 7.9 million and constitute the largest segment of the veteran population.

Ethnicity

Approximately 80% of veterans are White, 10.9% are Black, 5.6% are Hispanic; 1.4% are Asian/Pacific Islander; 0.8% are American Indian/Alaska Natives; and 1.3% are classified as "other."

Branch of Service

As of September 30, 2007, approximately 10.6 million veterans served in the Army; 5.4 million served in the Navy; 4.3 million served in the Air Force; 2.4 million served in the Marines; 700 thousand were from the Reserve Forces; and 215 thousand served in a non-defense capacity.

Operation Enduring Freedom/Operation Iraqi Freedom (OEF/OIF)

Statistics for veterans of Operation Enduring Freedom/Operation Iraqi Freedom (OEF/OIF) include 48% Active Duty and 52% Reserve/National Guard service members, including Army (65%); Air Force (12%); Navy (12%); and Marines (12%). The largest age group (52%) is 20–29 years old. Thirty-four percent of these veterans were deployed multiple times. Eighty-eight percent are men and 12% are women.

As of September 2007, 223,564 OEF/OIF veterans filed for disability claims. Sixty-nine percent of those veterans who filed disability claims received service-connected disability compensation awards.

VA SPECIAL PROGRAMS AND INITIATIVES

The VA also sponsors and participates in a number of special programs and initiatives, including those listed below.

Health Care Programs

Agent Orange Health Effects and Vietnam Veterans

Approximately 20 million gallons of herbicides were used in Vietnam between 1962 and 1971 to remove unwanted plant life and leaves which otherwise provided cover for enemy forces during the Vietnam Conflict. Shortly following their military service in Vietnam, some veterans reported a variety of health problems which they attributed to exposure to Agent Orange or other herbicides.

The VA has developed a comprehensive program to respond to these medical problems and concerns. The principal elements of this program include quality health care services, disability compensation for veterans with service-connected illnesses, scientific research and outreach and education.

The VA has set up an Agent Orange Helpline for veterans who believe they may be suffering from health problems related to exposure from Agent Orange, which can be reached by telephone (1-800-749-8397) or email: (GW/AOHelpline@vba.va.gov/).

Blind Rehabilitation Service

The Blind Rehabilitation Service endeavors to provide coordinated health care services for blinded veterans extending from their home environment to the local VA facility and to the appropriate rehabilitation setting. These services include adjustment to blindness counseling, patient and family education, benefits analysis, comprehensive residential inpatient training, outpatient rehabilitation services, the provision of assistive technology, and research.

Cancer Program

The VA and the National Cancer Institute (NCI) are working together to make healthcare better for veterans by providing wide access to NCI-sponsored studies of the diagnosis, prevention, and treatment of cancer. Through this program, veterans are able to take advantage of some of the most promising advances in cancer research.

Cold Injury Prevention Program

The VA provides information designed to prevent and manage cold weather injuries in the field. Leaders and soldiers are advised that prevention of cold injuries is vital to sustaining combat power. In cold environments, leaders are made aware of the signs and symptoms of cold injuries. Prevention, early detection, and immediate evacuation are the leader initiatives through which cold injuries should be managed in the field.

Diabetes Prevention Program

The VA provides information and services designed to prevent and manage diabetes.

Flu Program

Information, policy, and management of the flu and flu vaccine issues for the VA is provided through a team of VA programs within the Veterans Health Administration (VHA). The VA takes seriously the threat influenza poses to veterans,.Influenza vaccination in the VA is a priority.

Gulf War Veterans' Health Program

The VA operates an Information Helpline to provide assistance to veterans, their families and others about VA health care programs related to Gulf War service. Gulf War veterans, including those who served in Operations Desert Shield, Desert Storm, and Iraqi Freedom, who need assistance in locating their nearest VA Medical Center, or who have general health questions regarding Gulf service, may call the VA Gulf War Veterans Information Helpline (1-800-PGW-VETS).

Health Care Programs for Elderly and Chronically Ill Veterans

The VA Office of Geriatrics and Extended Care provides quality care to aging and chronically ill veterans, including but not limited to geriatric primary care; home and community-based long-term care; community residential care; hospice and palliative care; and VA nursing home care.

HIV/AIDS/Hepatitis Program

The VA is the largest single provider of HIV care and Hepatitis C care in the United States. In fiscal year 2000, nearly 19,000 veterans received care for HIV disease by the VA and to date, nearly 70,000 veterans who use VA health care services have tested positive for hepatitis C.

Kidney Disease Program

The VA Medical-Surgical Service assures that top quality acute health care is available, immediately accessible and efficiently provided to all eligible veterans as clinically indicated. The VA National Transplant Program started providing solid organ transplants to veteran patients in 1961.

The first kidney transplant was performed at the VA Medical Center in Denver, Colorado. Since then, the VA National Transplant Program has expanded services to provide veteran patients with heart transplant services in 1980, bone marrow in 1982, liver in 1989, and lung in 1991. Most transplants are performed in specific VA medical centers across the country. VA also utilizes several VA sharing agreements with University affiliates and local emergency contracts for critical heart and liver cases.

Mental Health Strategic Healthcare Group

The Veterans Health Administration (VHA) Mental Health Strategic Healthcare Group provides general inpatient psychiatric services at 132 medical centers as well as mental health outpatient services in 689 medical centers and community-based outpatient clinics. In addition, readjustment counseling services are available for veterans and their families at 209 centers across the nation.

Mental health services are available in primary care clinics, VA nursing homes, and residential care facilities where veterans receive health care. Veterans with a serious mental illness are seen at facilities and clinics where specialized programs, such as mental health intensive case management, day centers, work programs and psychosocial rehabilitation are provided.

Mental Illness Research, Education and Clinical Centers

The Mental Illness Research, Education and Clinical Centers (MIRECC) were established by Congress with the goal of bringing best practices in mental health care into the clinical settings of the VA. The MIRECCs conduct research and produce clinical educational programs and products, but generally provide direct clinical treatment to veterans only in the context of research protocols. Therefore, veterans should seek treatment at their local VA medical centers.

National Center for Post-Traumatic Stress Disorder

The National Center for Post-Traumatic Stress Disorder (NCPTSD) conducts research, education and training on PTSD and stress-related disorders in order to advance the clinical care and social welfare of veterans.

National Center for Patient Safety

The National Center for Patient Safety (NCPS) was established in 1999 to reduce and prevent inadvertent harm to patients as a result of their care throughout the Veterans Health Administration. Patient safety managers at 153 VA hospitals and patient safety officers at 21 VA regional headquarters participate in the program.

Office of Nursing Services

The Office of Nursing Services provides leadership and guidance to the VA nursing workforce and promotes awareness of current nursing practices, products, and services in order to provide the best nursing care to veterans.

Polytrauma System of Care

Polytrauma care is for veterans and returning service members with injuries to more than one physical region or organ system, one of which may be life threatening, and which results in physical, cognitive, psychological, or psychosocial impairments and functional disability. Some examples of polytrauma include: (1) traumatic brain injury; (2) hearing loss; (3) amputations; (4) fractures; (5) burns; and (6) visual impairment.

The Polytrauma Rehabilitation Centers provide comprehensive, high-quality, and inter-disciplinary care to VA patients. Teams of physicians from every relevant field plan and administer an individually tailored rehabilitation plan to help the patient recover as much as possible.

Prosthetics and Sensory Aids Service

The VA Prosthetics and Sensory Aids Service provides specialized quality patient care by furnishing properly prescribed prosthetic equipment, sensory aids and devices in the most economical and timely manner. It serves as the pharmacy for assistive aids, and as the case manager for prosthetic equipment needs of the disabled veteran.

Recreation/Creative Arts Therapy Service

Using various modalities appropriate to the particular therapy approach involved, recreation/creative arts therapists seek to achieve and maintain optimal levels of independence, productivity, and well being through therapeutic art, dance, music, drama, or recreation activities and services.

These therapists evaluate history, interests, aptitudes, and skills of VA patients by interviews, inventories, tests, and measurements, and use such findings, along with medical records, and therapy orders of physicians, to develop and implement recreation therapy or creative arts therapy activities for individual patients.

These therapy approaches are directed toward achieving such therapeutic objectives as achieving and maintaining optimal levels of independence, productivity, and well being, and re-entry of the veteran into the mainstream of community life.

Social Work Program

Social workers are available to help veterans with most of their needs, including but not limited to crisis management, case management, discharge planning, and will also advocate on behalf of the veteran.

Social workers are located in every VA Medical Center, Vet Center and in many Community Based Clinics.

War-Related Illness and Injury Study Center

The War Related Illness and Injury Study Center (WRIISC) was developed to address those veterans who have deployment health questions or difficult to diagnosis illnesses or injuries. These centers evolved from the Gulf War Referral Centers that were developed by the VA in the 1990s to address the health concerns of Gulf War veterans. The WRIISC specializes in all combat related illnesses and injuries regardless of conflict.

An evaluation at the WRIISC is appropriate for combat veterans with debilitating symptoms that remain unexplained after medical examinations by the local VA medical center. Combat veterans with medically unexplained illnesses may request a referral from their VA physician to the WRIISC for evaluation.

Advisory Committees

Advisory Committees carefully and systematically review, evaluate, and advise the VA on a broad range of issues affecting policies and programs. The public, in return, is afforded an opportunity to participate actively in the VA's decision-making process.

Center for Faith-Based and Community Initiatives

The Center for Faith-Based and Community Initiatives provides information, resources and tools to help faith-based and community groups compete for funding on a level playing field with other organizations.

Center for Women Veterans: Programs & Initiatives for Women Veterans

The primary mission of the Center for Women Veterans is to: (1) ensure that VA programs and services are responsive to the gender-specific needs of women veterans; and (2) assure that women veterans receive benefits and services on a par with male veterans, encounter no discrimination in their attempt to access them, and are treated with the respect, dignity, and understanding by VA service providers.

Debt Management Center

The Debt Management Center's primary mission is to collect debt resulting from an individual's participation in VA benefit programs in the most efficient and cost effective means possible while maintaining compassionate, high quality service to veterans and their families.

Homeless Assistance Programs & Initiatives

The homeless program promotes the development and provision of housing and other supportive services. Homeless veterans achieve residential stability, increase their skill levels and/or income, and obtain greater self-determination.

VA Medical Training Program

The VA manages the largest medical education and health professions training program in the United States. VA facilities are affiliated with 107 medical schools, 55 dental schools and more than 1,200 other schools across the country. Each year, about 90,000 health professionals are trained in VA medical centers. More than half of the physicians practicing in the United States had some of their professional education in the VA health care system.

Records Center & Vault

In addition to general records storage, the vault specializes in providing customized storage and personalized services designed to meet client requirements.

VA Franchise Fund

The VA Franchise Fund provides information technology, debt collection, accounting, finance and payroll, law enforcement training, identification badges and access cards design and production, and records storage and retrieval services.

VA Vets Center Program

The VA Vets Center Program operates a system of 232 community based counseling centers located in all fifty states, the District of Columbia, Guam, Puerto Rico and the U.S. Virgin Islands. Vets Centers provide readjustment counseling and outreach services to all veterans who served in any combat zone. Services are also available for their family members for military related issues. There is no cost to the veteran or family.

The Vets Centers are staffed by small multi-disciplinary teams of dedicated providers, many of which are combat veterans themselves, and can be reached at the following toll-free telephone numbers: 1-800-905-4675 (Eastern)/1-866-496-8838 (Pacific).

A Directory of Veterans Centers can be found in Appendix 8 of this Almanac.

Veterans Industries

Veterans Industries is a vocational rehabilitation program that provides temporary and permanent staffing for manufacturing, warehouse construction, and office support, as well as outsource support in assembly, packaging, sorting, grading, reclaiming, and recycling.

VA ORGANIZATIONS

The VA is made up of a number of organizations, all of which work together to provide well-earned benefits to the nation's veterans and their dependents.

Veterans Benefits Administration

The Veterans Benefits Administration (VBA) provides benefits and services to the veteran population through 58 VA regional offices. Some of the benefits and services provided by the VBA to veterans and their dependents include compensation and pension, education, loan guaranty, and insurance.

Veterans Health Administration

The Veterans Health Administration (VHA) manages one of the largest health care systems in the United States, operating 157 hospitals nationwide. The VHA's mission is to provide efficient, accessible health care to veterans in their areas. The VHA also conducts research and education, and provides emergency medical preparedness.

National Cemetery Administration

The National Cemetery Administration (NCA) is responsible for providing burial benefits to veterans and eligible dependents. The NCA manages 120 National Cemeteries nationwide, provides grave markers worldwide, administers the State Cemetery Grants Program that complements the National Cemeteries network, and provides Presidential Memorial Certificates to the next of kin of deceased veterans.

Board of Contract Appeals

The Department of Veterans Affairs Board of Contract Appeals considers and determines appeals from decisions of contracting officers pursuant to the Contract Disputes Act of 1978.

Board of Veterans' Appeals

The Board of Veterans' Appeals (BVA) reviews benefit claims determinations made by local VA offices and issues decision on appeals. The Board members, attorneys experienced in veterans' law and in reviewing benefit claims, are the only ones who can issue Board decisions.

Center for Women Veterans

The mission of the Center for Women Veterans is to ensure women veterans have access to VA benefits and services, to ensure that VA health care and benefits programs are responsive to the gender-specific needs of women veterans, to perform outreach to improve women veterans awareness of VA services, benefits and eligibility, and to act as the primary advisor to the Secretary for Veterans Affairs on all matters related to programs, issues, and initiatives for and affecting women veterans.

Office of Acquisition & Material Management

The Office of Acquisition & Material Management (OA&MM) is responsible for overseeing the acquisition, storage, and distribution of supplies, services, and equipment used by VA facilities and other Government agencies. OA&MM manages pharmaceuticals, medical supplies and equipment, and nonperishable subsistence through its procurement system.

Office of Alternative Dispute Resolution and Mediation

The Office of Alternative Dispute Resolution (ADR) and Mediation provides effective training and consulting in conflict resolution and ADR, with an emphasis on mediation, to VA organizations and employees.

Office of Budget

The Office of Budget is the focal point for the Departmental Budget Formulation and Execution, the Capital Investment Board and Performance Reporting.

Office of Public Affairs & Intergovernmental Affairs

The Office of Public Affairs & Intergovernmental Affairs (OPIA) has two major offices, Public Affairs and Intergovernmental Affairs. The primary mission of Public Affairs is to provide information to the nation's veterans and their eligible dependents and survivors through news media concerning available VA benefits and programs. Intergovernmental Affairs interacts with federal, state, and local government agencies and officials in developing and maintaining a positive and productive relationship.

Office of Congressional Affairs

The Office of Congressional Affairs (OCA) is the principal point of contact between the VA and Congress and is the oversight and coordinating body for the VA's Congressional relations. The office serves in an advisory capacity to the Secretary and Deputy Secretary as well as other VA managers concerning policies, programs, and legislative matters in which Congressional committees or individual members of Congress have expressed an interest.

Office of Employment Discrimination Complaint Adjudication

The Office of Employment Discrimination Complaint Adjudication (OEDCA) ensures fairness, integrity, and trust throughout the complaint adjudication phase of the Equal Employment Opportunity complaint resolution process.

Office of Financial Management

The goal of the Office of Financial Management (OFM) is to improve the quality of the VA's financial services through the development of sound financial policies and the promotion of efficient financial management systems, operations, policies, and practices.

Office of the General Counsel

The Office of the General Counsel (OGC) identifies and meets the legal needs of the VA.

Office of Human Resources & Administration

The function of the Office of Human Resources & Administration (HR&A) includes human resources management, administrative policies and functions, equal opportunity policies and functions, and security and law enforcement.

Office of Information & Technology

The function of the Office of Information & Technology (OIT) includes integrated business and information technology (IT) planning; security and contingency planning to protect information and privacy across VA systems and networks; reviews to evaluate the performance of IT programs; review and approval of IT acquisitions; facilitation of intra- and intergovernmental partnerships; educating and informing the Department of IT, initiatives and legislation; and sharing lessons learned.

Office of the Inspector General

The Office of the Inspector General (IG) provides service to veterans, VA employees, and citizens concerned with good government.

Office of Occupational Safety & Health

The Office of Occupational Safety & Health ensures that the VA complies with requirements of the Federal Occupational Safety and Health Administration (OSHA), Joint Commission for Accreditation of Healthcare Organizations (JCAHO), and VA standards.

Office of Policy, Planning and Preparedness

The Office of Policy, Planning and Preparedness (OPP): (1) facilitates, coordinates and validates the VA's policy development and formulation processes; (2) coordinates the VA's strategic planning process and implementation of the Government Performance and Results Act requirements; (3) supports the identification, development, analysis, and review of issues affecting veterans' programs; (4) links and supplements the actuarial and quantitative analysis capabilities of the VA in support of major policy inquiries; (5) serves as the VA's focal point for access to and availability of official data; (6) coordinates the independent evaluation of the VA program performance; and (7) fosters quality management techniques and procedures throughout the VA.

Office of Regulation Policy and Management

The Office of Regulation Policy and Management is responsible for the centralized management, control, and coordination of all VA regulations, and for devising and implementing new procedures to centralize control and improve Secretarial oversight, management, drafting efficiency, policy resolution, impact analysis, and coordination of diverse VA regulations.

Office of Small & Disadvantaged Business Utilization

The Office of Small & Disadvantaged Business Utilization (OSDBU) advocates for the maximum practicable participation of small disadvantaged, veteran-owned, women-owned, and empowerment zone businesses in contracts awarded by the VA and in subcontracts, which are awarded by VA's prime contractors.

VA RESEARCH

In 2006, Congress appropriated $412 million for VA research, and an additional $357 million in the medical care research efforts. Non-VA sources, such as the National Institutes of Health, other government agencies, and pharmaceutical companies, provided an additional $882 million in funding for VA research.

VA research focuses on areas of concern to veterans. VA research has earned an international reputation for excellence in areas such as aging, chronic disease, prosthetics and mental health. VA scientists have won many awards, including the Nobel Prize and the Lasker Award.

VA investigators played key roles in developing the cardiac pacemaker, the CT scan, radioimmunoassay, and improvements in artificial limbs. In fact, the "Seattle Foot," developed in the VA, allows those with amputations to run and jump. In addition, the first liver transplant in the world was performed by a VA surgeon-researcher. VA clinical trials have also established the effectiveness of new treatments for tuberculosis, schizophrenia and high blood pressure.

Special VA "centers of excellence" conduct leading-edge research in areas of prime importance to veterans, such as neurotrauma, prosthetics, spinal cord injury, hearing and vision loss, alcoholism, and stroke. In addition to studies focused on recent veterans of operations Iraqi Freedom and Enduring Freedom, research continues on issues of special concern to veterans of earlier conflicts, such as the Gulf War and Vietnam War.

CHAPTER 2:
DISABILITY COMPENSATION AND
PENSION BENEFITS

IN GENERAL

In fiscal year 2006, the VA provided $34.4 billion in disability compensation, death compensation and pension to 3.6 million people. In 2007, the VA processed nearly 825,000 claims for disability benefits and added almost 250,000 new beneficiaries to the compensation and pension rolls.

As of March 31, 2008, 2.9 million veterans were receiving VA disability compensation, including 272,425 veterans who were rated 100% disabled, and 318,801 veterans were receiving a VA pension.

DISABILITY COMPENSATION

Disability compensation is a benefit paid to a veteran because of an injury or disease that occurred while the soldier was on active duty, or an injury or disease that was made worse by active military service. Disability compensation is also paid to certain veterans disabled from VA health care. Disability compensation benefits are tax-free.

Eligibility

A veteran may be eligible for disability compensation if he or she has a service-related disability and was discharged under other than dishonorable conditions.

Amount of Benefits

The amount of basic benefit currently ranges from $117 to over $3000 per month, depending on the extent of disability. The veteran may be paid additional amounts if he or she has any of the following:

1. Very severe disabilities or loss of limb(s);

2. A spouse, child(ren), or dependent parent(s); or

3. A seriously disabled spouse.

Application Process

In order to apply for disability compensation, the veteran must file *an Application for Compensation and/or Pension* (VA Form 21-526), along with any required documentation, which may include the veteran's discharge papers; dependency records, e.g., marriage and birth certificates; and medical evidence.

A sample Application for Compensation and/or Pension (VA Form 21-526) can be found in Appendix 9 of this Almanac.

VETERANS PENSION

A VA pension is a benefit paid to: (1) wartime veterans who have limited or no income, and who are age 65 or older; or (2) wartime veterans under 65 who are permanently and totally disabled.

Veterans who are more seriously disabled may qualify for Aid and Attendance benefits or Housebound benefits, as explained below. These are benefits that are paid in addition to the basic pension rate.

Eligibility

In general, a veteran is eligible for a pension if:

1. The veteran was discharged from service under conditions other than dishonorable;

2. The veteran served at least 90 days of active military service, one day of which was during a war time period, as set forth below. However, if the veteran entered active duty after September 7, 1980, he or she must have served at least 24 months, or the full period for which called or ordered to active duty;

3. The veteran's countable family income is below the yearly limit set by law; and

4. The veteran is age 65 or older, or permanently and totally disabled not due to the veteran's own willful misconduct.

The VA will review the veteran's application and determine whether he or she is eligible for a pension. If the veteran does not initially qualify, he or she may reapply if there are unreimbursed medical expenses during the twelve-month period after the VA receives the claim that brings the veteran's countable income below the yearly income limit. This includes expenses paid for medical services or products for which the veteran will not be reimbursed by Medicare or private medical insurance.

A veteran cannot receive a VA non-service connected pension and service-connected compensation at the same time. However, if the veteran applies for a pension and is awarded payments, the VA will pay whichever benefit is the greater amount.

Countable Income

Countable income includes income received by the veteran and his or her dependents, if any, from most sources. It includes earnings, disability and retirement payments, interest and dividends, and net income from farming or business. The VA may grant an exception in hardship cases.

There is no set limit on how much net worth a veteran and his or her dependents can have, but net worth cannot be excessive. Net worth refers to the net value of the assets of the veteran and his or her dependents. Net worth includes such assets as bank accounts, stocks, bonds, mutual funds and any property other than the veteran's residence.

The decision as to whether a claimant's net worth is excessive depends on the facts of each individual case. All net worth should be reported to the VA. The VA will determine if a claimant's assets are sufficiently large enough that the claimant could live off these assets for a reasonable period of time.

The VA's needs-based programs are not intended to protect substantial assets or build up an estate for the benefit of heirs.

Exclusions and Deductions

There are certain exclusions and deductions that may be considered to reduce the veteran's countable income, as follows:

1. Public assistance such as Supplemental Security Income is not considered income.

2. Many other specific sources of income are not considered countable income. Nevertheless, all income should be reported. The VA will exclude any income that the law allows.

3. A portion of unreimbursed medical expenses paid by the claimant after the VA receives the claimant's pension claim may be deducted.

4. Certain other expenses, such as a veteran's education expenses and, in some cases, a portion of the educational expenses of a child over 18 are deductible.

Veteran's Pension Calculation

The annual pension is calculated by first totaling all of the veteran's countable income. Then any deductions are subtracted from that total. The remaining countable income is deducted from the appropriate annual pension limit, which is determined by the number of dependents, if any, and whether or not the veteran is entitled to Housebound or Aid and Attendance benefits. This amount is then divided by 12 and rounded down to the nearest dollar. This is the amount of the monthly payment.

Application Process

In order to apply for a pension, the veteran must file *an Application for Compensation and/or Pension* (VA Form 21-526), along with any required documentation, such as dependency records, e.g., marriage and birth certificates.

A sample Application for Compensation and/or Pension (VA Form 21-526) can be found in Appendix 9 of this Almanac.

AID AND ATTENDANCE AND HOUSEBOUND BENEFITS

Aid and Attendance Benefits

Aid and Attendance (A&A) benefits are paid to a veteran in addition to the monthly pension. A&A benefits may not be paid unless the veteran is eligible for a pension. A veteran may be eligible for A&A if:

1. The veteran requires the aid of another person in order to perform personal functions required in everyday living, such as bathing, feeding, dressing, attending to the wants of nature, adjusting prosthetic devices, or protecting the veteran from the hazards of his or her daily environment;

2. The veteran is bedridden such that his or her disability requires that the veteran remain in bed apart from any prescribed course of convalescence or treatment;

3. The veteran is a patient in a nursing home due to mental or physical incapacity; or

4. The veteran is blind, or so nearly blind as to have corrected visual acuity of 5/200 or less, in both eyes, or concentric contraction of the visual field to 5 degrees or less.

Housebound Benefits

Housebound benefits are paid to a veteran in addition to the monthly pension. Like A&A benefits, Housebound benefits may not be paid unless the veteran is eligible for a pension. A veteran may be eligible for Housebound benefits if:

1. The veteran has a single permanent disability evaluated as 100% disabling and, due to such disability, the veteran is permanently and substantially confined to his or her immediate premises; or

2. The veteran has a single permanent disability evaluated as 100% disabling and another disability, or disabilities, evaluated as 60% or more disabling.

A veteran cannot receive both Aid and Attendance benefits and Housebound benefits at the same time.

Applying for Aid and Attendance or Housebound Benefits

In order to apply for Aid and Attendance benefits or Housebound benefits, the veteran must write to the VA regional office having jurisdiction over his or her claim. This is the same office where the claim for pension benefits was initially filed.

The claim should be supported by a report from an attending physician that validates the need for Aid and Attendance or Housebound type care. The report should be in sufficient detail to determine whether there is a disease or injury producing physical or mental impairment, loss of coordination, or conditions affecting the ability to dress and undress, to feed oneself, to attend to sanitary needs, and to keep oneself ordinarily clean and presentable.

In addition, it is necessary to determine whether the veteran is confined to the home or immediate premises. The report should also indicate how well the veteran can get around, where the veteran goes, and what the veteran is able to do during a typical day.

PERIODS OF WARTIME SERVICE FOR VA BENEFITS ELIGIBILITY

World War I

For World War I, wartime service extends from April 6, 1917, through November 11, 1918, inclusive. If the veteran served with the United States military forces in Russia, the ending date is April 1, 1920. Service after November 11, 1918 and before July 2, 1921 is considered World War I service if the veteran served in the active military, naval, or air service after April 5, 1917 and before November 12, 1918.

World War II

For World War II, wartime service extends from December 7, 1941 through December 31, 1946, inclusive. If the veteran was in service on December 31, 1946, continuous service before July 26, 1947 is considered World War II service.

Korean Conflict

For the Korean Conflict, wartime service extends from June 27, 1950 through January 31, 1955, inclusive.

Vietnam Era

For the Vietnam Era, wartime service extends from February 28, 1961 through May 7, 1975, inclusive, in the case of a veteran who served in the Republic of Vietnam during that period. Wartime service extends from August 5, 1964 through May 7, 1975, inclusive, in all other cases.

Persian Gulf War

For the Persian Gulf War, wartime service extends from August 2, 1990 through a date to be prescribed by Presidential proclamation or law.

Future Dates

For future dates, wartime service extends from the date of any future declaration of war by the Congress through a date prescribed by Presidential proclamation or concurrent resolution of the Congress.

CHAPTER 3:
HEALTH CARE BENEFITS

IN GENERAL

Health care is perhaps the most important of all benefits provided to veterans by the VA. The VA's health care system includes 155 medical centers, with at least one in each state, Puerto Rico and the District of Columbia. The VA operates more than 1,400 sites of care, including 872 ambulatory care and community-based outpatient clinics, 135 nursing homes, 45 residential rehabilitation treatment programs, 209 Veterans Centers and 108 comprehensive home-care programs. These VA health care facilities provide medical, surgical and rehabilitative care.

A Directory of VA Medical Centers can be found in Appendix 10 of this Almanac.

During the last ten years, the VA has provided more medical services to veterans and their family members than at any time during the VA's long history. By the end of fiscal year 2006, 78% of all disabled and low-income veterans had enrolled with the VA for health care, and 65% of them were treated by the VA. In 2006, VA inpatient facilities treated 773,600 patients, and the VA's outpatient clinics registered over 60 million visits.

As of fiscal year 2007, there were 7.8 million enrollees in the VA health care system, and the Veterans Health Administration (VHA) provided health care services to approximately 5.5 million patients. The VHA health care and research budget constituted 43% of the VA's total obligations in fiscal year 2007.

The VHA has also enhanced its overall mental health resources by over $500 million in fiscal year 2007 to meet the influx of veterans with mental and emotional health care needs. The VA hired suicide prevention counselors at each of its 153 medical centers to help support the national suicide prevention hot line. The hot line is manned by mental health professionals who are trained to help veterans cope with emotional crises. The hot line is available 365 days a year, 24 hours a day.

The VA provides health care and benefits to more than 100,000 homeless veterans each year. The VA actively engages these veterans in outreach, medical care, benefits assistance and transitional housing. The VA has also made more than 300 grants for transitional housing, service centers and vans for outreach and transportation to state and local governments, tribal governments, non-profit community and faith-based service providers.

Programs for alcoholism, drug addiction and post-traumatic stress disorder have been expanded in recent years, along with attention to environmental hazards. In addition, there are more than 90,000 active volunteers in the VA's Voluntary Service who donate 13 million hours each year to bring companionship and care to hospitalized veterans.

MEDICAL BENEFITS PACKAGE

As set forth below, the VA provides veterans with a Medical Benefits Package, a standard enhanced health benefits plan available to all enrolled veterans. This plan emphasizes preventive and primary care, and offers a full range of outpatient and inpatient services within the VA health care system.

The VA Medical Benefits Package provides the following health care services to all enrolled veterans.

Preventive Care Services

Preventive care services include immunizations, physical examinations, health care assessments, screening tests, and health education programs.

Ambulatory Diagnostic and Treatment Services

Ambulatory—i.e., outpatient—diagnostic and treatment services include:

1. Emergency outpatient care in VA facilities;

2. Medical services;

3. Surgical services, including reconstructive and plastic surgery as a result of disease or trauma;

4. Chiropractic care;

5. Mental health services;

6. Bereavement counseling; and

7. Substance abuse services.

Hospital Diagnostic and Treatment Services

Hospital—i.e., inpatient—diagnostic and treatment services include:

1. Emergency inpatient care in VA facilities;

2. Medical services;

3. Surgical services, including reconstructive and plastic surgery as a result of disease or trauma;

4. Mental health services; and

5. Substance abuse services.

Medications and Supplies

Medications and supplies available to enrolled veterans include prescription medications, over-the-counter medications, medical supplies, and surgical supplies. Generally, the medications and supplies must be prescribed by a VA provider and be available under the VA's national formulary system, which is set forth on the VA Web site (http://www.pbm.va.gov/).

In general, the VA does not pay for medications and supplies written by a non-VA physician. An exception may exist for veterans with special eligibility, such as veterans receiving Aid and Attendance or Housebound benefits, or who are approved by a VA health care facility.

ELIGIBILITY

Eligibility for most veterans' health care benefits is based solely on active military service in the Army, Navy, Air Force, Marines, or Coast Guard, and discharge under other than dishonorable conditions.

Reservists and National Guard members who were called to active duty by a Federal Executive Order may qualify for VA health care benefits. Returning service members, including Reservists and National Guard members who served on active duty in a theater of combat operations, have special eligibility for hospital care, medical services, and nursing home care for two years following discharge from active duty.

THE ENROLLMENT SYSTEM

To receive VA health care benefits, most veterans must enroll in the program. When a veteran enrolls, he or she is placed in a priority group or category that helps the VA manage health care services within its budget, and ensures quality care for those enrolled. The priority system ensures that veterans with service-connected disabilities and those below the low-income threshold are able to be enrolled in the VA's health care system.

The VA enrollment system also allows health care benefits to become portable throughout the entire VA system. Thus enrolled veterans who are traveling or who spend time away from their primary treatment facility may obtain care at any VA health care facility across the country without the worry of having to reapply.

Some veterans are exempted from having to enroll including: (1) veterans with a service-connected disability of 50% or more; (2) veterans who were discharged from the military within one year but have not yet been rated for a VA disability benefit; and (3) veterans seeking care for only a service-connected disability.

Veterans with service-connected disabilities receive priority access to care for hospitalization and outpatient care.

APPLYING FOR BENEFITS

A veteran can enroll in the program and apply for VA health care, nursing home, domiciliary, or dental benefits by completing an *Application for Health Benefits* (VA Form 10-10EZ). The application form may be obtained by: (1) visiting, calling, or writing any health care facility or Veterans Benefits Office; (2) calling the VA's Health Benefits Service Center (877-222-8387); or (3) accessing the online application at the VA Web site (www.va.gov/1010EZ.htm/).

A sample Application for Health Benefits (VA Form 10-10EZ) can be found in Appendix 11 of this Almanac.

Once the application for enrollment in the VA health care system is processed, the VA will send the veteran a letter informing him or her of the enrollment priority group assignment and whether he or she was enrolled. The letter will also give the veteran instructions on how to appeal the decision if he or she does not agree with it.

Veterans who are enrolled will remain enrolled without having to reapply for benefits annually. However, some veterans will need to update their financial information yearly to keep their enrollment priority current. The VA will contact these veterans when it is time to update their financial information.

Required Evidence

To reduce processing time, the veteran may submit the following paperwork:

1. A copy of the veteran's discharge papers if he or she is not currently receiving benefits from the VA; or

2. Military service records indicating that the veteran received a Purple Heart Medal; or

3. Evidence that the veteran received hostile fire or imminent danger pay, or a combat medal, after November 11, 1998.

Duty to Assist—The Veterans Claims Act of 2000 and Duty to Assist

The Veterans Claim Act of 2000 and Duty to Assist requires the VA to obtain any records in the VA's possession, or within any other Federal agency. The law also mandates that the VA tell the claimant what evidence is needed to support their claim. The VA now must make several efforts to obtain any evidence identified by the claimant.

By law, the burden of proof falls on the veteran or dependent. Even though the VA is now required to look for evidence, this may take many months. The veteran can help speed up the claims process if he or she can obtain supporting evidence. Evidence may include:

1. The veteran's statements, especially those of combat veterans claiming a "combat related" injury or illness;

2. Statements from friends, relatives or anyone that has knowledge of your disability and its relationship to service; or

3. Medical evidence.

HEALTH CARE APPOINTMENTS

If the veteran applies for VA health care in person at any VA medical center, he or she can request an appointment for medical care at the time of application. Alternatively, the veteran can request an appointment on their application and when the application is processed, an appointment will be scheduled. The veteran will be notified, in writing, of his or her eligibility for medical care and the appointment date and time. Veterans with service-connected disabilities will be given priority in scheduling.

Priority Scheduling for Veterans with Service-Connected Disabilities

The VA will provide priority access to care for: (1) a veteran who needs care for a service-connected disability; or (2) a veteran who has a

50% or higher service-connected disability and needs care for any condition.

The VA will schedule a primary care evaluation for a veteran with a service-connected disability within 30 days of his or her desired date. If the veteran's outpatient appointment cannot be scheduled within this timeframe, the VA will arrange to have the veteran seen within 30 days at another VA health care facility, or obtain the services on a fee basis, under a sharing agreement or contract at the VA's expense.

All other veterans will be scheduled for a Primary Care appointment as soon as one becomes available.

LONG TERM CARE

Long Term Care benefits provide for a range of long-term care services, including nursing home care, domiciliary care, adult day health care, geriatric evaluation and respite care.

In order to apply for long term care benefits, nonservice-connected and zero percent service-connected enrolled veterans with income over the single pension rate must submit an *Application for Extended Care Services* (VA Form 10-10EC) in addition to the Application for Health Benefits. The original application, along with the supporting documentation, should be mailed to the veteran's local VA health care facility.

VA Form 10-10EC is used to measure the current income and assets of the veteran's family in order to determine if the veteran will be charged co-pays for long-term care.

Veterans with a compensable service-connected disability are exempt from paying co-pays for long-term care.

SPECIAL AND LIMITED HEALTH CARE BENEFITS

Some health care benefits are offered only to certain veterans, or to veterans under special situations. Some of the most important of these special benefits include those listed below.

Agent Orange Health Effects and Vietnam Veterans

Vietnam veterans exposed to Agent Orange while in Vietnam are eligible for cost-free hospital care, medical services, and nursing home care for any disability that may be associated with the exposure. This special treatment authority is limited to the following veterans:

1. Veterans who served on active duty in the Republic of Vietnam during the period beginning on January 9, 1962, and ending on May 7, 1975; and

2. Veterans who have conditions for which the National Academy of Sciences found evidence of a possible association with herbicide exposure. Those conditions include: (1) Adult-onset (Type 2) diabetes; (2) Chronic lymphocytic leukemia; (3) Hodgkin's disease; (4) Multiple myeloma; (5) Non-Hodgkin's lymphoma; (6) Acute and subacute peripheral neuropathy; (7) Porphyria cutanea tarda; (8) Chloracne; (9) Prostate cancer; (10) Respiratory cancers; and (11) Soft-tissue sarcoma.

Extensive medical examinations are offered at all VA medical centers for eligible concerned veterans who may have been exposed to Agent Orange or other herbicides during their military service. Veterans with conditions recognized by the VA as associated with Agent Orange or herbicide exposure are eligible for priority enrollment.

The VA has set up an Agent Orange Helpline for veterans who believe they may be suffering from health problems related to exposure from Agent Orange, which can be reached by telephone (1-800-749-8397) or e-mail: (GW/AOHelpline@vba.va.gov/).

In addition to veterans who served in Vietnam or Korea during the specified times, the VA will provide registry examinations to any U.S. veteran who may have been exposed to dioxin, or other toxic substance in a herbicide or defoliant, during the conduct of, or as a result of, the testing, transporting or spraying of herbicides for military purposes. Facilities will make every effort to schedule an examination within 30 days of the request date.

Vietnam veterans' children with the birth defect spina bifida are eligible for certain benefits and services. In addition, the VA now provides certain benefits, including health care, for children with birth defects who were born to female Vietnam veterans. These programs are administered by the Health Administration Center.

Automobile Assistance

A veteran may qualify for automobile assistance for this VA benefit if he or she has:

1. A service connected loss or permanent loss of use of one or both hands or feet; or

2. A permanent impairment of vision of both eyes to a certain degree; or

3. Entitlement to compensation for ankylosis—i.e., immobility—of one or both knees or one or both hips.

The VA provides a one time payment of not more than $11,000 toward the purchase of an automobile or other vehicle. The VA also pays for adaptive equipment and for repair, replacement or reinstallation required because of disability.

Beneficiary Travel

The VA currently reimburses eligible veterans 28.5 cents per mile for travel to the nearest VA health care facility that can provide their needed care. Veterans traveling for their Compensation and Pension (C&P) exams are also reimbursed $.285 per mile. However, veterans are reimbursed $.17 per mile if, through no fault of their own, they have to return to the VA to repeat a lab test, x-ray or other exam in order to complete their C&P exam.

In most cases, travel benefits are subject to a deductible of $7.77 one-way or $15.54 round trip. Upon reaching $46.62 in deductibles, travel payments made for the balance of that particular month will be free of deductible charges.

A veteran qualifies for this benefit if:

1. The veteran has a service-connected rating of 30% or more;

2. The veteran is traveling for treatment of a service-connected condition;

3. The veteran receives a VA pension;

4. The veteran has an income that does not exceed the maximum annual VA pension rate;

5. The veteran is traveling for a scheduled compensation or pension examination; or

6. The veteran is in an authorized Vocational Rehabilitation Program.

In addition, the veteran may qualify for Special Mode Transportation, e.g., an ambulance, wheelchair van, etc., if:

1. The veteran's medical condition requires an ambulance or a specially equipped van; and

2. The veteran meets one of the eligibility criteria listed above; and

3. The veteran's travel is pre-authorized, unless authorization is not required because of an emergency where any delay would be hazardous to life or health.

Bereavement Counseling

VA health care facilities offer bereavement counseling to veterans and their family members who are receiving VA health care benefits.

Bereavement counseling is also provided to parents, spouses and children of Armed Forces personnel who died in the service of their country. Family members of reservists and National Guardsmen who die while on duty are also eligible for bereavement counseling. Counseling is provided at Vet Centers.

Blind Veterans Services

Blind veterans may be eligible for services at a VA medical center, or for admission to a VA blind rehabilitation center or clinic. Services for blind veterans include:

1. A total health and benefits review by a VA Visual Impairment services team;

2. Adjustment to blindness training;

3. Home improvements and structural alterations to homes;

4. Specially adapted housing and adaptations;

5. Low vision aids and training in their use;

6. Electronic and mechanical aids for the blind, including adaptive computers and computer-assisted devices such as reading machines and electronic travel aids;

7. Guide dogs, including the expense of training the veteran to use the dog and the cost of the dog's medical care; and

8. Talking books, tapes and Braille literature.

Dental Care

Eligibility for VA dental benefits is based on very specific guidelines and differs significantly from eligibility requirements for medical care. A veteran is eligible for outpatient dental treatment if he or she meets one of the following criteria:

1. If the veteran has a service-connected compensable dental disability or condition, he or she is eligible for any needed dental care;

2. If the veteran is a former prisoner of war, he or she is eligible for any needed dental care;

3. If the veteran has a service-connected disability rated 100% disabling or is unemployable due to service-connected conditions, he or she is eligible for any needed dental care;

4. If the veteran is participating in a VA vocational rehabilitation program, he or she is eligible for dental care needed to complete the program;

5. If the veteran has a service connected and/or noncompensable dental condition or disability that existed at the time of discharge or release from a period of active duty of 90 days or more during the Persian Gulf War era, he or she is eligible for one-time dental care if the veteran applies for dental care within 180 days of separation from active duty, and his or her certificate of discharge does not indicate that all appropriate dental treatment had been rendered prior to discharge;

6. If the veteran has a service-connected noncompensable dental condition or disability resulting from combat wounds or service trauma, he or she is eligible for needed care for the service-connected condition;

7. If the veteran has a dental condition clinically determined by the VA to be currently aggravating a service-connected medical condition, he or she is eligible for dental care to resolve the problem;

8. If the veteran is receiving outpatient care or scheduled for inpatient care and requires dental care for a condition complicating a medical condition currently under treatment, he or she is eligible for dental care to resolve the problem; and

9. Certain veterans enrolled in a VA Homeless Program for 60 consecutive days or more may receive certain medically necessary outpatient dental services.

Domiciliary Care

Domiciliary care is a residential rehabilitation program that provides short-term rehabilitation and long-term health maintenance to veterans who require minimal medical care as they recover from medical, psychiatric or psychosocial problems. Most domiciliary patients return to the community after a period of rehabilitation.

The VA may provide domiciliary care to veterans whose annual income does not exceed the maximum annual Improved Disability VA Pension Rate, or to veterans who have been determined to have no adequate means of support.

Domiciliary care is provided by VA and state homes. The VA also provides a number of psychiatric residential rehabilitation programs, including ones for veterans coping with post-traumatic stress disorder and substance abuse, and compensated work therapy or transitional residences for homeless chronically mentally ill veterans and veterans recovering from substance abuse.

Emergency Care in Non-VA Facilities

Emergency care in non-VA facilities is provided as a safety net for veterans under specific conditions. A veteran is eligible if the non-VA emergency care is for a service-connected condition or, if enrolled, the veteran has been provided care by a VA clinician or provider within the past 24 months and has no other health care coverage.

In addition, it must be determined that the VA health care facilities were not feasibly available; that a delay in medical attention would have endangered the veteran's life or health, and that the veteran is personally liable for the cost of the services.

Extended Care

The VA provides institutional long term care to eligible veterans through VA Nursing Homes, Community Nursing Homes, State Veterans Homes, and Domiciliaries. For extended care services, veterans may be subject to a co-pay determined by information contained in the veteran's application for extended care.

Eyeglasses and Hearing Aids

A veteran is eligible for hearing aids and eyeglasses if he or she: (1) receives an increased pension for regular aid and attendance or being permanently housebound; (2) receives compensation for a service-connected disability; (3) is a former prisoner of war; and/or (4) received a Purple Heart medal.

Otherwise, hearing aids and eyeglasses will be provided only in special circumstances, and not for normally occurring hearing or vision loss.

Gulf War Illnesses

Gulf War veterans from Operations Desert Shield, Desert Storm, and Iraqi Freedom, are eligible for a complete physical exam under the Persian Gulf Registry program. Veterans with conditions recognized by the VA as associated with Gulf War service are eligible for priority enrollment.

Home Health Services

Skilled home care is provided by the VA or through contract agencies to veterans that are homebound with chronic diseases. Available home health services include nursing, physical/occupational therapy, and social services.

Home Improvement and Structural Alterations (HISA)

The VA provides grants to assist in making certain home improvements or structural alterations that are medically necessary.

Homeless Programs

The VA offers special programs and initiatives specifically designed to help homeless veterans live as independently as possible.

Ionizing Radiation Exposure Treatment and Registry Examination

The VA offers Ionizing Radiation Registry Examinations at no charge to any veteran who participated in a radiation risk activity. In addition, veterans with certain conditions recognized by the VA as associated with radiation exposure are eligible for priority enrollment.

Maternity Care

The VA will provide maternity care including labor and delivery to female veterans, but is unable to provide care to the child after birth.

Military Sexual Trauma Counseling

The VA provides counseling and treatment to help male and female veterans overcome psychological trauma resulting from sexual trauma while serving on active duty. Veterans will receive care at no charge for conditions related to military sexual trauma.

Non-VA Health Care Services

The VA may authorize veterans to receive care at a non-VA health care facility when the needed services are not available at the VA health care facility, or when the veteran is unable to travel the distance to the VA health care facility. Non-VA care must be authorized by the VA in advance. Veterans may also obtain services not covered in the benefits package through private health care providers at their own expense.

Nose/Throat Radium Treatment

Veterans who served as an aviator in the active military, naval, or air service before the end of the Korean conflict, or received submarine training in active naval service before January 1, 1965, may have received nasopharyngeal radium treatment (NPR) while in the military. Some veterans who received this treatment may have head and/or neck cancer that may be related to the exposure. These veterans are provided care for this condition at no cost.

Nursing Home Care

The VA's nursing home programs include VA-operated nursing home care units, contract community nursing homes and state homes. More than 90% of the VA's medical centers provide home and community based outpatient long-term care programs. Veterans eligible for VA nursing home care include:

1. Any veteran who has a service-connected disability rating of 70% or more;

2. A veteran who is rated 60% service-connected and is unemployable or has an official rating of "permanent and total disabled;"

3. A veteran with combined disability ratings of 70% or more;

4. A veteran whose service-connected disability is clinically determined to require nursing home care;

5. Nonservice-connected veterans and those officially referred to as "zero percent, noncompensable, service-connected" veterans who require nursing home care for any nonservice-connected disability and who meet income and asset criteria; or

6. If space and resources are available, other veterans on a case-by-case basis with priority given to service-connected veterans and those who need care for post-acute rehabilitation, respite, hospice, geriatric evaluation and management, or spinal cord injury.

Project 112/SHAD Participants

Project 112 is the name of the overall program for both shipboard and land-based biological and chemical testing that was conducted by the United States military between 1962 and 1973. Project SHAD was the shipboard portion of these tests, which were conducted to determine: (1) the effectiveness of shipboard detection of chemical and biological warfare agents; (2) the effectiveness of protective measures against these agents; and (3) the potential risk to American forces posed by these weapons.

The VA provides a physical examination to veterans who participated in SHAD. Veterans with conditions recognized by the VA as associated with Project SHAD are eligible for priority enrollment. Veterans receive care at no charge for conditions related to exposure.

Veterans may call the SHAD Helpline (800-749-8387) or send an e-mail to the VA (SHADHELPLINE@vba.va.gov/) for information on obtaining a medical evaluation or filing a claim for disability benefits related to exposure.

Prosthetic Aids

Enrolled veterans receiving VA care for any condition may receive medically necessary VA prosthetic appliances, equipment and devices, such as artificial limbs, orthopedic braces and shoes, wheelchairs, crutches and canes, and other durable medical equipment and supplies. Certain veterans who are not enrolled are also eligible for prosthetic items including: (1) veterans needing prosthetic items for a service-connected disability; and (2) veterans with a service-connected disability rated 50% or more.

Readjustment Counseling

Veterans who served on active duty in a war or conflict may apply for counseling to assist in readjusting to civilian life. Counseling is provided at Vet Centers.

Women Veterans Services

Women veterans are eligible for the same medical benefit package as all veterans. In addition, the Women's Program provides women's gender-specific health care such as: (1) hormone replacement therapy; (2) breast care; (3) gynecological care; (4) maternity care; and (5) limited infertility treatment, excluding in-vitro fertilization.

The Sexual Trauma Treatment Center is also affiliated with the Women's Clinic, providing treatment for the psychological effects of sexual trauma.

CO-PAYS AND CHARGES

There is no monthly premium required to use VA health care, however, a veteran may have to agree to pay co-pays. Along with their enrollment confirmation and priority group assignment, enrollees will receive information regarding their co-pay requirements, if applicable.

Means Test

While many veterans qualify for cost-free health care services based on a compensable service-connected condition or other qualifying factor, most veterans are required to complete an annual financial assessment or means test to determine if they qualify for cost-free services. From the amounts reported on the Financial Worksheet, the VA will calculate and inform the veteran of his or her income-based benefits.

Certain nonservice-connected veterans and 0% noncompensable service-connected veterans are asked to report gross household income and net worth from the previous calendar year. Current year income and net worth can be considered when there is a hardship.

Veterans whose gross household income and net worth exceed the established threshold, as well as those who choose not to complete the financial assessment, must agree to pay the required co-pays to become eligible for VA health care services.

New veterans who apply for enrollment after January 16, 2003, and who decline to provide income information, are not eligible for enrollment.

Income Verification

The VA verifies the veteran's gross household income by matching the financial data provided with financial records maintained by the IRS and SSA. If the matching process reveals that the veteran's gross household income is higher than the threshold, he or she will be provided an opportunity to review the IRS and SSA data and provide additional information regarding the difference.

At the end of the income verification process, if it is determined that the veteran's gross household income is higher than the threshold: (1) his or her priority group assignment will be changed; he or she will be required to pay co-pay; (2) the facilities that provided the veteran's care will be notified to bill the veteran for services provided during the period covered by his or her income assessment; and (3) the veteran will be provided with his or her due process and appeal rights.

Private Health Care Insurance

All veterans applying for VA medical care are required to provide information on their health insurance coverage, including coverage provided under policies of their spouses. Veterans are not responsible for paying any remaining balance of the VA's insurance claim not paid or covered by their health insurance, and any payment received by the VA may be used to offset "dollar for dollar" a veteran's VA co-pay responsibility.

Exempt Services

Some of the services exempt from inpatient and outpatient co-pays include:

1. Special registry examinations offered by VA to evaluate possible health risks associated with military service;

2. Counseling and care for military sexual trauma;

3. Compensation and pension examination requested by VBA;

4. Care that is part of a VA-approved research project;

5. Care related to a VA-rated service connected disability;

6. Readjustment counseling and related mental health services for (PTSD);

7. Emergency treatment at other than VA facilities;

8. Care for cancer of head or neck caused from nose or throat radium treatments given while in the military;

9. Publicly announced VA public health initiatives i.e. health fairs;

10. Care related to service for veterans who served in combat or against a hostile force during a period of hostilities after November 11, 1998;

11. Laboratory services such as flat film radiology services and electrocardiograms;

12. Preventive screenings, e.g., hypertension, hepatitis C, tobacco, alcohol, colorectal cancer, etc.; and

13. Immunizations, e.g., such as influenza and pneumococcal.

Co-pay Waivers and Alternatives

If a veteran cannot afford to pay the co-pays, there are three options he or she may pursue:

1. Request a waiver of the co-pays you currently owe. To request a waiver, you must submit proof that you cannot financially afford to make payments to the VA. Contact the Revenue Coordinator at the VA health care facility where you receive care for more information.

2. Request a hardship determination. Current financial information must be submitted and a decision will be made based on the information provided. Contact the Enrollment Coordinator at the local VA for more information.

3. Request a compromise. A compromise is an offer and acceptance of a partial payment in settlement and full satisfaction of the debt as it exists at the time the offer is made. Most compromise offers that are accepted must be for a lump sum payment payable in full 30 days from the date of acceptance of the offer. Contact the Enrollment Coordinator at the local VA for more information.

VETERANS INDENTIFICATION CARD

The VA provides a Veterans Identification Card (VIC) to eligible veterans for use at VA health care facilities. Once the veteran's eligibility for VA medical benefits is verified and he or she has a picture taken at the local VA medical facility, the card will be mailed within 5 to 7 days.

The VIC does not contain any sensitive, identifying information such as a social security number or date of birth on the face of the card. The VIC displays the following special eligibility indicators: Service Connected, Purple Heart, and Former POW.

The VIC cannot be used as a credit or an insurance card and it does not authorize or pay for care at non-VA facilities.

If a VIC is lost, the VA should be contacted and a new card requested.

MY HEALTHEVET PROGRAM

In 2004, the VA launched a Web site that allows registered veterans to access health and benefits information, reorder prescriptions, view appointments and maintain health records. The online prescription refill service is one of the most popular additions to the Web site. The prescription refill service filled over 1.5 million prescriptions online in its first year.

As set forth below, the Personal Health Journal section of the Web site allows veterans to use self-assessment tools, such as medical events, military health history, and tracking information, to help manage their medical wellbeing. The Web site also provides health information, and links to Federal and VA health benefits and resources.

In the future, veterans who register with the Web site will be able to view appointments, co-pay balances, and key portions of their medical records online.

The Personal Health Journal

The Personal Health Journal provides many features for managing and tracking one's personal health information.

Personal Information

The Personal Health Journal helps the veteran keep track of personal information, such as contact information, emergency contacts, health care providers, treatment locations, and health insurance information.

Wallet ID Card

The wallet ID Card allows the veteran to print personal information on a handy pre-formatted wallet card for easy reference.

Military Health History

The veteran can record important events from their military service, including exposures he or she may have experienced and assignments related to the veteran's health history.

Medications

The veteran can record the name, starting and ending date, prescription number, and dosage of his or her prescription medications as well as any over-the-counter drugs, and/or herbals and supplements he or she may be using.

Allergies

The veteran can keep track of his or her allergies by logging the date, severity, reaction, diagnosis and any comments.

Tests

The veteran can keep track of any tests taken by logging the test name, date of test, location where the test was performed, the provider's name, results, and any comments.

Medical Events

The veteran can keep track of illnesses, accidents or other events by logging their date, treatment prescribed, or comments regarding the medical event.

Health eLogs

The veteran can track his or her health readings including blood pressure, blood sugar, cholesterol, body temperature, body weight, heart rate, and pain levels.

MEDICAL BENEFITS FOR FAMILY MEMBERS

The VA offers limited medical benefits for family members of eligible veterans. These include the following programs:

Civilian Health and Medical Program of VA (CHAMPVA)

The Civilian Health and Medical Program of VA (CHAMPVA) program provides reimbursement for most medical expenses of eligible family members. The CHAMPVA In-house Treatment Initiative (CITI) is a voluntary program that allows for the treatment of CHAMPVA beneficiaries at VA medical centers.

CHAMPVA is managed by the VA's Health Administration Center (800-733-8387), and representatives can be reached Monday through Friday from 8:05 AM to 7:30 PM ET.

Eligibility

To be eligible for CHAMPVA, an individual cannot be eligible for TRICARE/CHAMPUS and must be in one of the following categories:

1. The spouse or child of a veteran who has been rated permanently and totally disabled for a service-connected disability by a VA regional office, or

2. The surviving spouse or child of a veteran who died from a VA-rated service connected disability, or

3. The surviving spouse or child of a veteran who was, at the time of death, rated permanently and totally disabled from a service connected disability, or

4. The surviving spouse or child of a military member who died in the line of duty, not due to misconduct; however, in most of these cases, these family members are eligible for TRICARE, not CHAMPVA.

Benefits

In general, the CHAMPVA program covers most health care services and supplies that are medically and psychologically necessary. Upon confirmation of eligibility, the applicant will receive program materials that specifically address covered and non-covered services and supplies.

General Exclusions

Like all health programs there are certain services and supplies that are not covered by the CHAMPVA, including:

1. Services and supplies obtained as part of a grant, study, or research program.

2. Services and supplies not provided in accordance with accepted professional medical standards or related to experimental/investigational or unproven procedures or treatment regimens.

3. Care for which the beneficiary is not obligated to pay, such as services obtained at a health fair.

4. Care provided outside the scope of the provider's license or certification.

5. Services or supplies above the appropriate level required to provide the necessary medical care.

6. Services by providers suspended or sanctioned by any federal agency.

7. Services provided by a member of the beneficiary's immediate family or person living in his or her household.

Medicare Impact

CHAMPVA is always the secondary payer to Medicare. If an applicant is eligible for CHAMPVA, under age 65 and enrolled in both Medicare Parts A and B, SSA documentation of enrollment in both Parts A and B is required.

For benefits to be extended past age 65, the applicant must meet the following conditions:

1. If the beneficiary was 65 or older prior to June 5, 2001, and was otherwise eligible for CHAMPVA, and was entitled to Medicare Part A coverage, then the beneficiary will be eligible for CHAMPVA without having to have Medicare Part B coverage.

2. If the beneficiary turned 65 on/or before June 5, 2001, and has Medicare Parts A and B, he or she must keep both Parts to be eligible.

3. If the beneficiary turned 65 on or after June 5, 2001, he or she must be enrolled in Medicare Parts A and B to be eligible.

4. The beneficiary is not required to enroll in Medicare Part D in order to become or remain CHAMPVA eligible.

New and Expectant Parents

If the beneficiary is expecting a baby and needs to establish CHAMPVA eligibility for his or her new child, the following must be accomplished before submitting an application:

1. The beneficiary must obtain a social security number for the newborn by applying to the nearest Social Security Administration office.

2. The beneficiary must establish dependency of the newborn to the veteran sponsor by contacting the local VA regional office.

Remarried Widows/Widowers

Eligibility for CHAMPVA ends at midnight on the date of a beneficiary's remarriage if he or she remarries prior to age 55. If the beneficiary remarries on or after their 55th birthday, The Veterans Benefit Act of 2002 (Public Law 107-330) allows the beneficiary to keep his or her CHAMPVA benefits.

If the widow or widower of a qualifying sponsor remarries, and the remarriage is later terminated by death, divorce, or annulment, he or she may reestablish CHAMPVA eligibility. The beginning date of re-eligibility is the first day of the month after termination of the remarriage, or December 1, 1999, whichever date is later. To reestablish CHAMPVA eligibility, copies of the marriage certificate and death, divorce, or annulment documents, as appropriate, must be provided.

Spina Bifida Program

Children of Vietnam Veterans born with spina bifida may be eligible for specific benefits through the VA health care system.

Children of Women Vietnam Veterans Program

Biological children of women veterans who served in Vietnam during the period beginning February 28, 1961 and ending May 7, 1975 may be eligible for monetary allowances if their birth defects are associated with the mother's service in Vietnam and resulted in permanent physical or mental disability.

TRICARE

TRICARE is a health plan available to eligible military families. TRICARE was formerly known as CHAMPUS. The term TRICARE stands for the triple option benefit plan available for military families, as follows:

1. TRICARE Prime—Voluntary HMO option;

2. TRICARE Extra—PPO option. There is no enrollment or annual fees and discount cost-sharing rates; and

3. TRICARE Standard—Fee-for-service option with its normal cost-share.

Certain VA medical centers provide services to eligible TRICARE family members. TRICARE beneficiaries who utilize a participating VA medical center receive a reduced co-pay rate. However, these services may be limited and provided only on a space available basis.

TRICARE is a military health care program serving active duty service members, National Guard and Reserve members, retirees, their families, survivors and certain former spouses worldwide.

TRICARE offers several health plan options to meet the needs of its beneficiary population. Additionally, TRICARE offers two dental plans and several additional special programs. As a uniformed services member or family member, an individual is entitled to TRICARE benefits but must take specific steps to make sure he or she is eligible.

Eligible Persons

TRICARE is available to active duty service members and retirees of the seven uniformed services, their family members, survivors and others who are registered in the Defense Enrollment Eligibility Reporting System (DEERS). DEERS is a worldwide, computerized database of uniformed services members (sponsors), their family members, and others who are eligible for military benefits, including TRICARE.

All sponsors are automatically registered in DEERS. However, the sponsor must register eligible family members. Proper registration in the system is key to receiving timely and effective TRICARE benefits.

The uniformed services include the Army, Air Force, Navy, Marines, Coast Guard, Commissioned Corps of the Public Health Service, and the Commissioned Corps of the National Oceanic and Atmospheric Association.

TRICARE is also available to members of the National Guard and Reserves and their families. Benefits will vary depending on the sponsor's military status. The National Guard and Reserves include the Army National Guard, Army Reserve, Navy Reserve, Marine Corps Reserve, Air National Guard, Air Force Reserve, and Coast Guard Reserve.

Persons Not Eligible

The following persons are not eligible for TRICARE:

1. Persons not enrolled in DEERS, although one may be able to register retroactively.

2. Persons entitled to Medicare Part A who do not have Medicare Part B coverage, except for: (a) family members of active duty service members because Medicare Part B is not required until the sponsor retires; and (b) beneficiaries enrolled in the U.S. Family Health Plan because Medicare Part B is not required for U.S. Family Health Plan enrollment.

3. Dependent parents and parents-in-law; however, they may be able to obtain care at a military treatment facility (MTF) if there is space available.

4. Persons who are eligible for benefits under the Civilian Health and Medical Program of the Department of Veterans Affairs (CHAMPVA).

CHAPTER 4:
VETERANS GROUP LIFE INSURANCE

IN GENERAL

The VA operates one of the largest life insurance programs in the world, and directly administers six life insurance programs. In addition, the VA supervises the Servicemembers' Group Life Insurance and the Veterans' Group Life Insurance programs. These programs provide $1.1 trillion in insurance coverage to 4.1 million veterans, active-duty members, reservists and Guardsmembers, plus 3.1 million spouses and children. The average basic insurance amount is $240,000.

The Traumatic Injury Protection program under Servicemembers' Group Life Insurance provides coverage to active-duty personnel who sustain traumatic brain injuries that result in severe losses. Benefit amounts range from $25,000 to $100,000, depending on the loss. This program covers 2.3 million members.

In 2006, the VA life insurance programs returned $422 million in dividends to 1.2 million veterans holding some of these VA life insurance policies, and paid an additional $1.1 billion in death claims. There were approximately 1.7 million life VA veteran life insurance beneficiaries as of September 30, 2007.

In 2008, the VA expects to pay 1.2 million veterans insurance policy holders $369 million in dividends. The VA will also pay $2.5 billion in life insurance beneficiary claims to 105,000 survivors of veterans and service members.

SERVICEMEMBERS' GROUP LIFE INSURANCE

Servicemembers' Group Life Insurance (SGLI) is a program of low cost group life insurance for service members on active duty, ready reservists, members of the National Guard, members of the Commissioned Corps of the National Oceanic and Atmospheric Administration and the

Public Health Service, cadets and midshipmen of the four service academies, and members of the Reserve Officer Training Corps.

As set forth below, service members with SGLI coverage have two options available to them upon release from service. Service members can: (1) convert their full-time SGLI coverage to term insurance under the Veterans' Group Life Insurance (VGLI) program; or (2) convert to a permanent plan of insurance with one of the participating commercial insurance companies.

ELIGIBILITY FOR VETERANS GROUP LIFE INSURANCE

A veteran is eligible for VGLI if the veteran is:

1. An SGLI insured service member who is being released from active duty or active duty for training under a call or order to duty that does not specify a period of less than 31 days;

2. A service member of the Ready Reserves insured under SGLI who is being separated or released from drilling assignment;

3. A service member assigned to the Individual Ready Reserve (IRR) or to the Inactive National Guard (ING) of a branch of service;

4. A service member of the Public Health Service (PHS) or Inactive Reserve Corps (IRC); or

5. A service member who had part-time SGLI and who, while performing duty or traveling directly to or from duty, suffered an injury or disability that rendered the member uninsurable at standard premium rates.

AMOUNT OF COVERAGE

VGLI coverage is issued in multiples of $10,000 up to a maximum of $400,000 of group term life insurance for veterans. However, a veteran's VGLI coverage cannot exceed the amount of SGLI coverage they had in force at the time of separation from service.

VGLI provides for life insurance only and does not provide for disability or other supplementary benefits. VGLI has no cash, loan, paid-up or extended insurance values and does not pay dividends.

PERIOD OF COVERAGE

VGLI coverage begins on the 121st day following the veteran's separation from service. If the veteran receives an extension of SGLI for 2 years due to disability, VGLI coverage begins on the day following the end of the 2-year period.

If a veteran applies for VGLI coverage after the 120-day period, his or her VGLI coverage will begin on the date the VGLI application, premium and proof of good health are received by OSGLI.

A veteran can keep VGLI coverage for life, as long as he or she continues to pay the applicable premiums.

PREMIUM PAYMENTS

VGLI premiums are based upon the separating member's age. There are several age brackets of premium rates. As of July 1, 2008, VGLI premium rates were reduced for veterans ages 30 to 64, the group that comprises 85% of those insured under the program.

Premium payments are made directly to OSGLI as follows:

1. By check or money order;

2. By allotment from military retirement pay;

3. By automatic deduction from VA Disability Compensation Benefits; or

4. By debit or credit card on the Internet, or using the OSGLI toll-free telephone number.

The first premium must be sent with the VGLI application directly to OSGLI, even if the veteran chooses to pay by allotment or by automatic deduction. After the application has been approved, subsequent premiums are due monthly beginning the month after the insurance becomes effective.

If the veteran chooses to pay premiums directly, he or she will receive premium statements either monthly, quarterly, semi-annually or annually. If the veteran chooses to pay his or her premiums on a basis other than monthly, he or she will receive a discount.

If payments are not made by the due date, or within a 60-day grace period, the VGLI coverage will lapse. If VGLI coverage lapses, a notification of the lapse and a reinstatement form will be sent, and the veteran has 5 years from the date of the unpaid premium to reinstate VGLI coverage.

If the veteran applies for reinstatement within 6 months of the lapse, he or she will only need to provide evidence that he or she is in the same state of health on the date of reinstatement as the date of lapse. Otherwise, the veteran will need to provide proof of good health.

CONVERTING SGLI COVERAGE TO VGLI COVERAGE

Within approximately 45 to 60 days following the veteran's separation from service, he or she should receive an application for VGLI from OSGLI.

A veteran has one year and 120 days from his or her date of separation from service to apply for VGLI. After this, the veteran is no longer eligible for VGLI.

There are different criteria for applying within 120 days from the date of separation, or after 120 days from the date of separation, as set forth below.

Application Within 120 Days Following Separation

If the VGLI application is submitted within 120 days following separation from service:

1. The veteran does not need to provide proof of good health; and

2. The veteran must enclose the first month's premium with the application.

Application Between 120 Days and 1 Year and 120 Days Following Separation

If the VGLI application is submitted between 120 days after separation from service and one year and 120 days after separation from service:

1. The veteran needs to provide proof of good health. The application may be disapproved if the veteran is not in good health.

2. The veteran must enclose the first month's premium with his or her application.

To apply for VGLI, an eligible veteran must submit an *Application for Veterans' Group Life Insurance* (Form SGL 8714) to the OSGLI, along with the required premium.

A sample Application for Veterans' Group Life Insurance (Form SGL 8714) can be found in Appendix 12 of this Almanac.

ACCELERATED BENEFITS OPTION

The VGLI program offers an accelerated benefits option to terminally ill policyholders. An insured is considered to be terminally ill if he or she has a written medical prognosis of 9 months or less to live.

All terminally ill policyholders will be eligible to take up to 50% of their VGLI coverage in a lump sum. In addition, many commercial life insurance companies offer accelerated benefits in their policies. Accelerated benefits, paid prior to death, are not available for payment to survivors.

In order to obtain accelerated benefits under this provision, the policyholder must submit the *Servicemember/Veteran Accelerated Benefit Option Form* (Form SGL 8284) to the OSGLI.

POLICY BENEFICIARY

Designating a Beneficiary

A veteran who applies for VGLI coverage can name any person, firm, corporation, or legal entity as the beneficiary of the VGLI policy. To change the beneficiary, the veteran must complete, sign and submit a *Beneficiary Designation* (Form SGL 8721) to the OSGLI.

Death Claims

Upon the policyholder's death, the beneficiary files a claim for VGLI proceeds by submitting a *Claim for Death Benefits* (Form SGL 8283) to the OSGLI. The beneficiary should include a copy of the death certificate with the claim form.

The proceeds are paid to the beneficiary either in one lump sum or in 36 equal installments, according to how the policyholder specified that the payments were to be paid. If the insured specified that the proceeds were to be paid in one lump sum, or did not specify a method of payment, the beneficiary may choose to receive either 36 equal installments or one lump sum. However, if the insured specified that the proceeds were to be paid in 36 equal installments, the beneficiary may not choose to be paid in one lump sum.

A beneficiary may not assign or transfer VGLI proceeds to another person. In addition, VGLI proceeds are not subject to claims of creditors of the insured or creditors of the beneficiary.

Further, VGLI proceeds are exempt from taxation. Any installment interest or delayed settlement interest that a beneficiary receives in addition to the proceeds is also exempt from taxation and does not need to be reported to the Internal Revenue Service.

Alliance Accounts

An Alliance Account is an interest bearing draft account with an account book similar to a checking account. An Alliance account is opened for VGLI beneficiaries. Insurance proceeds are deposited in the beneficiary's name and the beneficiary can write drafts for any amount up to the full amount of the proceeds. The Alliance Account is designed to give the beneficiary time to make important financial decisions, while their funds are secure and earn continuous interest.

Beneficiary Financial Counseling Services

The Beneficiary Financial Counseling Services (BFCS) is an extra benefit offered to beneficiaries of VGLI policies. As a beneficiary, one can take advantage of free professional financial advice through this program.

CONVERTING VGLI COVERAGE TO COMMERCIAL LIFE INSURANCE

VGLI policyholders can convert their VGLI coverage to an individual commercial life insurance policy at any time. In order to convert VGLI coverage, the policyholder must:

1. Select a company from the Participating Companies listing;

2. Apply to a local sales office of the company selected;

3. Obtain a letter—known as a VGLI Conversion Notice—from the Office of Servicemembers' Group Life Insurance (OSGLI) verifying coverage; and

4. Give a copy of the VGLI Conversion Notice to the agent who takes the application.

A List of VGLI Participating Insurance Companies can be found in Appendix 13 of this Almanac.

VGLLI policyholders may convert their coverage to a commercial policy at standard premium rates, without having to provide proof of good health. The conversion policy must be a permanent policy, such as a whole life policy.

Other types of policies, such as term, variable life, or universal life insurance are not allowed as conversion policies. In addition, supplementary policy benefits such as accidental death and dismemberment, or waiver of premium for disability, are not considered part of the conversion policy.

THE OFFICE OF SERVICEMEMBERS' GROUP LIFE INSURANCE

Questions about Veterans' Group Life Insurance should be directed to the Office of Servicemembers' Group Life Insurance (OSGLI) as follows:

Toll-free telephone: 1-800-419-1473

Toll-free fax numbers:

1. Death and accelerated benefits claims only: 1-877-832-4943

2. All other fax inquiries: 1-800-236-6142

E-mail:

1. Death and accelerated benefits claims only: osgli.claims@prudential.com

2. All other inquiries: osgli@prudential.com

General Correspondence:

Office of Servicemembers' Group Life Insurance
80 Livingston Avenue
Roseland, New Jersey 07068-1733

New VGLI Applications and VGLI Reinstatements:

OSGLI
P.O. Box 41618
Philadelphia, PA 19176-9913

CHAPTER 5:
EDUCATION AND VOCATIONAL
REHABILITATION BENEFITS

IN GENERAL

Since 1944, when the first GI Bill began, more than 21.8 million veterans, service members and family members have received $75.6 billion in GI Bill benefits for education and training. The number of GI Bill recipients includes 7.8 million veterans from World War II, 2.4 million from the Korean War and 8.2 million post-Korean and Vietnam era veterans, plus active duty personnel.

Since the dependents program was enacted in 1956, the VA has also assisted in the education of more than 775,000 dependents of veterans whose deaths or total disabilities were service-connected.

The Veterans' Educational Assistance Program (VEAP) was established in 1977. Since the Vietnam era, there have been approximately 2.7 million veterans, service members, reservists and National Guardsmen who have participated in the VEAP.

In 2006, the VA helped pay for the education or training of 331,557 veterans and active-duty personnel, 89,852 reservists and National Guardsmen and 75,460 survivors. As of fiscal year 2007, there were 523,344 education beneficiaries. Twenty percent of those students were first time recipients of VA education benefits.

MONTGOMERY GI BILL—ACTIVE DUTY

The Montgomery GI Bill (MGIB) was established in 1985. The Montgomery GI Bill—Active Duty program provides up to 36 months of education benefits to eligible veterans for the following programs:

1. College

2. Technical or Vocational Courses

3. Correspondence Courses

4. Apprenticeship/Job Training

5. Flight Training

6. High-tech Training

7. Licensing & Certification Tests

8. Entrepreneurship Training

9. Certain Entrance Examinations

Eligibility

A veteran is eligible for MGIB benefits if he or she: (1) has an Honorable Discharge; (2) has a high school diploma or GED equivalency certificate, or in some cases 12 hours of college credit; and (3) meets the requirements of one of the categories listed below.

Category I—Requirements

1. The veteran entered active duty for the first time after June 30, 1985;

2. The veteran had his or her military pay reduced by $100 a month for first 12 months; and

3. The veteran continuously served for 3 years, or 2 years, if that is what the veteran first enlisted for; or 2 years, if the veteran entered the Selected Reserve within a year of leaving active duty and served 4 years (referred to as the "2 by 4" Program).

Category II—Requirements

1. The veteran entered active duty before January 1, 1977;

2. The veteran served at least 1 day between 10/19/84 and 6/30/85, and stayed on active duty through 6/30/88, (or 6/30/87, if the veteran entered the Selected Reserve within 1 year of leaving active duty and served 4 years); and

3. On 12/31/89, the veteran had entitlement left in a Vietnam Era Veterans Educational Assistance Program (VEAP) account.

Category III—Requirements

1. The veteran is not eligible for MGIB benefits under Category I or II;

2. The veteran was on active duty on 9/30/90 and (a) separated involuntarily after 2/2/91; or (b) involuntarily separated on or after 11/30/93; or (c) voluntarily separated under either the Voluntary

Separation Incentive (VSI) or Special Separation Benefit (SSB) program; and

3. Before separation, the veteran had military pay reduced by $1200.

Category IV—Requirements

1. The veteran was on active duty on 10/9/96, and had money remaining in a Vietnam Era Veterans Educational Assistance Program (VEAP) account on that date; and elected MGIB benefits by 10/9/97; or

2. The veteran entered full-time National Guard duty under Title 32, USC, between 7/1/85, and 11/28/89, and elected MGIB benefits during the period 10/9/96 through 7/8/97; and

3. The veteran had military pay reduced by $100 a month for 12 months or made a $1200 lump-sum contribution.

Amount of Benefits

The monthly benefit paid under this program is based on: (a) the type of training the veteran takes; (b) the veteran's length of service; (c) the veteran's category; and (d) if DOD put extra money in your MGIB Fund (called "kickers").

The veteran usually has 10 years to use their MGIB benefits. In some cases, the time limit may be shorter or longer depending on the circumstances.

Buy-up Program

Some service members may contribute up to an additional $600 to the MGIB benefits to receive increased monthly benefits. For an additional $600 contribution, the veteran may receive up to $5400 in additional MGIB benefits. However, the additional contribution must be made while on active duty.

Application Process

In order to apply for MGIB benefits, the veteran must submit an *Application for Education Benefits* (VA Form 22-1990).

Additional information about the MGIB benefits program may be obtained by calling the following toll-free telephone number: 1-888-GI-BILL-1.

A sample Application for Education Benefits (VA Form 22-1990) can be found in Appendix 14 of this Almanac.

MONTGOMERY GI BILL—SELECTED RESERVE

The Montgomery GI Bill—Selected Reserve (MGIB-SR) program provides up to 36 months of education benefits to members of the Selected Reserve.

The Selected Reserve includes: (1) Army Reserve; (2) Navy Reserve; (3) Air Force Reserve; (4) Marine Corps Reserve; (5) Coast Guard Reserve; (6) Army National Guard; and (7) Air National Guard.

This education assistance program may be used for the following programs:

1. Degree programs

2. Certificate and correspondence courses

3. Cooperative training

4. Independent study programs

5. Apprenticeship and on-the-job training programs

6. Vocational flight training programs.

7. Remedial, refresher and deficiency training are available under certain circumstances.

Eligibility

Eligibility for this program is determined by the Selected Reserve components. The Veterans Administration (VA) makes the payments under this program. To qualify, the service member must meet the following requirements:

1. The service member must have a six-year obligation to serve in the Selected Reserve signed after June 30, 1985. If the service member is an officer, he or she must have agreed to serve six years in addition to the original obligation. For some types of training, it is necessary to have a six-year commitment that begins after September 30, 1990;

2. The service member must complete his or her initial active duty for training (IADT);

3. The service member must meet the requirements to receive a high school diploma or GED equivalency certificate before completing IADT, and may not use 12 hours toward a college degree to meet this requirement; and

4. The service member must remain in good standing while serving in an active Selected Reserve unit.

If the service member's Reserve or National Guard unit was deactivated during the period October 1, 1991 through September 30, 1995, or he or she was involuntarily separated—e.g., due to a reduction in force—from Reserve or National Guard service during this same period, the service member retains eligibility for MGIB-SR benefits for the full 14 year eligibility period.

The service member also retains MGIB-SR eligibility if he or she is discharged from Selected Reserve service due to a disability that was not caused by misconduct.

If the service member's eligibility to this program began on or after October 1, 1992, his or her period of eligibility ends 14 years from the beginning date of eligibility, or on the day the service member leaves the Selected Reserve.

If the service member's eligibility to this program began prior to October 1, 1992, his or her period of eligibility ends 10 years from the beginning date of eligibility, or on the day the service member leaves the Selected Reserve.

The service member's benefit entitlement ends 14 years from the date of his or her eligibility for the program, or on the day the service member leaves the Selected Reserve.

One exception to the above rules exists if the service member is mobilized or recalled to active duty from his or her reserve status. If this occurs, the service member's eligibility may be extended for the amount of time he or she is mobilized plus four months. Therefore, even if the service member leaves the reserves after mobilization, he or she may have additional eligibility under the MGIB-SR program.

Application Process

The service member's unit will give the service member a *Notice of Basic Eligibility* (DD Form 2384-1) when he or she becomes eligible for the program. The unit will also code the service member's eligibility into the Department of Defense personnel system so that the VA may verify his or her eligibility.

The service member should make sure that his or her selected program is approved for VA training.

In order to apply for MGIB-SR benefits, the service member must submit an *Application for Education Benefits* (VA Form 22-1990) to the VA regional office with jurisdiction over the state where he or she will train.

If the service member has already started training, he or she should take the Application for Education Benefits and the Notice of Basic Eligibility to his or her school or employer, ask them to complete an *Enrollment Certification* (VA Form 22-1999), and have them send all three forms to the VA.

VA WORK-STUDY ALLOWANCE PROGRAM

A veteran who is a full-time or 3/4-time student in a college degree program, or a vocational or professional program, may be eligible for a VA work-study allowance.

Eligibility

The VA Work-Study Allowance Program is available to persons training under the following programs:

1. Montgomery GI Bill-Active Duty (MGIB) (38 U.S.C. Chapter 30);

2. Montgomery GI Bill-Selected Reserve (MGIB-SSR) (38 U.S.C. Chapter 1606);

3. REAP Participants;

4. Post-Vietnam Era Veteran's Educational Assistance Program (VEAP) (38 U.S.C. Chapter 32);

5. Dependents' Educational Assistance Program (38 U.S.C. Chapter 35); and

6. National Call to Service Participants.

The VA will select students for the work-study program based on different factors. Such factors include:

1. Disability of the student;

2. Ability of the student to complete the work-study contract before the end of his or her eligibility to education benefits;

3. Job availability within normal commuting distance to the student; and

4. High priority is given to a veteran who has a service-connected disability rated by the VA at 30% or more.

The number of applicants selected for the work-study program depends on the availability of VA-related work at the applicant's school or at VA facilities in the applicant's area.

Amount of Benefits

The student is eligible to earn an hourly wage equal to the federal minimum wage or the student's state minimum wage, whichever is greater. If the student is in a work-study program at a college or university, the school may pay the difference between the amount the VA pays and the amount the school normally pays other work-study students doing the same job.

The student may elect to be paid in advance for 40% of the number of hours in his or her work-study agreement, or for 50 hours, whichever is less. After the student has completed the hours covered by the first payment, the VA will pay the student each time he or she completes 50 hours of service.

He or she can arrange with the VA to work any number of hours during enrollment, however, the total number of hours worked cannot be more than 25 times the number of weeks in the student's enrollment period. The student may work during or between periods of enrollment.

Type of Work

Services performed under a VA work-study program must be related to VA work, and depends on the student's interests and the type of work available. Examples of VA-related work include:

1. Processing VA paperwork at school or at VA offices.

2. Performing outreach services under the supervision of a VA employee.

3. Performing services at VA medical facilities or the offices of the National Cemetery Administration.

Application Process

In order to apply for VA work-study allowance, the applicant must submit an *Application for Work-Study Allowance* (VA Form 22-8691) to the VA Regional Processing Office that handles the applicant's education claim.

Additional information about the VA Work-Study Allowance Program may be obtained by calling the following toll-free telephone number: 1-888-442-1455.

A sample Application for Work-Study Allowance (VA Form 22-8691) can be found in Appendix 15 of this Almanac.

SURVIVORS' AND DEPENDENTS' EDUCATION ASSISTANCE PROGRAM (DEA)

Dependents' Educational Assistance provides education and training opportunities to eligible dependents of certain veterans. The program offers up to 45 months of education benefits.

This education assistance program may be used for the following programs:

1. Degree and certificate programs.

2. Apprenticeship and on-the-job training programs.

3. An eligible spouse may take a correspondence course.

4. Remedial, deficiency, and refresher courses may be approved under certain circumstances.

Eligibility

In order to be eligible for the program, the applicant must be the son, daughter, or spouse of:

1. A veteran who died or is permanently and totally disabled as the result of a service-connected disability that arises out of active service in the Armed Forces.

2. A veteran who died from any cause while such service-connected disability was in existence.

3. A service member missing in action or captured in the line of duty by a hostile force.

4. A service member forcibly detained or interned in the line of duty by a foreign government or power.

5. A service member who is hospitalized or receiving outpatient treatment for a service-connected permanent and total disability and is likely to be discharged for that disability.

Period of Eligibility

Son or Daughter

A son or daughter who wishes to receive benefits for attending school or job training must be between the ages of 18 and 26. In certain instances, it is possible to begin before age 18 and to continue after age 26.

Marriage is not a bar to this benefit. If the son or daughter is in the Armed Forces, he or she may not receive this benefit while on active duty. To pursue training after military service, his or her discharge must not be under dishonorable conditions.

The VA can extend the period of eligibility by the number of months and days equal to the time spent on active duty. This extension cannot generally go beyond one's 31st birthday, however, there are some exceptions.

Spouse

A spouse's benefits end 10 years from: (1) the date the VA determines the spouse is eligible; or (2) the date of death of the veteran.

For surviving spouses—i.e., spouses of service members who died on active duty—benefits end 20 years from the date of the service member's death.

Application Process

In order to apply for DEA benefits, the applicant must submit an *Application for Survivors' and Dependents' Educational Assistance* (VA Form 22-5490). A parent or guardian must sign the application on behalf of a son or daughter who is under legal age.

A sample Application for Survivors' and Dependents' Educational Assistance (VA Form 22-5490) can be found in Appendix 16 of this Almanac.

If a school or training establishment has already been chosen, the application should be sent to the VA Regional Processing Office in the region of the school's physical address. If a school or training establishment has not yet been chosen, the application should be sent to the VA Regional Processing Center in the region of the applicant's home address.

Eastern Region

The VA Regional Office for the Eastern Region includes Connecticut, Delaware, District of Columbia, Maine, Maryland, Massachusetts, New Hampshire, New Jersey, New York, Ohio, Pennsylvania, Rhode Island, Vermont, Virginia, West Virginia, and Foreign Schools. The address is as follows:

VA Regional Office—Eastern Region
P.O. Box 4616
Buffalo, New York 14240-4616

Central Region

The VA Regional Office for the Central Region includes Colorado, Iowa, Illinois, Indiana, Kansas, Kentucky, Michigan, Minnesota, Missouri,

Montana, Nebraska, North Dakota, South Dakota, Wisconsin, and Wyoming. The address is as follows:

VA Regional Office—Central Region
P.O. Box 66830
St. Louis, Missouri 63166-6830

Western Region

The VA Regional Office for the Western Region includes Alaska, Arkansas, Arizona, California, Hawaii, Idaho, Louisiana, New Mexico, Nevada, Oklahoma, Oregon, Philippines, Texas, Utah, Washington. The address is as follows:

VA Regional Office—Western Region
P.O. Box 8888
Muskogee, Oklahoma 74402-8888

Southern Region

The VA Regional Office for the Southern Region includes Alabama, Florida, Georgia, Mississippi, North Carolina, Puerto Rico, South Carolina, Tennessee, and the U.S. Virgin Islands. The address is as follows:

VA Regional Office—Southern Region
P.O. Box 100022
Decatur, Georgia 30031-7022

VOCATIONAL REHABILITATION

The VA's vocational rehabilitation program provides services to enable veterans with service-connected disabilities achieve maximum independence in daily living and, to the maximum extent feasible, obtain and maintain employment.

During fiscal years 1998 through 2006, 79,031 program participants achieved rehabilitation by obtaining and maintaining suitable employment. Additionally, during that same period, 15,548 participants achieved rehabilitation through maximum independence in daily living.

Vocational Rehabilitation and Employment Service

The mission of the VA Vocational Rehabilitation and Employment Service (VR&E) is to deliver timely and effective vocational rehabilitation services to veterans with service-connected disabilities. The goal is to help injured service members and veterans with disabilities transition from military service, through successful rehabilitation, to suitable employment.

Services provided by the VR&E program include:

1. Comprehensive rehabilitation evaluation to determine abilities, skills, interests, and needs;

2. Vocational counseling and rehabilitation planning;

3. Employment services such as job-seeking skills, resume development, and other work readiness assistance;

4. Assistance in finding and keeping a job, including the use of special employer incentives;

5. If needed, training such as On the Job Training (OJT), apprenticeships, and non-paid work experiences;

6. If needed, post-secondary training at a college, vocational, technical or business school;

7. Supportive rehabilitation services including case management, counseling, and referral; and

8. Independent living services.

Eligibility and Entitlement

To receive services, a veteran must be found both eligible and entitled. To receive an evaluation for VR&E services, a veteran must: (1) have received, or will receive, a discharge that is other than dishonorable; (2) have a service-connected disability rating of at least 10%; and (3) submit a completed application for VR&E services.

The basic period of eligibility in which VR&E services may be used is 12 years from the latter of: (1) the date of separation from active military service; or (2) the date the veteran was first notified by the VA of a service-connected disability rating.

After eligibility is established, the veteran is scheduled to meet with a Vocational Rehabilitation Counselor for a comprehensive evaluation to determine whether the veteran has an employment handicap and is entitled to services. The comprehensive evaluation includes:

1. An assessment of the veteran's interests, aptitudes, and abilities;

2. An assessment of whether service-connected disabilities impair the veteran's ability to find and/or hold a job using the occupational skills he or she has already developed; and

3. Vocational exploration and goal development.

Entitlement to services is established if: (1) the veteran is within his or her 12 year basic period of eligibility; (2) the veteran has a 20% or greater service-connected disability rating; and (3) it is determined that the veteran has an employment handicap.

If the service-connected disability rating is less than 20%, or if the veteran is beyond the 12-year basic period of eligibility, then a serious employment handicap must be found to establish entitlement to VR&E services.

Once the determination is made that the veteran is entitled to VR&E services, the veteran and Vocational Rehabilitation Counselor work together to identify the veteran's employment or independent living goal and develop an individualized rehabilitation plan to achieve the goal.

A rehabilitation plan is an individualized, written outline of the services, resources and criteria that will be used to achieve successful rehabilitation. It is an agreement that is signed by the veteran and the Vocational Rehabilitation Counselor, and is reviewed annually to determine whether any changes may be needed.

After the plan is developed and signed, the Vocational Rehabilitation Counselor (VRC) or a case manager will continue to work with the veteran to implement the plan to achieve suitable employment or independent living.

Vocational and Educational Counseling

Vocational Rehabilitation and Employment Service provides vocational-educational counseling to veterans and certain dependents. Individuals who are eligible for vocational-educational counseling include the following:

1. Transitioning service members who are within six months prior to discharge from active duty, or within one year following discharge from active duty;

2. Current beneficiaries of vocational-educational counseling assistance participating in certain G.I. Bill programs; and

3. Veterans and qualified dependents who are eligible for educational assistance under certain G.I. Bill programs.

The VR&E program can provide a wide range of vocational and educational counseling services to service members still on active duty, as well as veterans and dependents who are eligible for one of the VA's educational benefit programs. These services are designed to help an individual choose a vocational direction and determine the course needed to achieve the chosen goal.

A sample Application for Vocational-Educational Counseling (VA Form 28-8832) can be found in Appendix 17 of this Almanac.

Services for Disabled Children of Vietnam and Korean Veterans

In addition, the VR&E program also provides educational and vocational counseling benefits for eligible dependent children of Vietnam veterans born with certain birth defects, or children of Vietnam or Korean veterans born with spina bifida. In order to be eligible for the program, the child must be: (1) the biological child of a veteran who served in Vietnam or on the Korean demilitarized zone during certain periods in the 1960s or 1970s; and (2) conceived after the veteran served some time in one of those two places.

CHAPTER 6:
HOME FINANCING BENEFITS

IN GENERAL

From 1944, when the VA began helping veterans purchase homes under the original GI Bill, through December 2006, more than 18 million VA home loan guaranties have been issued, with a total value of $911 billion. The VA ended fiscal year 2006 with almost 2.3 million active home loans, reflecting amortized loans totaling $203.2 billion. In fiscal year 2006, the VA guaranteed 135,151 loans valued at $23.5 billion. Also during fiscal year 2006, the VA's programs for specially adapted housing helped 550 disabled veterans with grants totaling more than $24.6 million.

The VA guarantees an average of 11,109 loans a month for veterans, and currently guarantees 2.2 million active home loans to veterans, totaling $243 billion. Over half of the VA home loan guarantees went to first time home buyers. Approximately 90% of the loans use the "no down payment" feature that makes the VA loan guaranty so effective.

The VA Loan Guaranty Service is the organization within the Veterans Benefits Administration charged with the responsibility of administering the home loan program. The main purpose of the VA home loan program is to help veterans finance the purchase of homes with favorable loan terms and at a rate of interest which is usually lower than the rate charged on other types of mortgage loans.

FEATURES OF THE VA HOME LOAN

VA home loans offer the following important features:

1. The VA ensures that all veterans are given an equal opportunity to buy homes with VA assistance, without regard to their race, color, religion, sex, handicap, familial status, or national origin;

2. There is no down payment unless: (a) a down payment is required by the lender; (b) the purchase price is more than the reasonable value of the property as determined by the VA; or (c) the loan is made with graduated payment features;

3. The loan has a freely negotiable fixed interest rate competitive with conventional mortgage interest rates;

4. The buyer is informed of the estimated reasonable value of the property;

5. There are limitations on closing costs;

6. The mortgage is an assumable mortgage. For loans closed on or after March 1, 1988, the assumption must be approved in advance by the lender or VA;

7. There are long repayment terms;

8. There is the right to prepay without penalty;

9. For houses inspected by the VA during construction, the home buyer receives a warranty from the builder and VA assistance in trying to obtain the builder's cooperation in correcting any justified construction complaint; and

10. Forbearance is extended to VA homeowners experiencing temporary financial difficulty.

It is important to be aware that the VA guarantees the loan, not the condition of the property. The VA appraisal is not intended to be a home inspection. Therefore, the buyer is advised to hire a professional to inspect the property and make sure that any problems are addressed before buying the house.

APPLYING FOR A VA HOME LOAN

Requirements for VA Loan Approval

In order to obtain a VA loan, there are a number of requirements, as set forth below:

1. The applicant must be an eligible veteran who has available home loan entitlement;

2. The loan must be for an eligible purpose;

3. The purchase price should not exceed the appraised value of the house or the applicant will have to pay the difference;

4. The veteran must occupy the property as his or her home within a reasonable period of time after closing the loan;

5. The veteran must have enough income to meet the new mortgage payments on the loan, cover the costs of owning a home, take care of other obligations and expenses, and still have enough income left over for family support; and

6. The veteran must have a good credit record.

Application Process

In order to arrange for a veteran's guaranteed loan:

1. The veteran must find the property;

2. The veteran must go to a lender and submit the application for the loan;

3. The veteran must present his or her discharge or separation papers and/or a Certificate of Eligibility;

4. The property must be appraised and an estimate of the property's reasonable value must be determined; and

5. If the application is approved, the veteran is given the home loan.

Amount of the Loan

A veteran may generally borrow up to the reasonable value of the property or the purchase price, whichever is less, plus the funding fee, if required. There is no maximum VA loan amount, except that the loan cannot exceed the lesser of the appraised value or purchase price, plus the VA funding fee and energy efficient improvements, if applicable.

For certain refinancing loans, the maximum loan is limited to 90% of the value of the property, plus the funding fee, if required.

The VA loan must be repaid. If the veteran fails to make the payments as agreed, the lender can foreclose on the property and the veteran may lose their home. If the lender takes a loss, the VA must pay the guaranty to the lender.

Eligible Loan Purposes

VA home loans may be used for the following eligible purposes:

1. To buy a home.

2. To buy a townhouse or condominium unit in a project approved by the VA.

3. To build a home.

4. To repair, alter, or improve a home.

5. To simultaneously purchase and improve a home.

6. To improve a home through installment of a solar heating and/or cooling system or other energy efficient improvements.

7. To buy a manufactured home and/or lot.

8. To buy and improve a lot on which to place a manufactured home which you already own and occupy.

9. To refinance a manufactured home loan in order to acquire a lot.

Refinancing Loans

The following refinancing loans are available under the VA guaranteed home loan program:

1. The loan may be used to pay off the mortgage and/or other liens of record on the veteran's home. In most cases, the loan may not exceed 90% of the reasonable value of the property as determined by an appraisal, plus the funding fee, if required. The loan may include funds for any purpose which is acceptable to the lender, plus closing costs, including a reasonable number of discount points. A veteran must have available home loan entitlement. An existing loan on a manufactured home may not be refinanced with a VA-guaranteed loan except as set forth below

2. The loan may be used to refinance an existing VA loan to obtain a lower interest rate. Use of additional loan entitlement is not required. The loan amount is limited to the balance of the old loan plus the closing costs, discount points, funding fee, and up to $6,000 in energy efficient improvements. An existing VA loan on a manufactured home may be refinanced to obtain a lower interest rate.

Loan Repayment Terms

The maximum VA home loan term is 30 years and 32 days; however, the term may never be for more than the remaining economic life of the property as determined by the appraisal. In addition, the maturity on the VA loan may be extended to reduce the monthly payment, if necessary, as long as the extension provides for complete repayment of the loan within the maximum period permitted for the type of loan.

A veteran may partially or fully pay off a VA loan at any time, without penalty. However, partial payments may not be less than 1 monthly installment or $100, whichever is less.

If a veteran dies before the loan is paid off, the VA will not pay off the balance. The surviving spouse or other co-borrower must continue to make the payments. If there is no co-borrower, the loan becomes the obligation of the veteran's estate. Protection against this outcome may be obtained through mortgage life insurance, which must be purchased from private insurance sources.

The VA will guarantee home loans with the following repayment plans:

Traditional Fixed-Payment Mortgage

This type of mortgage loan calls for equal monthly payments for the life or term of the loan. Each monthly payment reduces a certain portion of the principal owed on the loan and pays interest accrued to date.

Graduated Payment Mortgage (GPM)

This repayment plan provides for smaller-than-normal monthly payments for the first few years, which gradually increase each year, and then level off after the end of the "graduation period" to larger-than-normal payments for the remaining term of the loan. The reduction in the monthly payment in the early years of the loan is accomplished by delaying a portion of the interest due on the loan each month and by adding that interest to the principal balance.

Buydowns

The builder of a new home or seller of an existing home may "buy down" the veteran's mortgage payments by making a large lump-sum payment up front at closing that will be used to supplement the monthly payments for a certain period.

Growing Equity Mortgage (GEM)

This repayment plan provides for a gradual annual increase in the monthly payments with all of the increase applied to the principal balance. The annual increases in the monthly payment may be fixed, or tied to an appropriate index. The increases to the monthly payment result in an early payoff of the loan in about 11 to 16 years for a typical 30-year mortgage.

Adjustable Rate Mortgages (ARM)

ARM loans are typically made at an initial interest rate lower than market rate; however, the interest rate can be adjusted up or down during the life of the loan. A one-year ARM allows for annual adjustments of no more than 1% and a lifetime cap of 5%. Hybrid ARM loans allow for an initial fixed rate for a period of at least 3 years, followed by annual adjustments. Depending on the length of the fixed rate period, the initial adjustment can be up to 2% and the lifetime cap is either 5% or 6%.

Down Payment Requirements

For the Traditional Fixed-Payment Mortgage, Buydown Loans, and Growing Equity Mortgage, the VA does not require a down payment if the purchase price or cost is not more than the reasonable value of the property as determined by the VA, although the lender may require a down payment. If the purchase price or cost is more than the reasonable value, the difference must be paid in cash from the veteran's own resources.

For the Graduated Payment Mortgage, the maximum loan amount may not be for more than the reasonable value of the property or the purchase price, whichever is less. Because the loan balance will be increasing during the first years of the loan, a down payment is required to keep the loan balance from going over the reasonable value or the purchase price.

Interest Rates

The interest rate on VA loans can be negotiated based on prevailing rates in the mortgage market. Once a loan is made, the interest rate set in the note will stay the same for the life of the loan. However, if interest rates go down, and you still own and occupy the property with a previously secured VA loan, you may apply for a new VA loan to refinance the previous loan at a lower interest rate without using any additional entitlement.

Closing Costs

The VA regulates the closing costs that a veteran may be charged in connection with closing a VA loan. No commission or brokerage fees may be charged; however, the veteran may pay reasonable closing costs to the lender in connection with a VA-guaranteed loan.

Although some additional costs are unique to certain localities, the closing costs may include: (1) the VA appraisal; (2) credit report; (3) survey; (4) title services; (5) recording fees; (6) a 1% loan origination fee; and (7) discount points. The closing costs and origination charge may not be included in the loan, except in VA refinancing loans.

In addition to negotiating the interest rate with the lender, veterans may negotiate the payment of discount points and other closing costs with the seller.

Funding Fee

Veterans must also pay a VA funding fee at the time of loan closing. The fee may be included in the loan and paid from loan proceeds. The fee is not required from veterans in receipt of service-connected compensation, or who would be but for receipt of military retired pay, or surviving spouses of veterans who died in service or from service-connected causes.

THE VA LOAN GUARANTY

The loans guaranteed by the VA are made by private lenders such as banks, savings and loan associations, or mortgage companies. The VA guaranty, which protects the lender against loss, encourages the lender to make a loan with terms favorable to the veteran.

The veteran applies for the loan with the lender. If the loan is approved, the VA guarantees the loan at the closing. The guaranty means the lender is protected against loss if the veteran fails to repay the loan

The amount of the VA guaranty is calculated as follows:

1. The VA will guarantee up to 50% of a home loan up to $45,000.

2. For loans between $45,000 and $144,000, the minimum guaranty amount is $22,500, with a maximum guaranty, of up to 40% of the loan up to $36,000, subject to the amount of entitlement a veteran has available.

3. For loans of more than $144,000 made for the purchase or construction of a home, or to purchase a residential unit in a condominium, or to refinance an existing VA-guaranteed loan for interest rate reduction, the maximum guaranty is the lesser of 25% or $104,250, which is 25% of the Freddie Mac conforming loan limit for a single family residence for 2007. This figure will change yearly.

SERVICE ELIGIBILITY

A veteran is eligible for a VA loan if his or her service falls within the following categories:

Wartime Service

Wartime service includes service during the following periods:

1. World War II (September 16, 1940 to July 25, 1947).

2. The Korean Conflict (June 27, 1950 to January 31, 1955).

3. The Vietnam Era (August 5, 1964 to May 7, 1975, or beginning February 28, 1961 for individuals who served in the Republic of Vietnam).

4. The Persian Gulf War (August 2, 1990 to present). Eligibility requires service for 2 years or the full period for which the veteran was called to active duty. The exceptions set forth below for service between September 7, 1980 and August 1, 1990 also apply except the veteran need only serve 90 days instead of the 181 days required.

In addition, the veteran must have served at least 90 days on active duty and been discharged or released under other than dishonorable conditions. If the veteran served less than 90 days, he or she may be eligible if discharged because of a service-connected disability.

Peacetime Service

Peacetime service includes service during the following periods:

1. July 26, 1947 to June 26, 1950.

2. February 1, 1955 to August 4, 1964; or

3. May 8, 1975 to September 7, 1980 (enlisted), or to October 16, 1981 (officer), the veteran must have served at least 181 days of continuous active duty and been discharged or released under conditions other than dishonorable. If the veteran served less than 181 days, he or she may be eligible if discharged because of a service-connected disability.

Service Between September 7, 1980 or October 16, 1981 and August 1, 1990

If the veteran's entire period of service was between September 7, 1980 (enlisted) or October 16, 1981 (officer) and August 1, 1990, the following apply:

1. The veteran must have completed 24 months of continuous active duty or the full period (at least 181 days) for which the veteran was called or ordered to active duty, and been discharged or released under conditions other than dishonorable.

2. The veteran may also be determined eligible if he or she: (a) was discharged for a service-connected disability; or (b) was discharged for the convenience of the Government after completing at least 20 months of a 2-year enlistment; or (c) completed 181 days of active duty and:

(i) the veteran was discharged because of a hardship; or

(ii) the veteran was determined to have a service-connected compensable disability; or

(iii) the veteran was discharged or released from active duty for a medical condition which preexisted service and has not been determined to be service-connected; or

(iv) the veteran received an involuntary discharge or release from active duty for the convenience of the Government as a result of a reduction in force; or

(v) the veteran was discharged or released from active duty for a physical or mental condition not characterized as a disability and not the result of misconduct, but which did interfere with the veteran's performance of duty.

Active Duty Service Personnel

If a service member is now on active duty, eligibility can be established after having served on continuous active duty for at least 90 days. Upon discharge or release from active duty, eligibility must be reestablished.

Members of the Selected Reserve

Individuals who are not otherwise eligible and who have completed at least 6 years in the Reserves or National Guard, or have been discharged because of a service-connected disability, are eligible for a loan if:

1. He or she has been discharged with an honorable discharge; or

2. He or she has been placed on the retired list; or

3. He or she has been transferred to an element of the Ready reserve other than the Selected Reserve; or

4. He or she continues to serve in the Selected Reserve.

Other Types of Service

Other types of service that satisfy eligibility for a home loan include:

1. Certain United States citizens who served in the armed forces of a government allied with the United States in World War II.

2. Unmarried surviving spouses of the above-described eligible persons who died as the result of service or service-connected injuries.

3. A surviving spouse who remarried on or after attaining age 57, and on or after December 16, 2003.

4. The spouse of any member of the Armed Forces serving on active duty who is listed as missing in action, or is a prisoner of war and has been so listed for a total of more than 90 days.

Individuals with service as members in certain other organizations, services, programs and schools may also be eligible. Questions about whether a certain service qualifies for home loan benefits should be referred to the VA Regional Loan Center.

CERTIFICATE OF ELIGIBILITY

If the VA determines that the applicant is eligible and qualified for a home loan, a Certificate of Eligibility will be issued. The loan applicant can request the Certificate of Eligibility from the VA, by completing a *Request for a Certificate of Eligibility* (VA Form 26-1880).

A sample Request for Certificate of Eligibility (VA Form 26-1880) can be found in Appendix 18 of this Almanac.

The form should be submitted along with either the originals or legible copies of the veteran's most recent discharge or separation papers which show active duty dates and type of discharge.

If the service member is still on active duty, and has not been previously discharged from active duty, he or she must submit a statement of service which includes the name of the issuing authority, and signed by or at the direction of an appropriate official. The statement must include the veteran's date of entry on active duty and the duration of any time lost.

The Request for Certificate of Eligibility should be mailed to:

The Winston-Salem Eligibility Center
P.O. Box 20729
Winston-Salem, NC 27120.

The Winston-Salem Eligibility Center also maintains a toll free number (888-244-6711) for persons seeking information on eligibility.

ENTITLEMENT

The present maximum entitlement is $36,000, or up to $89,912 for certain loans over $144,000. The entitlement of $36,000 may, however, be reduced if the veteran's entitlement has been used before to get a VA loan. The amount of remaining entitlement can be determined by subtracting the amount of entitlement used from the current maximum available entitlement of $36,000. Home loan entitlement does not expire.

If a veteran has used all or part of the entitlement, he or she can get that entitlement back to purchase another home if the following conditions for "restoration" are met:

1. The property has been sold and the loan has been paid in full.

2. A qualified veteran-transferee (buyer) must agree to assume the outstanding balance on the loan and agree to "substitute" his or her entitlement for the same amount of entitlement the veteran originally used to get the loan. However, the buyer must meet the occupancy, income, and credit requirements of the law.

3. For one time only, if the veteran has repaid the prior VA loan in full but has not yet disposed of the property securing that loan, the entitlement used in connection with that loan may be restored.

4. Any loss suffered by the VA as a result of guaranty of the loan must be repaid in full before the entitlement used on the loan can be restored.

Restoration of entitlement is not automatic. The veteran must apply for restoration by completing and returning the Request for Certificate of Eligibility, as set forth above.

CHAPTER 7:
DEPENDENT AND SURVIVOR BENEFITS

IN GENERAL

The Department of Veterans Affairs (VA) offers a wide range of benefits and services for the surviving spouse, dependent children and dependent parents of deceased veterans and military servicemembers.

In fiscal year 2006, approximately 533,000 spouses, children, and parents of deceased veterans received VA benefits. This total includes 156,320 survivors of Vietnam era veterans and 250,432 survivors of World War II veterans. In addition, there are three survivors of Civil War veterans, and approximately 200 children and widows of Spanish-American War veterans still receiving VA survivor benefits.

DEPENDENCY AND INDEMNITY COMPENSATION

Dependency and Indemnity Compensation (DIC) is a monthly benefit paid to eligible survivors of:

1. A military service member who died while on active duty;

2. A veteran whose death resulted from a service-related injury or disease; or

3. A veteran whose death resulted from a non service-related injury or disease, and who was receiving, or was entitled to receive VA Compensation for a service-connected disability that was rated as totally disabling:

(a) for at least 10 years immediately before death;

(b) since the veteran's release from active duty and for at least five years immediately preceding death; or

(c) for at least one year before death if the veteran was a former prisoner of war who died after September 30, 1999.

Eligibility

Surviving Spouse

The surviving spouse is eligible for DIC benefits if he or she:

1. Validly married the veteran before January 1, 1957;

2. Was married to a service member who died on active duty;

3. Married the veteran within 15 years of discharge from the period of military service in which the disease or injury that caused the veteran's death began or was aggravated;

4. Was married to the veteran for at least one year; or

5. Had a child with the veteran;

and the surviving spouse cohabited with the veteran continuously until the veteran's death or, if separated, was not at fault for the separation; and the surviving spouse is not currently married.

However, a surviving spouse who remarries on or after December 16, 2003, and on or after attaining age 57, is entitled to continue to receive DIC.

Surviving Child

The surviving child is eligible for DIC benefits if:

1. The child is not included on the surviving spouse's DIC;

2. The child is unmarried; and

3. The child is under age 18, or between the ages of 18 and 23 and attending school.

However, certain helpless adult children are entitled to DIC.

Surviving Parent

The surviving parent may be eligible for an income-based benefit.

Application Process

To apply for surviving spouse/child DIC benefits, an *Application for Dependency and Indemnity Compensation, Death Pension and Accrued Benefits by Surviving Spouse or Child* (VA Form 21-534) is generally completed by the Casualty Assistance Officer and submitted on behalf of the survivor. The form needs special processing and should be mailed or faxed, along with a Report of Casualty (DD Form 1300) to:

The Department of Veterans Affairs
Regional Office and Insurance Center

P.O. Box 8079
Philadelphia, PA 19101
Fax: (215) 381-3084.

To apply for surviving parents' DIC benefits, an application for benefits (VA Form 21-535) should be mailed to the VA regional office that serves the area where the parents reside.

Amount of Benefit

Presently, the basic monthly rate of DIC is $1,091 for an eligible surviving spouse. The rate is increased for each dependent child, and also if the surviving spouse is housebound or in need of aid and attendance, as discussed below. The VA also adds a transitional benefit of $250 to the surviving spouse's monthly DIC if there are children under age 18.

DEATH PENSION

A death pension is a needs-based benefit paid to an unremarried surviving spouse, or an unmarried child of a deceased wartime veteran.

Eligibility

An individual may be eligible to receive a death pension if:

1. The deceased veteran was discharged from service under other than dishonorable conditions;

2. The deceased veteran served at least 90 days of active military service, one day of which was during a war time period, as set forth below. However, if the veteran entered active duty after September 7, 1980, he or she must have served at least 24 months, or the full period for which called or ordered to active duty;

3. The claimant is the surviving spouse or unmarried child of the deceased veteran; and

4. The claimant's countable family income is below the yearly limit set by law.

Age Restriction

The unremarried spouse may be any age. However, in order for the veteran's child to be eligible for a death pension, the child must be:

1. Under the age of 18; or

2. In school and under the age of 23; or

3. Incapable of self-support before reaching the age of 18.

Countable Income

For purposes of a death pension, countable income includes income received from most sources by the surviving spouse and any eligible children. It includes earnings, disability and retirement payments, interest and dividends, and net income from farming or business.

Certain expenses such as unreimbursed medical expenses may be excluded from the claimant's annual income to lower the total countable income.

There is no set limit on how much net worth a surviving spouse and his or her children can have, but net worth cannot be excessive. The decision as to whether a claimant's net worth is excessive depends on the facts of each individual case.

Net worth includes the net value of the assets of the surviving spouse and his or her children. It includes such assets as bank accounts, stocks, bonds, mutual funds and any property other than the surviving spouse's residence.

All net worth should be reported to the VA. The VA will determine if a claimant's assets are sufficiently large that the claimant could live off these assets for a reasonable period of time.

The VA's needs-based programs are not intended to protect substantial assets or build up an estate for the benefit of heirs.

Exclusions and Deductions

There are certain exclusions and deductions that may be considered to reduce the claimant's countable income, as follows:

1. The final expenses of the veteran's last illness and burial paid by the surviving spouse or eligible children is deductible.

2. Public assistance such as Supplemental Security Income is not considered income.

3. Many other specific sources of income are not considered income. Nevertheless, all income should be reported. The VA will exclude any income that the law allows.

4. A portion of unreimbursed medical expenses paid by the claimant after the VA receives the pension claim may be deducted.

5. Certain other expenses, such as a surviving spouse's educational expenses and, in some cases, a portion of the educational expenses of a child over 18 are deductible.

Death Pension Calculation

The annual death pension is calculated by first totaling all of the countable income. Then any deductions are subtracted from that total. The remaining countable income is deducted from the appropriate annual rate of payment established by Congress. The difference is then divided by 12 and rounded down to the nearest dollar. This is the amount of the monthly payment.

Application Process

In order to apply for a death pension, the claimant must file an *Application for Dependency and Indemnity Compensation, Death Pension and Accrued Benefits by Surviving Spouse or Child* (VA Form 21-534), along with any required documentation, such as dependency records, e.g., marriage and birth certificates.

The completed application and any required documentation must be sent to the VA regional office that serves the claimant's area of residence.

A sample Application for Dependency and Indemnity Compensation, Death Pension and Accrued Benefits by Surviving Spouse or Child (VA Form 21-534) can be found in Appendix 19 of this Almanac.

AID AND ATTENDANCE AND HOUSEBOUND BENEFITS

Aid and Attendance is a benefit paid to a survivor in addition to the monthly pension when:

1. The claimant requires the aid of another person in order to perform personal functions required in everyday living, such as bathing, feeding, dressing, attending to the wants of nature, adjusting prosthetic devices, or protecting himself/herself from the hazards of his/her daily environment;

2. The claimant is bedridden, in that his or her disability or disabilities requires that he or she remain in bed apart from any prescribed course of convalescence or treatment;

3. The claimant is a patient in a nursing home due to mental or physical incapacity; or

4. The claimant is blind or so nearly blind as to have corrected visual acuity of 5/200 or less in both eyes, or concentric contraction of the visual field to 5 degrees or less.

Housebound benefits are paid to a claimant when the claimant is substantially confined to his or her immediate premises because of permanent disability.

The survivor may not receive Aid and Attendance benefits and Housebound benefits at the same time.

To apply for Aid and Attendance or Housebound benefits, the claimant must write to the VA regional office where the survivor filed a claim for pension benefits. The claimant should include copies of any evidence, such as a report from an attending physician, which validates the claimant's need for Aid and Attendance or Housebound type care.

The report should be in sufficient detail to determine whether there is disease or injury producing physical or mental impairment, loss of coordination, or conditions affecting the ability to dress and undress, to feed oneself, to attend to sanitary needs, and to keep oneself ordinarily clean and presentable.

In addition, it is necessary to determine whether the claimant is confined to the home or immediate premises. Whether the claim is for Aid and Attendance or Housebound, the report should indicate how well the individual gets around, where the individual goes, and what he or she is able to do during a typical day.

SURVIVORS' AND DEPENDENTS' EDUCATIONAL ASSISTANCE (DEA)

Survivors' and Dependents' Educational Assistance (DEA) provides payment of a monthly education or training allowance to the spouse and children of a veteran who died of a service-connected disability. Eligible persons can receive up to 45 months of benefits. Professional, educational and vocational counseling will be provided to eligible children and surviving spouses without charge upon request.

Survivors' and Dependents' Educational Assistance (DEA) is discussed more fully in Chapter 5, "Education and Vocational Rehabilitation Benefits," of this Almanac.

In addition, work-study employment is a benefit available to eligible survivors while pursuing a program of education or training under Dependent's Educational Assistance. To apply for work-study employment, an Application for Work-Study Allowance (VA Form 22-8691) should be submitted.

HOME LOAN GUARANTY PROGRAM

The surviving spouse of a veteran who died in service or as the result of a service-connected disability may be eligible for a guaranteed loan from a private lender. The loan may be used to: (1) purchase, construct or improve a home; (2) purchase a manufactured home and/or lot; or

(3) to refinance existing mortgages or other liens of record on a dwelling owned and occupied by the surviving spouse as his or her home. There is no time limit to use this benefit.

To apply for a VA Home Loan Guaranty, a Request for Determination of Loan Guaranty Eligibility (VA Form 26-1817) should be sent to the VA Loan Eligibility Center that serves the applicant's location.

BURIAL BENEFITS

Burial benefits, including a headstone or grave marker is available for the grave of veterans and their eligible dependents who are buried in a military post, state veteran cemetery, or VA national cemetery. In addition, a Presidential Memorial Certificate is issued to recognize the service of deceased veterans who were discharged under honorable conditions. Eligible recipients include the veteran's next of kin or other loved one.

Burial benefits are discussed more fully in Chapter 8, "Burial Rights and Memorial Benefits," of this Almanac.

LIFE INSURANCE BENEFITS AND FINANCIAL COUNSELING

Beneficiaries of a deceased veteran's life insurance proceeds under Servicemembers Group Life Insurance (SGLI) or Veterans Group Life Insurance (VGLI) are eligible for financial counseling, including a detailed step-by-step financial plan and access to financial counselors for one year.

Servicemembers and Veterans Group Life Insurance is discussed more fully in Chapter 4, "Veterans Group Life Insurance," of this Almanac.

BEREAVEMENT COUNSELING

Bereavement Counseling is available to parents, spouses and children of Armed Forces personnel who died in the service of their country. Also eligible are family members of reservists and National Guardsmen who die while on duty.

VOCATIONAL REHABILITATION & EMPLOYMENT SERVICES (VR&E)

Vocational Rehabilitation & Employment Services (VR&E) provide a wide range of vocational and educational counseling services to survivors and dependents who are eligible for one of the VA's educational benefit programs.

VR&E services are discussed more fully in Chapter 5, "Education and Vocational Rehabilitation Benefits," of this Almanac.

MEDICAL BENEFITS FOR FAMILY MEMBERS

Limited medical benefits are available for family members of eligible veterans. These include the Civilian Health and Medical Program of VA (CHAMPVA) and TRICARE.

The CHAMPVA and TRICARE programs are discussed more fully in Chapter 3, "Health Care Benefits," of this Almanac.

Children of Vietnam Veterans

Biological children of Vietnam Veterans born with spina bifida may be eligible for specific benefits through the VA health care system through the Spina Bifida program.

Biological children of women veterans who served in Vietnam during the period beginning February 28, 1961 and ending May 7, 1975 may be eligible for monetary allowances if their birth defects are associated with the mother's service in Vietnam and resulted in permanent physical or mental disability.

CHAPTER 8:
BURIAL RIGHTS AND MEMORIAL BENEFITS

HISTORY AND BACKGROUND

On July 17, 1862, Congress enacted legislation authorizing the president to purchase cemetery grounds for soldiers who die in the service of the country. Fourteen national cemeteries were established that first year, including one in Sharpsburg, Maryland, where 4,476 Union soldiers were laid to rest after the one-day Battle of Antietam.

By 1870, nearly 300,000 Union soldiers had been buried in 73 national cemeteries. Most of the cemeteries were located in the Southeast, near Civil War battlefields and campgrounds. All honorably discharged Union veterans became eligible for burial in 1873. In the late nineteenth century, cemeteries associated with military posts on the western frontier were added.

In the 1930s, new national cemeteries were established to serve veterans living in metropolitan areas such as New York, Baltimore, Minneapolis, San Diego, San Francisco and San Antonio. In addition, cemeteries associated with battlefields, such as Gettysburg and Antietam, were transferred from U.S. Army control to the National Park Service because of their historical significance.

In 1973, the U.S. Army transferred 82 national cemeteries to the VA, which now manages them through its National Cemetery Administration (NCA). Presently, there are 141 national cemeteries. Through the NCA, the VA maintains more than 2.9 million gravesites at 125 of the national cemeteries in 39 states and Puerto Rico, which total more than 17,000 acres of land. Just over half of this land is undeveloped and, along with available gravesites in developed acreage, have the potential to provide more than four million gravesites.

A Directory of VA National Cemeteries can be found in Appendix 20 of this Almanac.

STATISTICS

In 2006, the VA national cemeteries conducted 96,800 interments. That number is likely to increase to 109,000 in 2008.

More than three million people, including veterans of every war and conflict, from the Revolutionary War to the war in Iraq and Afghanistan, are buried in VA national cemeteries.

More than 300 recipients of the Medal of Honor are buried in VA national cemeteries.

Since 1973, annual interments in VA national cemeteries have increased by more than 175%, from 36,400 to nearly 101,200 in 2007, including dependents. Interments are expected to increase annually through 2009.

In 2007, more than 656,000 veterans in the U.S. and Puerto Rico died, and 100,200 interments were conducted, nearly 69% of which were in the 20 busiest national cemeteries. As of Sept. 30, 2007, eight national cemeteries each contained more than 100,000 occupied gravesites, collectively accounting for 40% of all VA gravesites.

On average, only 12% of U.S. veterans choose burial in VA national and state veterans cemeteries, however, as new veterans cemeteries open, this percentage is expected to increase. In 1999 and 2003, Congress directed the VA to establish 12 new national cemeteries. Six have since opened in Oklahoma, Pennsylvania, Michigan, Georgia, California and Florida. The other six will be located near large populations of veterans who currently do not have access to a burial site, and will be located in Alabama, California, Pennsylvania, South Carolina, and two in Florida.

The largest national cemetery is located in Calverton, New York, and contains 1,045 acres. The smallest national cemetery is located in Hampton, Virginia at the VA Medical Center, and contains .03 acres.

The 14 oldest national cemeteries were established in 1862. The newest national cemetery is South Florida National Cemetery in Lake Worth, Florida, which opened April 16, 2007.

Since 1973, the VA has provided more than 9.9 million headstones and markers. In 2007, the VA provided more than 361,000 headstones and markers. In addition, the VA has provided more than 423,000 Presidential Memorial Certificates to the loved ones of deceased veterans in 2007.

More than 8.1 million people visited VA national cemeteries in 2007.

BURIAL BENEFITS

Burial in a VA National Cemetery

Burial benefits available for veterans buried in a VA national cemetery include a gravesite in any of the 125 national cemeteries. In addition to providing a gravesite, the VA opens and closes the grave, provides a headstone or marker, a burial flag, a Presidential Memorial Certificate, and perpetually cares for the grave, at no cost to the veteran's family.

Burial benefits available for spouses and dependents buried in a national cemetery include burial with the veteran, perpetual care, and the spouse or dependent's name and date of birth and death will be inscribed on the veteran's headstone, at no cost to the family. Eligible spouses and dependents may be buried, even if they predecease the veteran.

Of the 125 national cemeteries, 65 are open to all interments; 20 can accommodate cremated remains and the remains of family members interred in the same gravesite as a previously deceased family member; and 40 will perform only interments of family members in the same gravesite as a previously deceased family member.

Burial in a Private Cemetery

Burial benefits available for veterans buried in a private cemetery include a government headstone or marker, a burial flag, and a Presidential Memorial Certificate, at no cost to the veteran's family. Some veterans may also be eligible for a burial allowance, as further discussed below.

If the veteran will be buried in a private cemetery, and a government headstone or marker will be requested for the veteran's grave, it is advisable to complete an Application for Standard Government Headstone or Marker for Installation in a Private or State Veterans' Cemetery (VA Form 40-1330), and place it with the military discharge papers for use at the time of need. Only an eligible veteran may receive a Government-furnished headstone or marker for placement in a private cemetery. Veteran's spouses and dependent children are not eligible.

A sample Application for Standard Government Headstone or Marker for Installation in a Private or State Veterans' Cemetery (VA Form 40-1330) can be found in Appendix 21 of this Almanac.

ELIGIBILITY

VA national cemetery directors have the primary responsibility for verifying eligibility for burial in VA national cemeteries. A determination of eligibility is usually made in response to a request for burial in a VA national cemetery. VA Regional Offices will also assist in determining eligibility for burial in a VA national cemetery.

Persons Eligible for Burial in a VA National Cemetery

Veterans with discharges "other than dishonorable," their spouses and dependent children are eligible for burial in a VA national cemetery, as set forth below.

Veterans and Members of the Armed Forces

1. Any member of the Armed Forces of the United States (Army, Navy, Air Force, Marine Corps, Coast Guard) who dies on active duty.

2. Any veteran who was discharged under conditions other than dishonorable. With certain exceptions, service beginning after September 7, 1980, as an enlisted person, and service after October 16, 1981, as an officer, must be for a minimum of 24 continuous months or the full period for which the person was called to active duty.

3. Any citizen of the United States who, during any war in which the United States has or may be engaged, served in the Armed Forces of any Government allied with the United States during that war, whose last active service was terminated honorably by death or otherwise, and who was a citizen of the United States at the time of entry into such service and at the time of his or her death.

Members of Reserve Components and Reserve Officers' Training Corps

1. Reservists and National Guard members who, at time of death, were entitled to retired pay, or would have been entitled, but are under the age of 60.

2. Members of reserve components, and members of the Army National Guard or the Air National Guard, who die while hospitalized

or undergoing treatment at the expense of the United States for injury or disease contracted or incurred under honorable conditions while performing active duty for training or inactive duty training, or undergoing such hospitalization or treatment.

3. Members of the Reserve Officers' Training Corps of the Army, Navy, or Air Force who die under honorable conditions while attending an authorized training camp or on an authorized cruise, while performing authorized travel to or from that camp or cruise, or, while hospitalized or undergoing treatment at the expense of the United States for injury or disease, contracted or incurred under honorable conditions while engaged in one of those activities.

4. Members of reserve components who, during a period of active duty for training, were disabled or died from a disease or injury incurred or aggravated in line of duty or, during a period of inactive duty training, were disabled or died from an injury or certain cardiovascular disorders incurred or aggravated in line of duty.

Commissioned Officers, National Oceanic and Atmospheric Administration

1. A Commissioned Officer of the National Oceanic and Atmospheric Administration with full-time duty on or after July 29, 1945.

2. A Commissioned Officer who served before July 29, 1945, and;

(a) the veteran who was assigned to an area of immediate military hazard as determined by the Secretary of Defense while in time of war, or in a Presidentially declared national emergency; or,

(b) the veteran who served in the Philippine Islands on December 7, 1941, and continuously in such islands thereafter.

Public Health Service

1. A Commissioned Officer of the Regular or Reserve Corps of the Public Health Service who served on full-time duty on or after July 29, 1945.

2. A Commissioned Officer of the Regular or Reserve Corps of the Public Health Service who performed full-time duty prior to July 29, 1945:

(a) in a time of war;

(b) on detail for duty with the Army, Navy, Air Force, Marine Corps, or Coast Guard; or,

(c) while the Service was part of the military forces of the United States pursuant to Executive Order of the President.

3. A Commissioned Officer serving on inactive duty training whose death resulted from an injury incurred or aggravated in the line of duty.

World War II Merchant Mariners

1. United States Merchant Mariners with oceangoing service during the period of armed conflict, December 7, 1941 to December 31, 1946.

2. United States Merchant Mariners who served on blockships in support of Operation Mulberry during World War II.

The Philippine Armed Forces

1. Any Philippine veteran who was a citizen of the United States or an alien lawfully admitted for permanent residence in the United States at the time of their death; and resided in the United States at the time of their death; and,

(a) the veteran who served before July 1, 1946, in the organized military forces of the Government of the Commonwealth of the Philippines, while such forces were in the service of the Armed Forces of the United States pursuant to the military order of the President dated July 26, 1941.

(b) the veteran who enlisted between October 6, 1945, and June 30, 1947, with the Armed Forces of the United States with the consent of the Philippine government, and who died on or after December 16, 2003.

Spouses and Dependents

The spouse or surviving spouse of an eligible veteran is eligible for interment in a national cemetery even if that veteran is not buried or memorialized in a national cemetery. In addition, the spouse or surviving spouse of a member of the Armed Forces of the United States whose remains are unavailable for burial is also eligible for burial.

The surviving spouse of an eligible veteran who had a subsequent remarriage to a non-veteran and whose death occurred on or after January 1, 2000, is eligible for burial in a national cemetery, based on his or her marriage to the eligible veteran.

The minor children of an eligible veteran are eligible for burial in a national cemetery. For purpose of burial in a national cemetery, a minor child is a child who is unmarried and: (1) under 21 years of age; or (2) under 23 years of age and pursuing a full-time course of instruction at an approved educational institution.

The unmarried adult child of an eligible veteran is eligible for burial in a national cemetery. For purpose of burial in a national cemetery, an unmarried adult child is defined as a child of any age who became permanently physically or mentally disabled and incapable of self-support before reaching 21 years of age, or before reaching 23 years of age if pursuing a full-time course of instruction at an approved educational institution. Proper supporting documentation must be provided.

Persons Who are Not Eligible for Burial in a VA National Cemetery

Persons who are generally not eligible for burial in a VA national cemetery, as determined by the VA national cemetery director, are set forth below.

Disqualifying Discharge

A veteran whose only separation from the Armed Forces was under dishonorable conditions, or whose character of service results in a bar to veterans' benefits, is not eligible for burial in a national cemetery.

Discharge from Draft

A person who was ordered to report to an induction station, but was not actually inducted into military service, is not eligible for burial in a national cemetery.

Person Found Guilty of a Capital Crime

Interment or memorialization in a national cemetery is prohibited if a person is convicted of a federal capital crime and sentenced to death or life imprisonment, or is convicted of a state capital crime, and sentenced to death or life imprisonment without parole.

Federal officials are authorized to deny burial in veterans cemeteries to persons who are shown by clear and convincing evidence to have committed a federal or state capital crime but were not convicted of such crime because of flight to avoid prosecution or by death prior to trial.

Subversive Activities

Any person convicted of subversive activities after September 1, 1959 has no right to burial in a national cemetery.

Active or Inactive Duty for Training

A person whose only service is active duty for training or inactive duty training in the National Guard or Reserve Component, unless the individual meets the eligibility criteria set forth above, has no right to burial in a national cemetery.

Former Spouses

A former spouse of an eligible individual whose marriage to that individual has been terminated by annulment or divorce, if not otherwise eligible, is not eligible for burial in a national cemetery.

Other Family Members

Family members other than eligible spouses or dependents, as set forth above, are not eligible for burial in a national cemetery.

VERIFYING VETERAN STATUS

In some cases, it may be necessary to verify whether a decedent was a veteran in order to provide him or her with proper VA burial rights. Verification requests for veteran status of an adult decedent should be made to the VA regional offices, VA medical facilities, or VA national cemeteries, or by calling the VA toll-free benefits number (1-800-827-1000).

A VA representative will be able to verify if the decedent was a veteran, and if he or she is eligible for VA burial benefits. The VA cannot verify the veteran status of unidentified remains, therefore, the Federal Bureau of Investigation (FBI) should be contacted for assistance in such a case.

The information needed for verification is the decedent's name and VA claim number. Otherwise, as much of the following information as possible will be useful: (1) social security number: (2) date of birth; (3) branch of military service; (4) service number; and (5) service dates.

If the VA representative is unable to fully verify the veteran's status from computer records, a process is activated to investigate further and follow up with the inquirer. If there is a claims file for the veteran, it will be reviewed. If necessary, assistance will be sought from the VA Records Management Center or the National Personnel Records Center where veterans' military records are stored.

The turnaround time for VA verification generally ranges from immediate to three days, and the result will be one of the following: (1) the decedent was a veteran, and eligible for VA burial monetary benefits; (2) the decedent was a veteran but ineligible for burial monetary benefits; and (3) there are no records identifying military service by the decedent.

ARRANGING FOR BURIAL IN A VA NATIONAL CEMETERY

To arrange for burial in a VA national cemetery, the person making the burial arrangements should have the funeral home contact the national cemetery in which burial is desired. Scheduling can be done seven days a week for interments on Mondays through Fridays.

If possible, the following information concerning the veteran should be provided when the cemetery is first contacted:

1. Full name and military rank;

2. Branch of service;

3. Social security number;

4. Service number;

5. VA claim number, if applicable;

6. Date and place of birth;

7. Date and place of death;

8. Date of retirement or last separation from active duty; and

9. A copy of any military separation documents, e.g., the Department of Defense Form 214 (DD-214).

The discharge documents must specify active military duty and show that the veteran's release from active duty was under other than dishonorable conditions.

Funeral services cannot be held at the VA national cemetery, however, a final committal service may be performed. The committal services are held in committal shelters located away from the gravesite. Burial will take place following the committal service. Floral arrangements may accompany the casket or urn from the committal shelter and will be placed on the grave after burial.

The same procedures are followed if the veteran's eligible spouse or dependent predeceases the veteran. In most cases, one gravesite is provided for the burial of all eligible family members and a single headstone or marker is provided. When both spouses are veterans, two gravesites and two headstones or markers may be provided, if requested.

THE BURIAL FLAG

A United States flag is provided, at no cost, to drape the casket or accompany the urn of a deceased veteran who served honorably in the U. S. Armed Forces. The flag is given to honor the memory of a veteran's military service to his or her country. Generally, the flag is given to the next-of-kin after it is used during the service. When there is no next-of-kin, a friend may request the burial flag.

For those VA national cemeteries with an Avenue of Flags, families of veterans buried in these national cemeteries may donate the burial flags of their loved ones to be flown on patriotic holidays. A Certificate of Appreciation is presented to the donor for providing the veteran's burial flag to a national cemetery.

To obtain a burial flag, an Application for United States Flag for Burial Purposes (VA Form 21-2008) should be submitted to the VA.

A sample Application for United States Flag for Burial Purposes (VA Form 21-2008) can be found in Appendix 22 of this Almanac.

HEADSTONES AND MARKERS

Upon request, and at no cost, the VA provides a Government headstone or marker for the unmarked grave of any deceased eligible veteran in any cemetery around the world, regardless of their date of death.

For eligible veterans that died on or after Nov. 1, 1990, the VA may also provide a headstone or marker for graves that are already marked with a private headstone or marker. When the grave is already marked, applicants will have the option to apply for either a traditional headstone or marker.

When burial or memorialization is in a national cemetery, state veterans' cemetery, or military base cemetery, a headstone or marker will be ordered by the cemetery officials based on inscription information provided by the next of kin or authorized representative.

Spouses and dependents are not eligible for a Government-furnished headstone or marker unless they are buried in a national cemetery, state veteran's cemetery, or military post/base cemetery.

PRESIDENTIAL MEMORIAL CERTIFICATES

A Presidential Memorial Certificate is an engraved paper certificate, signed by the current President, to honor the memory of honorably discharged deceased veterans. The VA administers the program, which was started in March 1962 by President John F. Kennedy, and has been continued by all subsequent Presidents.

Eligible recipients of the Presidential Memorial Certificate include the next of kin and loved ones of honorably discharged deceased veterans. More than one certificate may be provided. Eligible recipients may apply for a certificate in person at any VA regional office, or by U.S. mail or toll-free fax, along with a copy of the veteran's military discharge document (e.g., DD 214 or its equivalent) and death certificate to verify proof of honorable military service.

To obtain a certificate, an Application Presidential Memorial Certificate (VA Form 40-0247) should be submitted to the VA.

A sample Application for a Presidential Memorial Certificate (VA Form 40-0247) can be found in Appendix 23 of this Almanac.

MILITARY FUNERAL HONORS

The Department of Defense provides military funeral honors at the burials of veterans on request. Funeral honors can be given at private or government-operated cemeteries. Military funeral honors include the presence of an honors detail to fold and present the U.S. flag to the next of kin.

The law defines a military funeral honors detail as two or more uniformed military persons, with at least one being a member of the veteran's branch of military service. In addition, "Taps" will be played either by recording or by a bugler.

The VA staff at national cemeteries can also assist in arranging funeral honors at VA national cemeteries. When military honors are desired at a national cemetery, they are arranged by the funeral home in advance of the committal service.

BURIAL ALLOWANCE

The VA burial allowance is a partial reimbursement of an eligible veteran's burial and funeral costs. When the cause of death is not service-related, the reimbursement is generally described as two payments: (1) a burial and funeral expense allowance; and (2) a plot or interment allowance.

Eligibility

An individual is eligible for a VA burial allowance if: (1) he or she paid for a veteran's burial or funeral; and (2) there has been no reimbursement by another government agency or some other source; and (3) the veteran was discharged under conditions other than dishonorable.

In addition, at least one of the following conditions must be met:

1. The veteran died because of a service-related disability.

2. The veteran was receiving a VA pension or compensation at the time of his or her death.

3. The veteran was entitled to receive a VA pension or compensation, but decided not to reduce his/her military retirement or disability pay.

4. The veteran died while hospitalized by the VA, or while receiving care under a VA contract at a non-VA facility.

5. The veteran died while traveling under proper authorization and at VA expense to or from a specified place for the purpose of examination, treatment, or care.

6. The veteran had an original or reopened claim pending at the time of death and has been found entitled to compensation or pension from a date prior to the date or death.

7. The veteran died on or after October 9, 1996, while a patient at a VA-approved state nursing home.

Amount of Benefit

The amount of benefit depends on whether the veteran's death was service-related, as follows:

Service-Related Death

If the veteran's death was service-related, the VA will pay up to $2,000 toward burial expenses for deaths that occurred on or after September 11, 2001. The VA will pay up to $1,500 for deaths that occurred prior to September 10, 2001. If the veteran is buried in a VA national cemetery, some or all of the cost of transporting the deceased may be reimbursed.

Nonservice-Related Death

If the veteran's death was not service-related, the VA will pay up to $300 toward burial and funeral expenses and a $300 plot-interment allowance for deaths that occurred on or after December 1, 2001. The plot-interment allowance is $150 for deaths that occurred prior to December 1, 2001. If the death happened while the veteran was in a VA hospital or under a VA contracted nursing home care, some or all of the costs for transporting the veteran's remains may be reimbursed.

Applying for a Burial Allowance

To apply for a VA burial allowance, an Application for Burial Benefits (VA Form 21-530) should be submitted to the VA. Copies of the veteran's military discharge document (e.g., DD 214 or its equivalent), death certificate, and paid funeral and burial bills should be attached to the application.

A sample Application for Burial Benefits (VA Form 21-530) can be found in Appendix 24 of this Almanac.

CHAPTER 9:
THE BOARD OF VETERANS APPEALS

IN GENERAL

If a veteran disagrees with the decision made on his or her claim by the local VA office, the veteran can appeal the decision to the Board of Veterans' Appeals (BVA or Board). The BVA is a part of the U.S. Veterans Administration located in Washington, D.C.

An appeal is a request for the Board to review the decision the local VA office made on a claim. According to the VA, the two most common reasons an appeal is made include: (1) the VA denied benefits for a disability the veteran believes began while he or she was in service; or (2) the veteran's disability is more severe than the VA rated it.

Members of the Board, known as law judges, review benefit claims determinations made by local VA offices and issue decision on appeals. The law judges are attorneys who are experienced in veterans' law and in reviewing benefit claims. The law judges are assisted by staff attorneys. The staff attorneys are also trained in veterans' law, and review the facts of each appeal, however, the law judge are the only ones who can issue Board decisions.

THE APPEALS PROCESS

As discussed in this Almanac, to apply for benefits, a veteran must file a claim with his or her local VA office or VA medical facility. The local VA office makes a decision to either allow or deny the claim, and sends their decision to the veteran. If the veteran is not satisfied with the decision, he or she can appeal the decision to the Board.

Notice of Disagreement

The first step in appealing the decision is to file a Notice of Disagreement (NOD) with the local VA office that made the decision. The NOD is a statement that sets forth the reason the veteran disagrees with the decision, and his or her intention to appeal the decision.

The NOD must be sent within one year from the date the local VA office mailed their original decision. After the NOD is sent to the local VA office, the veteran can request a Decision Review Officer (DRO) from the local VA office to review the file and original decision. The DRO will review the entire file and can also hold a personal hearing on the claim.

Statement of the Case

After the local VA receives the NOD, it creates a Statement of the Case (SOC). The SOC is a detailed explanation of the evidence, laws, and regulations that the local VA office used in deciding the claim. The local VA office mails the SOC to the veteran, along with a Substantive Appeal Form (VA Form 9).

Filing the completed VA Form 9 is the last step in the appeal process. The form must state the benefit the veteran is seeking, as well as any errors contained in the accompanying SOC. In addition, the form must state whether the veteran wants a personal hearing, as discussed below.

The local VA office must receive the completed VA Form 9 within 60 days from the date the VA mailed the SOC, or within one year from the date that the VA mailed the original decision denying the claim, whichever is later.

THE PERSONAL HEARING

A personal hearing is a meeting among the VA official, the veteran who is appealing the claim, and the veteran's representative, if any. There are two types of personal hearings: (1) a hearing with an official from the local VA office; or (2) a hearing with a member of the Board.

To request a personal hearing with a local VA official, a written request must be sent to the local VA office. A request for a personal hearing with a member of the Board should be made when the VA Form 9 is submitted.

A personal hearing with a member of the Board may be conducted as follows:

1. The hearing can take place in Washington, D.C. at the BVA office.

2. A videoconference hearing can take place at the local VA office with the Board member in Washington, D.C. This is generally the quickest way to get a hearing with a Board member.

3. The hearing can take place at the local VA office with the Board member present.

The personal hearing is an informal proceeding. The veteran will be given an oath, and will tell the Board member whatever he or she believes is important regarding the claim and appeal. It is important to give as much detail as possible about any evidence the veteran wants the VA to consider.

The Board member may also ask additional questions about the claim. If the veteran has a representative at the hearing, the representative may ask questions that will assist the veteran in explaining his or her claim. Representatives from Veterans Service Organizations have offices in most local VA offices.

Additional evidence regarding the claim may be introduced at the hearing. The evidence will be added to the veteran's file and reviewed by the Board member when he or she decides the claim. The decision on the claim is not made at the hearing. A transcript of the hearing is made and sent to the BVA with the veteran's file. When the Board member receives all of the information, the file is reviewed and a decision is made.

THE DECISION

After the Board member reviews the file and makes a decision, the BVA sends a copy of the decision to the veteran. The decision will allow, deny, or remand the claim. If the claim is allowed or denied, the Board's decision is final. A remand is not a final decision.

Remand

If the BVA finds that it does not have enough information about the claim to make a decision, they will try to obtain more information. They may send the claim back to the local VA office for more information. This is known as a remand.

Denial

Although the Board's denial is final, the veteran still has several options to pursue: (1) Ask the local VA to reopen the claim; (2) File a motion asking the Board to reconsider the claim or review the case again alleging a "clear and unmistakable error" (CUE) in the Board decision; or (3) File an appeal with the U.S. Court of Appeals for Veterans Claims.

THE U.S. COURT OF APPEALS FOR VETERANS CLAIMS

The United States Court of Appeals for Veterans Claims is a national court of record, established under Article I of the Constitution of the United States. The Court has exclusive jurisdiction to provide judicial review of final decisions by the Board of Veterans Appeal. The Court is not part of the VA.

The Court provides veterans an impartial judicial forum for review of administrative decisions by the Board that are adverse to the veteran's claim of entitlement to benefits for service-connected disabilities, survivor benefits and other benefits such as education payments and waiver of indebtedness.

The Court is composed of seven judges who are appointed by the President with the advice and consent of the Senate. Many appeals are decided by only one of these judges. However, the Court may sit as a panel of three judges, or the entire Court may decide the case.

Filing the Appeal

If a veteran disagrees with the final decision of the Board and wants to appeal to the Court, he or she must file a written notice of appeal with the Clerk of the Court within 120 days after the date the Board mailed a copy of its final decision. That date is stamped on the front of the Board's decision. If the notice of appeal is not timely filed, the Board's decision becomes final and the Court cannot hear the appeal unless the veteran has filed a motion for reconsideration with the Board within 120 days of its original decision.

Filing a motion for reconsideration with the Board stops the clock on the time within which an appeal must be filed with the Court. If the motion for reconsideration is denied, the time to file an appeal with the Court begins again, and the notice of appeal must be filed with the Court within 120 days from the date of the letter denying the motion for reconsideration.

The notice of appeal is considered received by the Court on the date of a legible postmark if it is properly addressed and sent by the U.S. Postal Service, or the date it is actually received by the Court if it is sent by means other than the U.S. Postal Service or faxed. The appropriate filing fee, or a declaration of inability to pay the filing fee, must accompany the notice of appeal when it is filed.

Filing By Mail

The Notice of Appeal and filing fee or Declaration of Financial Hardship should be mailed to the following address:

Clerk of the Court
United States Court of Appeals for Veterans Claims
625 Indiana Avenue, NW, Suite 900
Washington, D.C. 20004-2950

Filing By Fax

Alternatively, the Notice of Appeal may be faxed to the Court (202-501-5848). If the Notice of Appeal is faxed, the filing fee or Declaration of Financial hardship must be mailed to the Court so that it receives it no later than 14 days after the fax is sent. It is advisable to contact the Court to confirm that the Notice of Appeal has been received.

The Appeal Process

The veteran filing the appeal of a Board decision is called the "appellant." The action is brought against the Secretary of Veterans Affairs, called the "appellee." The Court follows its own Rules of Practice and Procedure, which must be followed carefully or the appeal could be dismissed or delayed.

The appeal process begins when the Notice of Appeal is filed by the appellant. The lawyer representing the VA will designate the documents in the file that the lawyer believes are important for the Court to review, and will forward a copy of those documents to the appellant. This is known as the "Designation of the Record."

If the appellant believes that additional documents should be reviewed by the Court, but were not included in the Designation of the Record, the appellant may file those documents with the Court. This is known as the "Counter Designation of the Record."

The Designation of the Record and the Counter Designation of the Record are called the "Record on Appeal." After the Record on Appeal is filed with the Court, the Clerk of the Court will notify the appellant that the Record on Appeal has been filed. The appellant must then file a brief with the Court within 60 days of the date of that notice. If the appellant is unrepresented, he or she may file an informal brief using the Court's Informal Brief Form.

After the appellant files his or her brief, the VA lawyer has 60 days to file a brief on behalf of the Secretary of Veterans Affairs. Once that brief is filed, the appellant has 14 days to file an optional Reply Brief to respond to anything contained in the Secretary's brief.

After all of the briefs have been filed, the case is assigned to a judge. The judge will render a decision after reviewing all of the submitted documentation. It takes an average of one year from the date a notice of appeal is filed until a decision is made.

Finding a Representative

The appellant is not required to have a lawyer or other person represent the appellant before the Court. This is known as an unrepresented or "pro se" appellant. It should be noted, however, that the Secretary of Veterans Affairs will be represented by an attorney who has experience with the appeal process. Therefore, it is advisable for an appellant to have a qualified representative acting on his or her behalf before the Court.

In order to assist an unrepresented appellant, the Clerk of the Court maintains a list of individuals who have been admitted to practice before the Court and who have an interest in representing appellants. The Court makes no representation as to the qualifications of these individuals. Most representatives charge a fee, however, there are representatives who will only collect a fee if the appellant prevails in the case.

Veterans Consortium Pro Bono Program

The Veterans Consortium Pro Bono Program provides free attorneys to veterans and their qualifying family members who have an appeal pending at the U.S. Court of Appeals for Veterans Claims. If an appellant has filed an appeal with the Court, he or she can request assistance from The Veterans Consortium.

The Veterans Consortium recruits and trains volunteer attorneys to help appellants, free of charge, with their appeals at the Court. The Veterans Consortium does not provide general legal advice or information about the VA or the Court, nor does it provide legal advice or representation concerning a claim pending at the Board or at a local VA office.

The Veterans Consortium was created by a grant from the Legal Services Corporation (LSC), as authorized by the U.S. Congress. It is an ongoing cooperative effort by four national veterans' service organizations including the American Legion, the Disabled American Veterans, the

National Veterans Legal Services Program, and the Paralyzed Veterans of America.

Appellants can contact the Veterans Consortium Pro Bono Program to see if they meet the Pro Bono Program's eligibility requirements for free representation.

CHAPTER 10:
THE SERVICEMEMBERS CIVIL
RELIEF ACT

IN GENERAL

The Servicemembers Civil Relief Act (SCRA) is a federal statute passed by Congress and signed into law by President Bush on December 19, 2003. The SCRA allows military service members to suspend or postpone certain civil obligations so that the service member can devote his or her full attention to military duties. The original Soldiers' and Sailors' Civil Relief Act was passed during World War I. The statute was reenacted during World War II, and was later modified during Operation Desert Storm.

The SCRA amended the Soldiers' and Sailors' Civil Relief Act and was signed into law on December 19, 2003 as Public Law 108-189. The text of the Servicemembers Civil Relief Act can be found at 50 U.S.C. §§ 501–593.

The SCRA is designed to protect active duty service members, reservists who are in active federal service, and National Guardsmen who are in active federal service. Some of the benefits under the SCRA extend to dependents of active duty service members as well.

The SCRA can be a big help to service members in times of need. In fact, the United States Supreme Court has declared that the Act must be read with "an eye friendly to those who dropped their affairs to answer their country's call."

PROVISIONS

Under the SCRA, judicial and administrative transactions that may adversely affect a service member during their military service are temporarily suspended so that the service member can focus their energy on the defense of the United States and devote full attention to duty, and to relieve stress on the family members of those deployed service members.

As discussed below, the SCRA provides for forbearance and reduced interest on certain obligations incurred prior to military service, and it restricts default judgments against service members, and rental evictions of service members and all their dependents.

The provisions of the SCRA generally begin the day the service member receives his or her orders to active duty or deployment, and end when the service member is: (1) discharged from active duty; (2) within 90 days of discharge; or (3) when the service member dies.

Below are some of the most common forms of relief provided under the Act. The SCRA actually provides many more protections than those listed below, therefore, the reader is advised to consult the Act for more specific information.

INTEREST RATE CAPS

Under the SCRA, a service member can cap the interest rate at 6% for all obligations entered into before beginning active duty if military service materially affects his or her ability to meet the obligations. This includes, but is not limited to, interest rates on credit cards, mortgages, and even some student loans, except for federal guaranteed student loans.

To qualify for the interest rate cap, the service member has to show that:

1. He or she is now on active duty;

2. The obligation or debt was incurred prior to entry on active duty; and

3. Military service materially affects the members' ability to pay.

To begin the process, the service member needs to send a letter requesting relief under the SCRA, along with a copy of his or her current military orders, to the lender. The interest rate cap will apply from the first date of active-duty service, and lasts for the duration of active duty service.

The service member must provide written notice to the creditor, and a copy of the military order, not later than 180 days after the service member's termination or release from military service.

STAY OF JUDICIAL PROCEEDINGS

If a service member is served with a complaint indicating that he or she is being sued for some reason, the service member can obtain a "stay" or postponement of those proceedings if the service member's military service materially affects his or her ability to proceed in the case.

A stay can be used to stop the action altogether, or to hold up some phase of it. According to the SCRA, a service member can request a stay during any stage of the proceedings. However, the burden is on the service member to show that military service has materially affected his or her ability to appear in court.

In general, the service member can request a stay of the proceedings for a reasonable period of time, e.g., 30–60 days. It is unlikely that a court will allow the service member to put off the proceedings indefinitely. The stay can also be granted in administrative proceedings.

PROTECTION AGAINST DEFAULT JUDGMENTS

A default judgment is entered against a party who has failed to defend against a claim that has been brought by another party. To obtain a default judgment, a plaintiff must file a sworn affidavit stating that the defendant is not in the military service and has not requested a stay.

If a service member is sued while on active duty, fails to respond to the claim, and as a result a default judgment is obtained, the service member can reopen the default judgment. In order to do so, the service member must:

1. Demonstrate that the judgment was entered during the service member's military service, or within 30 days after he or she has left the service.

2. Write to the court requesting that the default judgment be reopened while he or she is still on active duty, or within 90 days of leaving the service.

3. Not have made any kind of appearance in court, through filing an answer or otherwise, prior to the default judgment being entered.

4. Indicate that the service member's military service prejudiced his or her ability to defend the case, and show that he or she had a valid defense to the action.

PROTECTION FROM EVICTION

If the service member is leasing a house or apartment, and the rent is below a certain amount, the SCRA can protect the service member from being evicted for a period of time, e.g., three months. The house or apartment must be occupied by either the active duty service member or the service member's dependents.

In addition, the service member must show that military service materially affects his or her ability to pay rent. If a landlord continues to try to evict the service member, or actually evicts the service member, he or she is subject to criminal sanctions such as fines or even imprisonment.

TERMINATION OF RESIDENTIAL LEASE

Prior to Military Service

The SCRA allows a service member who is entering active duty service to lawfully terminate a residential lease. To do so, the service member needs to show that:

1. The lease was entered into prior to the commencement of active duty service;

2. The lease was signed by or on behalf of the service member; and

3. The service member is currently in military service or was called to active-duty service for a period of 180 days or more.

In addition, the service member must provide the landlord with proper written notice, along with a copy of his or her military orders.

During Military Service

The SCRA allows a service member who receives permanent change of station orders or who is deployed for a period of 90 days or more to terminate a residential lease. The service member must provide the landlord with proper written notice, along with a copy of his or her military orders.

The termination of a lease that provides for monthly payment of rent will occur 30 days after the first date on which the next rental payment is due and payable, after the landlord receives proper written notice.

MORTGAGE PAYMENT RELIEF

The SCRA provides the service member temporary relief from making mortgage payments. To obtain relief, a service member must show that:

1. The mortgage was entered into prior to beginning active duty;

2. The property was owned prior to entry into military service;

3. The property is still owned by the service member; and

4. Military service materially affects the service member's ability to make the mortgage payments.

TERMINATION OF AUTOMOBILE LEASE

The SCRA allows a service member to terminate a pre-service automobile lease if he or she is called up for military service of 180 days or longer.

In addition, service members who sign automobile leases while on active-duty may be able to terminate an automobile lease if they are given orders for a permanent change of station outside the continental United States, and his or her deployment with the military unit is for a period of 180 days or longer.

PROTECTION FROM DOUBLE-TAXATION

If a service member's home state taxes military pay, the service member will have to pay those taxes. However, if the service member is assigned to another state, he or she will still legally be a "domiciliary" of the home state. The state to which the military assigns the service member cannot tax his or her military pay.

In addition, the SCRA prevents service members from a form of double taxation that can occur when they have a spouse who works and is taxed in a state other than the state in which they maintain their permanent legal residence. The SCRA prevents states from using the income earned by a service member in determining the spouse's tax rate when they do not maintain their permanent legal residence in that state.

ADDITIONAL PROTECTIONS

The SCRA actually provides many more protections than those listed above. Military legal assistance attorneys are available to provide guidance on the SCRA. Military personnel are advised to learn about the SCRA and the protections and benefits it provides for them and their families.

Selected provisions of the Servicemembers Civil Relief Act can be found in Appendix 25 of this Almanac.

APPENDIX 1:
VA BENEFIT CENTERS

STATE	ADDRESS/TELEPHONE
Alabama	Montgomery Regional Office 345 Perry Hill Rd. Montgomery, AL 36109 (800) 827-1000
Alaska	Anchorage Regional Office 2925 DeBarr Road Anchorage, AK 99508-2989 (800) 827-1000
Arizona	Phoenix Regional Office 3333 North Central Avenue Phoenix, AZ 85012 (800) 827-1000 Western Area Office 3333 North Central Avenue, Suite 3026 Phoenix, AZ 85012-2402 (800) 827-1000
Arkansas	North Little Rock Regional Office 2200 Fort Roots Drive, Building 65 North Little Rock, AR 72114-1756 (800) 827-1000
California	Los Angeles Regional Office Federal Building 11000 Wilshire Boulevard Los Angeles, CA 90024 (800) 827-1000 Oakland Regional Office 1301 Clay Street, Rm. 1300 North Oakland, CA 94612 (800) 827-1000

STATE	ADDRESS/TELEPHONE
	San Diego Regional Office 8810 Rio San Diego Drive San Diego, CA 92108 (800) 827-1000
Colorado	Denver Regional Office 155 Van Gordon St. Lakewood, CO 80228 (800) 827-1000
Connecticut	Hartford Regional Office 555 Willard Avenue Newington, CT 06111 (800) 827-1000
Delaware	Wilmington Regional Office 1601 Kirkwood Highway Wilmington, DE 19805 (800) 827-1000
District of Columbia	Washington D.C. Regional Office 1722 I Street N.W. Washington D.C., DC 20421 (800) 827-1000
Florida	St. Petersburg Regional Office 9500 Bay Pines Boulevard St. Petersburg, FL 33708 (800) 827-1000
Georgia	Atlanta Regional Office 1700 Clairmont Road Decatur, GA 30033 (800) 827-1000
Hawaii	Honolulu Regional Office 459 Patterson Road, E-Wing Honolulu, HI 96819-1522 (800) 827-1000
Idaho	Boise Regional Office 805 W. Franklin Street Boise, ID 83702 (800) 827-1000
Illinois	Chicago Regional Office 2122 W Taylor Street Chicago, IL 60612 (800) 827-1000

STATE	ADDRESS/TELEPHONE
Indiana	Indianapolis Regional Office 575 N Pennsylvania St. Indianapolis, IN 46204 (800) 827-1000
Iowa	Des Moines VA Regional Office 210 Walnut Street Des Moines, IA 50309 (800) 827-1000
Kansas	Wichita Regional Office 5500 E. Kellogg Wichita, KS 67211 (800) 827-1000
Kentucky	Louisville Regional Office 321 West Main Street, Suite 390 Louisville, KY 40202 (800) 827-1000
Louisiana	New Orleans Regional Office 701 Loyola Avenue New Orleans, LA 70113 (800) 827-1000
Maine	Togus VA Medical/Regional Office Center 1 VA Center Togus, ME 04330 (800) 827-1000
Maryland	Baltimore Regional Office 31 Hopkins Plaza Baltimore, MD 21201 (800) 827-1000
Massachusetts	Boston VA Regional Office JFK Federal Building Boston, MA 02203 (800) 827-1000
Michigan	Detroit Regional Office Patrick V. McNamara Federal Bldg. 477 Michigan Ave. Detroit, MI 48226 (800) 827-1000
Minnesota	St. Paul Regional Office 1 Federal Drive Fort Snelling St. Paul, MN 55111 (800) 827-1000

STATE	ADDRESS/TELEPHONE
Mississippi	Jackson Regional Office 1600 E. Woodrow Wilson Avenue Jackson, MS 39216 (800) 827-1000
Missouri	St. Louis Regional Office 400 South, 18th Street St. Louis, MO 63103 (800) 827-1000
Montana	Fort Harrison Medical and Regional Office William Street Fort Harrison, MT 59636 (800) 827-1000
Nebraska	Lincoln Regional Office 5631 South 48th Street Lincoln, NE 68516 (800) 827-1000
Nevada	Reno Regional Office 5460 Reno Corporate Drive Reno, NV 89511 (800) 827-1000
New Hampshire	Manchester Regional Office Norris Cotton Federal Bldg. 275 Chestnut St. Manchester, NH 03101 (800) 827-1000
New Jersey	Newark Regional Office 20 Washington Place Newark, NJ 07102 (800) 827-1000
New Mexico	Albuquerque Regional Office 500 Gold Avenue, S.W. Albuquerque, NM 87102 (800) 827-1000
New York	Buffalo Regional Office 130 S. Elmwood Avenue Buffalo, NY 14202-2478 (800) 827-1000 New York Regional Office 245 W Houston St. New York, NY 10014 (800) 827-1000

STATE	ADDRESS/TELEPHONE
North Carolina	Winston-Salem Regional Office Federal Building 251 N. Main Street Winston Salem, NC 27155 (800) 827-1000
North Dakota	Fargo Regional Office 2101 Elm Street Fargo, ND 58102-2417 (800) 827-1000
Ohio	Cleveland Regional Office A.J. Celebrezze Federal Building 1240 East 9th Street Cleveland, OH 44199 (800) 827-1000
Oklahoma	Central Area Office Federal Building 125 South Main Street Muskogee, OK 74401-7025 (800) 827-1000
Oregon	Portland Regional Office 1220 SW 3rd Avenue Portland, OR 97204 (800) 827-1000
Pennsylvania	Philadelphia Regional Office and Insurance Center 5000 Wissahickon Avenue Philadelphia, PA 19101 (800) 827-1000 Pittsburgh Regional Office 1000 Liberty Avenue Pittsburgh, PA 15222 (800) 827-1000
Phillipines	Manila Regional Office 1131 Roxas Blvd. Ermita 0930 Manila, PI 96440PI (011) (632) 528-6300
Puerto Rico	San Juan Regional Office 150 Carlos Chardon Avenue Hato Rey, PR 00918 (800) 827-1000

STATE	ADDRESS/TELEPHONE
Rhode Island	Providence Regional Office 380 Westminister Mall Providence, RI 02903 (800) 827-1000
South Carolina	Columbia Regional Office 1801 Assembly Street Columbia, SC 29201 (800) 827-1000
South Dakota	Sioux Falls Regional Office 2501 W 22nd St. Sioux Falls, SD 57117 (800) 827-1000
Tennessee	Nashville Regional Office 110 9th Avenue South Nashville, TN 37203 (800) 827-1000 Southern Area Office 3322 West End, Suite 408 Nashville, TN 37203 (800) 827-1000
Texas	Houston Regional Office 6900 Almeda Road Houston, TX 77030 TX (800) 827-1000 Waco Regional Office 1 Veterans Plaza 701 Clay Ave. Waco, TX 76799 (800) 827-1000
Utah	Salt Lake City Regional Office 550 Foothill Drive Salt Lake City, UT 84158 (800) 827-1000
Vermont	White River Junction Regional Office 215 North Main Street White River Junction, VT 05009 (800) 827-1000
Virginia	Roanoke Regional Office 210 Franklin Rd. SW Roanoke, VA 24011 (800) 827-1000

STATE	ADDRESS/TELEPHONE
Washington	Seattle Regional Office Federal Building 915 2nd Avenue Seattle, WA 98174 (800) 827-1000
West Virginia	Huntington Regional Office 640 Fourth Ave. Huntington, WV 25701 (800) 827-1000
Wisconsin	Milwaukee Regional Office 5400 West National Avenue Milwaukee, WI 53214 (800) 827-1000
Wyoming	Cheyenne VA Medical/Regional Office Center 2360 E. Pershing Blvd. Cheyenne, WY 82001 (800) 827-1000

Source: U.S. Veterans Administration.

APPENDIX 2:
DIRECTORY OF U.S. ARMY MILITARY
INSTALLATIONS

STATE	MILITARY FACILITIES
Alabama	Anniston Army Depot Tel: 256-235-7445 Fort Rucker Tel: 334-255-1110 Redstone Arsenal Tel: 256-876-2151
Alaska	Fort Greely Tel: 907-873-3284 Fort Richardson Tel: 907-384-1110 Fort Wainwright Tel: 907-353-1110
Arizona	Fort Huachuca Tel: 520-533-2330 Yuma Proving Ground Tel: 928-328-3287
Arkansas	Pine Bluff Arsenal Tel: 870-540-3217
California	DLI FLC Presidio Tel: 831-242-5119 Fort Irwin Tel: 760-380-1110
Colorado	Fort Carson Tel: 719-526-5811

STATE	MILITARY FACILITIES
District of Columbia	Fort McNair Tel: 703-545-6700 Walter Reed Army Medical Center Tel: 202-782-3501
Georgia	Fort Benning Tel: 706-545-2011 Fort Gordon Tel: 706-791-0110 Fort McPherson Tel: 404-464-2980 Fort Stewart Tel: 912-767-1411 Hunter Army Airfield Tel: 912-352-6521
Hawaii	Schofield/Shafter Tel: 808-471-7110
Illinois	Charles M. Price Support Center Tel: 618-452-4212 Rock Island Arsenal Tel: 309-782-6001
Kansas	Fort Leavenworth Tel: 913-684-4021 Fort Riley Tel: 785-239-2672
Kentucky	Fort Campbell Tel: 270-798-2151 Fort Knox Tel: 502-624-1181 U.S. Army Recruiting Command Tel: 502-626-1080
Louisiana	Fort Polk Tel: 337-531-2911
Maryland	Aberdeen Test Center Tel: 410-306-2353 Fort Detrick Tel: 301-619-8000 Fort Meade Tel: 301-677-6261

STATE	MILITARY FACILITIES
Massachussetts	Devens Reserve Training Area Tel: 978-796-3951 Soldiers Systems Center Tel: 508-233-4798
Missouri	Fort Leonard Wood Tel: 573-596-0131
New Jersey	Fort Dix Tel: 609-562-1011 Fort Monmouth Tel: 732-532-9000 Picatinny Arsenal Tel: 973-724-4939
New York	Fort Drum Tel: 315-772-6011 Fort Hamilton Tel: 718-630-4754 USMA West Point Tel: 845-938-4011 Watervliet Arsenal 518-266-5103
North Carolina	Fort Bragg Tel: 910-396-0011
Oklahoma	Fort Sill Tel: 580-442-8111 McAlester Army Ammunition Plant Tel: 918-420-7490
Pennsylvania	Carlisle Barracks Tel: 717-245-3131 Tobyhanna Army Depot Tel: 570-895-7000
Puerto Rico	Fort Buchanan Tel: 1-800-786-5315
South Carolina	Fort Jackson Tel: 803-751-1110

STATE	MILITARY FACILITIES
Texas	Fort Bliss Tel: 915-568-2121 Fort Hood Tel: 254-287-1110 Fort Sam Houston Tel: 210-221-1211 Red River Army Depot Tel: 903-334-4137
Utah	Dugway Proving Ground Tel: 435-831-2321 Tooele Army Depot Tel: 435-833-2852
Virginia	Fort Belvoir Tel: 703-545-6700 Fort Eustis Tel: 757-878-3638 Fort Lee Tel: 804-765-3000 Fort Monroe Tel: 757-727-8000 Fort Myer Tel: 202-685-3089 Fort Story Tel: 757-422-7305
Washington	Fort Lewis Tel: 235-967-1110
Wisconsin	Fort McCoy Tel: 608-388-2222

Source: Military Advantage.

APPENDIX 3:
DIRECTORY OF U.S. NAVY MILITARY INSTALLATIONS

STATE	MILITARY FACILITIES
California	Naval Base—Port Heuneme Tel: 805-989-1110 Naval Station—San Diego Tel: 619-556-1011 Naval Air Weapons Station—China Lake Tel: 760-939-9011 Naval Post Graduate School—Monterey Tel: 831-656-2441
Connecticut	Naval Submarine Base—New London Tel: 860-694-4636
District of Columbia	Naval District—Washington Tel: 703-545-6700
Florida	Naval Air Station—Jacksonville Tel: 904-542-8195 Naval Air Station—Key West Tel: 305-292-7556 Naval Air Station—Pensacola Tel: 850-452-0111 Naval Air Station—Whiting Field Tel: 850-623-7011 Naval Coastal Systems Station—Panama City Tel: 850-234-4011

STATE	MILITARY FACILITIES
	Naval Station—Mayport Tel: 904-270-5011 Naval Technical Training Center—Corry Station Tel: 850-452-2000
Georgia	Naval Air Station—Atlanta Tel: 678-655-5000 Naval Submarine Base—Kings Bay Tel: 912-573-2000
Hawaii	Naval Base—Oahu Tel: 808-473-4222 Naval Station—Barking Sands Tel: 808-334-4254 Naval Station—Pearl Harbor Tel: 808-471-2405
Illinois	Naval Training Command—Great Lakes Tel: 847-688-3500
Louisiana	Naval Aviation Station—New Orleans Tel: 504-678-3011 Naval Support Activity—New Orleans Tel: 504-678-2290
Maine	Naval Air Station—New Brunswick Tel: 207-921-1110
Maryland	Naval Air Station—Patuxent River Tel: 301-342-3000 Naval Security Group Activity—Fort Meade Tel: 301-688-6311 U.S. Naval Academy—Annapolis Tel: 410-293-1000
Mississippi	Naval Air Station—Meridian Tel: 601-679-2211 Naval Construction Battalion Center—Gulfport Tel: 228-871-2555 Naval Station—Pascagoula Tel: 228-761-2140
Nevada	Naval Air Station—Fallon Tel: 775-426-5161

STATE	MILITARY FACILITIES
New Hampshire	Naval Station—Portsmouth Tel: 207-438-1000
New Jersey	Naval Air Engineering Station—Lakehurst Tel: 732-323-2011 Naval Weapons Station—Earle Tel: 732-866-2500
New York	Naval Support Unit—Saratoga Springs Tel: 518-886-0200
Pennsylvania	Naval Air Station—Willow Grove Tel: 215-443-6033
Rhode Island	Naval Station—Newport Tel: 401-849-4500
South Carolina	Naval Weapons Station—Charleston Tel: 843-764-7480
Tennessee	Naval Support Activity Mid-South—Millington Tel: 901-874-5111
Texas	Naval Air Station—Corpus Christi Tel: 361-961-2811 Naval Air Station—Fort Worth Tel: 817-782-5000 Naval Air Station—Kingsville Tel: 361-516-6136 Naval Station—Ingleside Tel: 361-776-4201
Virginia	Naval Station—Dam Neck Tel: 757-433-6234 Naval Amphibious Base—Little Creek Tel: 757-462-7386 Naval Air Station—Oceana Tel: 757-433-2366 Naval Station—Norfolk Tel: 757-444-0000 Naval Support Activity Northwest—Hampton Roads Tel: 757-421-8000

STATE	MILITARY FACILITIES
	Naval Surface Warfare Center—Dahlgren Tel: 540-653-8531 Naval Weapons Station—Yorktown Tel: 757-887-4000 Surface Combat Systems Center—Wallops Island Tel: 757-824-1692
Washington	Naval Air Station—Whidbey Island Tel: 360-257-3331 Naval Station—Bremerton Tel: 360-476-3711 Naval Station—Everett Tel: 425-304-3000 Naval Base—Bangor Tel: 360-396-4840

Source: Military Advantage.

APPENDIX 4:
DIRECTORY OF U.S. AIR FORCE
MILITARY INSTALLATIONS

STATE	MILITARY FACILITIES
Alabama	Maxwell Gunter Air Force Base Tel: 334-953-1110
Alaska	Clear Air Station Tel: 907-585-6416 Eielson Air Force Base Tel: 907-377-1110 Elmendorf Air Force Base Tel: 907-552-1110
Arizona	Davis-Monthan Air Force Base Tel: 520-228-5690 Luke Air Force Base Tel: 623-856-1110
Arkansas	Little Rock Air Force Base Tel: 501-987-1110
California	Beale Air Force Base Tel: 530-634-1110 Edwards Air Force Base Tel: 661-277-2777 Los Angeles Air Force Base Tel: 562-363-1110 March Air Reserve Base Tel: 951-655-5350

STATE	MILITARY FACILITIES
	McClellan Air Force Base Tel: 916-643-4113
	Travis Air Force Base Tel: 707-424-1110
	Vandenberg Air Force Base Tel: 805-606-1110
Colorado	Buckley Air Force Base Tel: 720-847-9011
	Petersen Air Force Base Tel: 719-556-7011
	Schriever Air Force Base Tel: 719-567-1110
Delaware	Dover Air Force Base Tel: 302-677-3000
District of Columbia	Bolling Air Force Base Tel: 703-545-6700
Florida	Eglin Air Force Base Tel: 850-882-1110
	Huriburt Air Force Base Tel: 850-884-1110
	MacDill Air Force Base Tel: 813-828-1110
	Patrick Air Force Base Tel: 321-494-1110
	Tyndall Air Force Base Tel: 850-283-1110
Georgia	Moody Air Force Base Tel: 229-257-4211
	Robins Air Force Base Tel: 478-926-1113
Hawaii	Hickam Air Force Base Tel: 808-449-1110
Idaho	Mountain Home Air Force Base Tel: 208-828-2111
Illinois	Scott Air Force Base Tel: 618-256-1110

STATE	MILITARY FACILITIES
Indiana	Grissom Air Reserve Base Tel: 765-688-5211
Kansas	McConnell Air Force Base Tel: 316-759-6100
Louisiana	Barksdale Air Force Base Tel: 318-456-8400
Maryland	Andrews Air Force Base Tel: 301-981-1110
Massachusetts	Hanscom Air Force Base Tel: 781-377-4441
Mississippi	Columbus Air Force Base Tel: 662-434-7322 Keesler Air Force Base Tel: 228-377-1110
Missouri	Whiteman Air Force Base Tel: 660-687-1110
Montana	Malmstrom Air Force Base Tel: 406-731-1110
Nevada	Nellis Air Force Base Tel: 702-652-1110
New Jersey	McGuire Air Force Base Tel: 609-754-1100
New Mexico	Cannon Air Force Base Tel: 505-784-3311 Holloman Air Force Base Tel: 505-572-6511 Kirtland Air Force Base Tel: 505-846-0011
North Carolina	Pope Air Force Base Tel: 910-394-1110 Seymour Johnson Air Force Base Tel: 919-722-1110
North Dakota	Grand Forks Air Force Base Tel: 701-747-3000 Minot Air Force Base Tel: 701-723-1110

STATE	MILITARY FACILITIES
Ohio	Wright-Patterson Air Force Base Tel: 937-257-1110
Oklahoma	Altus Air Force Base Tel: 580-482-8100 Tinker Air Force Base Tel: 405-732-7321 Vance Air Force Base Tel: 580-213-5000
South Carolina	Charleston Air Force Base Tel: 843-963-4406 Shaw Air Force Base Tel: 803-895-1110
South Dakota	Ellsworth Air Force Base Tel: 605-385-1110
Tennessee	Arnold Air Force Base Tel: 615-454-3000
Texas	Brooks Air Force Base Tel: 210-536-1110 Dyess Air Force Base Tel: 325-696-5999 Goodfellow Air Force Base Tel: 325-654-1110 Kelly Air Force Base Tel: 210-925-1110 Lackland Air Force Base Tel: 210-671-1110 Laughlin Air Force Base Tel: 830-298-3511 Randolph Air Force Base Tel: 210-652-1110 Sheppard Air Force Base Tel: 940-676-2511
Utah	Hill Air Force Base Tel: 801-777-7221
Virginia	Langley Air Force Base Tel: 757-764-9990

STATE	MILITARY FACILITIES
Washington	Fairchild Air Force Base Tel: 509-247-1212 McChord Air Force Base Tel: 253-982-1110
Wyoming	Francis E. Warren Air Force Base Tel: 307-773-1110

Source: Military Advantage.

APPENDIX 5:
DIRECTORY OF U.S. MARINE CORPS
MILITARY INSTALLATIONS

STATE	MILITARY FACILITIES
Arizona	MCAS Yuma Tel: 928-269-2011
California	Camp Pendleton Tel: 760-725-4111 MCAGCC 29 Palms Tel: 760-830-6000 MCAS Miramar Tel: 858-577-1011 MCLB Barstow Tel: 760-577-6418 MCRD San Diego Tel: 619-524-8762
Georgia	MCLB Albany Tel: 229-639-5000
Hawaii	MCBH Kaneohe Bay Tel: 808-471-7110
Missouri	MCSA Kansas City Tel: 816-843-3652
North Carolina	Camp Lejeune Tel: 910-451-1113 MCAS Cherry Point Tel: 252-466-2811

STATE	MILITARY FACILITIES
	MCAS New River Tel: 910-451-1113
South Carolina	MCAS Beaufort Tel: 843-522-7100
	MCRD Parris Island Tel: 843-228-2976
Virginia	Henderson Hall Tel: 703-545-6700
	Quantico Tel: 703-784-2121

Source: Military Advantage.

APPENDIX 6:
DIRECTORY OF U.S. COAST GUARD
MILITARY INSTALLATIONS

STATE	MILITARY FACILITIES
Alaska	USCG - Kodiak Tel: 907-487-5760 USCG - Juneau Tel: 907-463-2123 USCG - Ketchikan Tel: 907-228-0211
California	USCG - Petaluma Tel: 707-765-7514
Florida	USCG - Miami Tel: 305-953-2100
Hawaii	USCG - Honolulu Tel: 808-842-2970
North Carolina	USCG - Elizabeth City Tel: 252-335-6229
Virginia	USCG - Hampton Roads Tel: 757-686-4030 USCG - Yorktown Tel: 757-898-2314

Source: Military Advantage.

APPENDIX 7:
THE VETERANS EMPLOYMENT OPPORTUNITIES ACT
[PUB. L. NO. 105-339, 10/31/98]

PUBLIC LAW 105-339

105th CONGRESS - 2d Session

S. 1021

AN ACT To amend title 5, United States Code, to provide that consideration may not be denied to preference eligibles applying for certain positions in the competitive service, and for other purposes.

Be it enacted by the Senate and House of Representatives of the United States of America in Congress assembled,

SECTION 1. SHORT TITLE.

This Act may be cited as the 'Veterans Employment Opportunities Act of 1998'.

SEC. 2. ACCESS FOR VETERANS.

Section 3304 of title 5, United States Code, is amended by adding at the end the following:

'(f)(1) Preference eligibles or veterans who have been separated from the armed forces under honorable conditions after 3 years or more of active service may not be denied the opportunity to compete for vacant positions for which the agency making the announcement will accept applications from individuals outside its own workforce under merit promotion procedures.

'(2) This subsection shall not be construed to confer an entitlement to veterans' preference that is not otherwise required by law.

'(3) The area of consideration for all merit promotion announcements which include consideration of individuals of the Federal workforce shall indicate that preference eligibles and veterans who have been separated from the armed forces under honorable conditions after 3 years or more of active service are eligible to apply. The announcements shall be publicized in accordance with section 3327.

'(4) The Office of Personnel and Management shall establish an appointing authority to appoint such preference eligibles and veterans.'.

SEC. 3. IMPROVED REDRESS FOR PREFERENCE ELIGIBLES.

(a) IN GENERAL—Subchapter I of chapter 33 of title 5, United States Code, is amended by adding at the end the following:

'Sec. 3330a. Preference eligibles; administrative redress

'(a)(1) A preference eligible who alleges that an agency has violated such individual's rights under any statute or regulation relating to veterans' preference may file a complaint with the Secretary of Labor.

'(2)(A) A complaint under this subsection must be filed within 60 days after the date of the alleged violation.

'(B) Such complaint shall be in writing, be in such form as the Secretary may prescribe, specify the agency against which the complaint is filed, and contain a summary of the allegations that form the basis for the complaint.

'(3) The Secretary shall, upon request, provide technical assistance to a potential complainant with respect to a complaint under this subsection.

'(b)(1) The Secretary of Labor shall investigate each complaint under subsection (a).

'(2) In carrying out any investigation under this subsection, the Secretary's duly authorized representatives shall, at all reasonable times, have reasonable access to, for purposes of examination, and the right to copy and receive, any documents of any person or agency that the Secretary considers relevant to the investigation.

'(3) In carrying out any investigation under this subsection, the Secretary may require by subpoena the attendance and testimony of witnesses and the production of documents relating to any matter under investigation. In case of disobedience of the subpoena or contumacy and on request of the Secretary, the Attorney General may apply to any district court of the United States in whose jurisdiction such disobedience or contumacy occurs for an order enforcing the subpoena.

'(4) Upon application, the district courts of the United States shall have jurisdiction to issue writs commanding any person or agency to comply with the subpoena of the Secretary or to comply with any order of the Secretary made pursuant to a lawful investigation under this subsection and the district courts shall have jurisdiction to punish failure to obey a subpoena or other lawful order of the Secretary as a contempt of court.

'(c)(1)(A) If the Secretary of Labor determines as a result of an investigation under subsection (b) that the action alleged in a complaint under subsection (a) occurred, the Secretary shall attempt to resolve the complaint by making reasonable efforts to ensure that the agency specified in the complaint complies with applicable provisions of statute or regulation relating to veterans' preference.

'(B) The Secretary of Labor shall make determinations referred to in subparagraph (A) based on a preponderance of the evidence.

'(2) If the efforts of the Secretary under subsection (b) with respect to a complaint under subsection (a) do not result in the resolution of the complaint, the Secretary shall notify the person who submitted the complaint, in writing, of the results of the Secretary's investigation under subsection (b).

'(d)(1) If the Secretary of Labor is unable to resolve a complaint under subsection (a) within 60 days after the date on which it is filed, the complainant may elect to appeal the alleged violation to the Merit Systems Protection Board in accordance with such procedures as the Merit Systems Protection Board shall prescribe, except that in no event may any such appeal be brought—

'(A) before the 61st day after the date on which the complaint is filed; or

'(B) later than 15 days after the date on which the complainant receives written notification from the Secretary under subsection (c)(2).

'(2) An appeal under this subsection may not be brought unless—

'(A) the complainant first provides written notification to the Secretary of such complainant's intention to bring such appeal; and

'(B) appropriate evidence of compliance with subparagraph (A) is included (in such form and manner as the Merit Systems Protection Board may prescribe) with the notice of appeal under this subsection.

'(3) Upon receiving notification under paragraph (2)(A), the Secretary shall not continue to investigate or further attempt to resolve the complaint to which the notification relates.

'(e)(1) This section shall not be construed to prohibit a preference eligible from appealing directly to the Merit Systems Protection Board from any action which is appealable to the Board under any other law, rule, or regulation, in lieu of administrative redress under this section.

'(2) A preference eligible may not pursue redress for an alleged violation described in subsection (a) under this section at the same time the preference eligible pursues redress for such violation under any other law, rule, or regulation.

'Sec. 3330b. Preference eligibles; judicial redress

'(a) In lieu of continuing the administrative redress procedure provided under section 3330a(d), a preference eligible may elect, in accordance with this section, to terminate those administrative proceedings and file an action with the appropriate United States district court not later than 60 days after the date of the election.

'(b) An election under this section may not be made—

'(1) before the 121st day after the date on which the appeal is filed with the Merit Systems Protection Board under section 3330a(d); or

'(2) after the Merit Systems Protection Board has issued a judicially reviewable decision on the merits of the appeal.

'(c) An election under this section shall be made, in writing, in such form and manner as the Merit Systems Protection Board shall by regulation prescribe. The election shall be effective as of the date on which it is received, and the administrative proceeding to which it relates shall terminate immediately upon the receipt of such election.

'Sec. 3330c. Preference eligibles; remedy

'(a) If the Merit Systems Protection Board (in a proceeding under section 3330a) or a court (in a proceeding under section 3330b) determines that an agency has violated a right described in section 3330a, the Board or court (as the case may be) shall order the agency to comply with such provisions and award compensation for any loss of wages or benefits suffered by the individual by reason of the violation involved. If the Board or court determines that such violation was willful, it shall award an amount equal to backpay as liquidated damages.

'(b) A preference eligible who prevails in an action under section 3330a or 3330b shall be awarded reasonable attorney fees, expert witness fees, and other litigation expenses.'.

(b) CLERICAL AMENDMENT—The table of sections at the beginning of chapter 33 of title 5, United States Code, is amended by adding after the item relating to section 3330 the following:

'3330a. Preference eligibles; administrative redress.
'3330b. Preference eligibles; judicial redress.
'3330c. Preference eligibles; remedy.'.

SEC. 4. EXTENSION OF VETERANS' PREFERENCE.

(a) AMENDMENT TO TITLE 5, UNITED STATES CODE—Paragraph (3) of section 2108 of title 5, United States Code, is amended by striking 'the Federal Bureau of Investigation and Drug Enforcement Administration Senior Executive Service, or the General Accounting Office;' and inserting 'or the Federal Bureau of Investigation and Drug Enforcement Administration Senior Executive Service;'.

(b) AMENDMENTS TO TITLE 3, UNITED STATES CODE—

(1) IN GENERAL—Chapter 2 of title 3, United States Code, is amended by adding at the end the following:

'Sec. 115. Veterans' preference

'(a) Subject to subsection (b), appointments under sections 105, 106, and 107 shall be made in accordance with section 2108, and sections 3309 through 3312, of title 5.

'(b) Subsection (a) shall not apply to any appointment to a position the rate of basic pay for which is at least equal to the minimum rate established for positions in the Senior Executive Service under section 5382 of title 5 and the duties of which are comparable to those described in section 3132(a)(2) of such title or to any other position if, with respect to such position, the President makes certification—

'(1) that such position is—

'(A) a confidential or policy-making position; or

'(B) a position for which political affiliation or political philosophy is otherwise an important qualification; and

'(2) that any individual selected for such position is expected to vacate the position at or before the end of the President's term (or terms) of office.

Each individual appointed to a position described in the preceding sentence as to which the expectation described in paragraph (2) applies shall be notified as to such expectation, in writing, at the time of appointment to such position.'.

(2) CLERICAL AMENDMENT—The table of sections at the beginning of chapter 2 of title 3, United States Code, is amended by adding at the end the following:

'115. Veterans' preference.'.

(c) LEGISLATIVE BRANCH APPOINTMENTS—

(1) DEFINITIONS—For the purposes of this subsection, the terms 'covered employee' and 'Board' shall each have the meaning given such term by section 101 of the Congressional Accountability Act of 1995 (2 U.S.C. 1301).

(2) RIGHTS AND PROTECTIONS—The rights and protections established under section 2108, sections 3309 through 3312, and

subchapter I of chapter 35, of title 5, United States Code, shall apply to covered employees.

(3) REMEDIES—

(A) IN GENERAL—The remedy for a violation of paragraph (2) shall be such remedy as would be appropriate if awarded under applicable provisions of title 5, United States Code, in the case of a violation of the relevant corresponding provision (referred to in paragraph (2)) of such title.

(B) PROCEDURE—The procedure for consideration of alleged violations of paragraph (2) shall be the same as apply under section 401 of the Congressional Accountability Act of 1995 (and the provisions of law referred to therein) in the case of an alleged violation of part A of title II of such Act.

(4) REGULATIONS TO IMPLEMENT SUBSECTION—

(A) IN GENERAL—The Board shall, pursuant to section 304 of the Congressional Accountability Act of 1995 (2 U.S.C. 1384), issue regulations to implement this subsection.

(B) AGENCY REGULATIONS—The regulations issued under subparagraph (A) shall be the same as the most relevant substantive regulations (applicable with respect to the executive branch) promulgated to implement the statutory provisions referred to in paragraph (2) except insofar as the Board may determine, for good cause shown and stated together with the regulation, that a modification of such regulations would be more effective for the implementation of the rights and protections under this subsection.

(C) COORDINATION—The regulations issued under subparagraph (A) shall be consistent with section 225 of the Congressional Accountability Act of 1995 (2 U.S.C. 1361).

(5) APPLICABILITY—Notwithstanding any other provision of this subsection, the term 'covered employee' shall not, for purposes of this subsection, include an employee—

(A) whose appointment is made by the President with the advice and consent of the Senate;

(B) whose appointment is made by a Member of Congress or by a committee or subcommittee of either House of Congress; or

(C) who is appointed to a position, the duties of which are equivalent to those of a Senior Executive Service position (within the meaning of section 3132(a)(2) of title 5, United States Code).

(6) EFFECTIVE DATE—Paragraphs (2) and (3) shall be effective as of the effective date of the regulations under paragraph (4).

(d) JUDICIAL BRANCH APPOINTMENTS—

(1) IN GENERAL—Subject to paragraphs (2) and (3), the Judicial Conference of the United States shall prescribe procedures to provide for—

(A) veterans' preference in the consideration of applicants for employment, and in the conduct of any reductions in force, within the judicial branch; and

(B) redress for alleged violations of any rights provided for under subparagraph (A).

(2) PROCEDURES—Under the procedures, a preference eligible (as defined by section 2108 of title 5, United States Code) shall be afforded preferences in a manner and to the extent consistent with preferences afforded to preference eligibles in the executive branch.

(3) EXCLUSIONS—Nothing in the procedures shall apply with respect to an applicant or employee—

(A) whose appointment is made by the President with the advice and consent of the Senate;

(B) whose appointment is as a judicial officer;

(C) whose appointment is required by statute to be made by or with the approval of a court or judicial officer; or

(D) whose appointment is to a position, the duties of which are equivalent to those of a Senior Executive Service position (within the meaning of section 3132(a)(2) of title 5, United States Code).

(4) DEFINITIONS—For purposes of this subsection, the term 'judicial officer' means a justice, judge, or magistrate judge listed in subparagraph (A), (B), (F), or (G) of section 376(a)(1) of title 28, United States Code.

(5) SUBMISSION TO CONGRESS; EFFECTIVE DATE—

(A) SUBMISSION TO CONGRESS—Not later than 12 months after the date of enactment of this Act, the Judicial Conference of the United States shall submit a copy of the procedures prescribed under this subsection to the Committee on Government Reform and Oversight and the Committee on the Judiciary of the House of Representatives and the Committee on Governmental Affairs and the Committee on the Judiciary of the Senate.

(B) EFFECTIVE DATE—The procedures prescribed under this subsection shall take effect 13 months after the date of enactment of this Act.

SEC. 5. VETERANS' PREFERENCE REQUIRED FOR REDUCTIONS IN FORCE IN THE FEDERAL AVIATION ADMINISTRATION.

Section 347(b) of the Department of Transportation and Related Agencies Appropriations Act, 1996 (109 Stat. 460) is amended—

(1) by striking 'and' at the end of paragraph (6);

(2) by striking the period at the end of paragraph (7) and inserting '; and'; and

(3) by adding at the end the following:

'(8) sections 3501-3504, as such sections relate to veterans' preference.'.

SEC. 6. FAILURE TO COMPLY WITH VETERANS' PREFERENCE REQUIREMENTS TO BE TREATED AS A PROHIBITED PERSONNEL PRACTICE FOR CERTAIN PURPOSES.

(a) IN GENERAL—Subsection (b) of section 2302 of title 5, United States Code, is amended—

(1) by striking 'or' at the end of paragraph (10);

(2) by redesignating paragraph (11) as paragraph (12); and

(3) by inserting after paragraph (10) the following:

'(11)(A) knowingly take, recommend, or approve any personnel action if the taking of such action would violate a veterans' preference requirement; or

'(B) knowingly fail to take, recommend, or approve any personnel action if the failure to take such action would violate a veterans' preference requirement; or'.

(b) DEFINITION; LIMITATION—Section 2302 of title 5, United States Code, is amended by adding at the end the following:

'(e)(1) For the purpose of this section, the term 'veterans' preference requirement' means any of the following provisions of law:

'(A) Sections 2108, 3305(b), 3309, 3310, 3311, 3312, 3313, 3314, 3315, 3316, 3317(b), 3318, 3320, 3351, 3352, 3363, 3501, 3502(b), 3504, and 4303(e) and (with respect to a preference eligible referred to in section 7511(a)(1)(B)) subchapter II of chapter 75 and section 7701.

'(B) Sections 943(c)(2) and 1784(c) of title 10.

'(C) Section 1308(b) of the Alaska National Interest Lands Conservation Act.

'(D) Section 301(c) of the Foreign Service Act of 1980.

'(E) Sections 106(f), 7281(e), and 7802(5) of title 38.

'(F) Section 1005(a) of title 39.

'(G) Any other provision of law that the Director of the Office of Personnel Management designates in regulations as being a veterans' preference requirement for the purposes of this subsection.

'(H) Any regulation prescribed under subsection (b) or (c) of section 1302 and any other regulation that implements a provision of law referred to in any of the preceding subparagraphs.

'(2) Notwithstanding any other provision of this title, no authority to order corrective action shall be available in connection with a prohibited personnel practice described in subsection (b)(11). Nothing in this paragraph shall be considered to affect any authority under section 1215 (relating to disciplinary action).'.

(c) REPEALS—

(1) SECTION 1599c OF TITLE 10, UNITED STATES CODE—

(A) REPEAL—Section 1599c of title 10, United States Code, is repealed.

(B) CLERICAL AMENDMENT—The table of sections at the beginning of chapter 81 of such title is amended by striking out the item relating to section 1599c.

(2) SECTION 2302(a)(1) OF TITLE 5, UNITED STATES CODE— Subsection (a)(1) of section 2302 of title 5, United States Code, is amended to read as follows:

'(a)(1) For the purpose of this title, 'prohibited personnel practice' means any action described in subsection (b).'.

(d) SAVINGS PROVISION—This section shall be treated as if it had never been enacted for purposes of any personnel action (within the meaning of section 2302 of title 5, United States Code) preceding the date of enactment of this Act.

SEC. 7. EXPANSION AND IMPROVEMENT OF VETERANS' EMPLOYMENT EMPHASIS UNDER FEDERAL CONTRACTS.

(a) COVERED VwwwETERANS—Section 4212 of title 38, United States Code, is amended—

(1) in subsection (a)—

(A) by striking out '$10,000' and inserting in lieu thereof '$25,000'; and

(B) by striking out 'special disabled veterans and veterans of the Vietnam era' and inserting in lieu thereof 'special disabled veterans, veterans of the Vietnam era, and any other veterans who served on active duty during a war or in a campaign or expedition for which a campaign badge has been authorized';

(2) in subsection (b), by striking out 'special disabled veteran or veteran of the Vietnam era' and inserting in lieu thereof 'veteran covered by the first sentence of subsection (a)'; and

(3) in subsection (d)(1), by striking out 'veterans of the Vietnam era or special disabled veterans' both places it appears and inserting in lieu thereof 'special disabled veterans, veterans of the Vietnam era, or other veterans who served on active duty during a war or in a campaign or expedition for which a campaign badge has been authorized'.

(b) PROHIBITION ON CONTRACTING WITH ENTITIES NOT MEETING REPORTING REQUIREMENTS—(1) Subchapter III of chapter 13 of title 31, United States Code, is amended by adding at the end the following:

'Sec. 1354. Limitation on use of appropriated funds for contracts with entities not meeting veterans' employment reporting requirements

'(a)(1) Subject to paragraph (2), no agency may obligate or expend funds appropriated for the agency for a fiscal year to enter into a contract described in section 4212(a) of title 38 with a contractor from which a report was required under section 4212(d) of that title with respect to the preceding fiscal year if such contractor did not submit such report.

'(2) Paragraph (1) shall cease to apply with respect to a contractor otherwise covered by that paragraph on the date on which the contractor submits the report required by such section 4212(d) for the fiscal year concerned.

'(b) The Secretary of Labor shall make available in a database a list of the contractors that have complied with the provisions of such section 4212(d).'.

(2) The table of sections at the beginning of chapter 13 of such title is amended by adding at the end the following:

'1354. Limitation on use of appropriated funds for contracts with entities not meeting veterans' employment reporting requirements.'.

SEC. 8. REQUIREMENT FOR ADDITIONAL INFORMATION IN ANNUAL REPORTS FROM FEDERAL CONTRACTORS ON VETERANS EMPLOYMENT.

Section 4212(d)(1) of title 38, United States Code, as amended by section 7(a)(3) of this Act, is further amended—

(1) by striking out 'and' at the end of subparagraph (A);

(2) by striking out the period at the end of subparagraph (B) and inserting in lieu thereof '; and'; and

(3) by adding at the end the following:

'(C) the maximum number and the minimum number of employees of such contractor during the period covered by the report.'.

APPENDIX 8:
VETERANS CENTERS

STATE	ADDRESS/TELEPHONE
Alabama	Birmingham Vet Center 1500 5th Avenue South Birmingham, AL 35233 (205) 731-0550 Mobile Vet Center 2577 Government Blvd. Mobile, AL 36606 (251) 478-5906 Montgomery Vet Center 215 Perry Hill Road, Bldg.6, 2nd Fl. Montgomery, AL 36109 (334) 272-4670
Alaska	Anchorage Vet Center 4201 Tudor Centre Dr., Suite 115 Anchorage, AK 99508 (907) 563-6966 Fairbanks Vet Center 540 4th Ave., Suite 100 Fairbanks, AK 99701 (907) 456-4238 Kenai Vet Center Red Diamond Center 43335 Kalifornsky Beach Rd. Soldotna, AK 99669 (907) 260-7640 Wasilla Vet Center 851 E. West Point Dr., Suite 111 Wasilla, AK 99654 (907) 376-4318

STATE	ADDRESS/TELEPHONE
Arizona	Chinle Vet Center P.O. Box 1934 Chinle, AZ 86503 (928) 674-3682 Hopi Vet Center P.O. Box 929 1 Main Street Hotevilla, AZ 86030 (928) 734-5166 Phoenix East Valley Vet Center 1303 South Longmore, Suite 5 Mesa, AZ 85202 (480) 610-6727 Phoenix Vet Center 77 E. Weldon, Suite 100 Phoenix, AZ 85012 (602) 640-2981 Prescott Vet Center 161 South Granite St., Suite B Prescott, AZ 86303 (928) 778-3469 Tucson Vet Center 3055 N. First Avenue Tucson, AZ 85719 (520) 882-0333
Arkansas	Little Rock Vet Center 201 W. Broadway Street, Suite A North Little Rock, AR 72114 (501) 324-6395
California	Pacific Western Regional Office 420 Executive Court North, Suite G Fairfield, CA 94534 (707) 646-2988 Chico Vet Center 280 Cohasset Road, Suite 100 Chico, CA 95928 (530) 899-8549 Concord Vet Center 1899 Clayton Rd., Suite 140 Concord, CA 94520 (925) 680-4526

STATE	ADDRESS/TELEPHONE
	Corona Vet Center 800 Magnolia Avenue, Suite 110 Corona, CA 82879 (951) 734-0525
	East Los Angeles Vet Center 5400 E. Olympic Blvd., Suite 140 Commerce, CA 90022 (323) 728-9966
	Fresno Vet Center 3636 North 1st St., Suite 112 Fresno, CA 93726 (559) 487-5660
	Los Angeles Veterans Resource Center 1045 W. Redondo Beach Blvd., Suite 150 Gardena, CA 90247 (310) 767-1221
	Modesto Vet Center 1219 N. Carpenter Rd., Suite 12 Modesto, CA 95351 (209) 569-0713
	Northbay Vet Center 6225 State Farm Drive, Suite 101 Rohnert Park, CA 94928 (707) 586-3295
	Oakland Vet Center 1504 Franklin St., Suite 200 Oakland, CA 94612 (510) 763-3904
	Orange County Vet Center 12453 Lewis St., Suite 101 Garden Grove, CA 92840 (714) 776-0161
	Peninsula Vet Center 2946 Broadway St. Redwood City, CA 94062 (650) 299-0672
	Redwoods Vet Center 2830 G Street, Suite A Eureka, CA 95501 (707) 444-8271
	Sacramento Vet Center 1111 Howe Avenue, Suite 390 Sacramento, CA 95825 (916) 566-7430

STATE	ADDRESS/TELEPHONE
	San Bernardino Vet Center 155 West Hospitality Lane, Suite 140 San Bernardino, CA 92408 (909) 890-0797
	San Diego Vet Center 2900 Sixth Avenue San Diego, CA 92103 (619) 294-2040
	San Francisco Vet Center 505 Polk Street San Francisco, CA 94102 (415) 441-5051
	San Jose Vet Center 278 North 2nd St. San Jose, CA 95112 (408) 993-0729
	San Marcos Vet Center One Civic Center Dr., Suite 140 San Marcos, CA 92069 (760) 744-6914
	Santa Cruz County Vet Center 1350 41st Ave., Suite 102 Capitola, CA 95010 (831) 464-4575
	Sepulveda Vet Center 9737 Haskell Ave. Sepulveda, CA 91343 (818) 892-9227
	Ventura Vet Center 790 E. Santa Clara St., Suite 100 Ventura, CA 93001 (805) 585-1860
	West Los Angeles Vet Center 5730 Uplander Way, Suite 100 Culver City, CA 90230 (310) 641-0326
Colorado	4A Western Mountain Regional Office 789 Sherman Street, Suite 570 Denver, CO 80203 (303) 393-2897
	Boulder Vet Center 2336 Canyon Blvd., Suite 103 Boulder, CO 80302 (303) 440-7306

STATE	ADDRESS/TELEPHONE
	Colorado Springs Vet Center 416 E. Colorado Avenue Colorado Springs, CO 80903 (719) 471-9992 Denver Vet Center 7465 East First Avenue, Suite B Denver, CO 80230 (303) 326-0645 Ft. Collins Vet Center Outstation 1100 Poudre River Dr. Ft. Collins, CO 80524 (970) 221-5176 Grand Junction Vet Center 2472 F. Road, Unit 16 Grand Junction, CO 81505 (970) 245-4156 Colorado Springs Vet Center 509 E. 13th St., Rm. 18 Pueblo, CO 81001 (719) 546-6666
Connecticut	Hartford Vet Center 25 Elm Street, Suite A Rocky Hill, CT 06067 (860) 563-8800 New Haven Vet Center 141 Captain Thomas Blvd. West Haven, CT 06516 (203) 932-9899 Norwich Vet Center 2 Cliff St. Norwich, CT 06360 (860) 887-1755
Delaware	Wilmington Vet Center 1601 Kirkwood Highway Wilmington, DE 19805 (302)-994-1660
District of Columbia	Washington Vet Center 1250 Taylor St., NW Washington, D.C. 20011 (202) 726-5212

STATE	ADDRESS/TELEPHONE
Florida	Southeast Regional Office VA Medical Center, Bldg. T203 Bay Pines, FL 33744 (727) 398-9343 Fort Lauderdale Vet Center 713 NE 3rd Ave. Ft. Lauderdale, FL 33304 (954) 356-7926 Ft. Myers Vet Center Lee County Veterans Service Office 2072 Victoria Ave. Ft. Myers, FL 33901 (239) 938-1100 Gainesville Vet Center 105 NW 75th Street, Suite #2 Gainesville, FL 32607 (352) 331-1408 Jacksonville Vet Center 300 East State St., Suite J Jacksonville, FL 32202 (904) 232-3621 Key Largo Vet Center Outstation 105662 Overseas Hwy. Key Largo, FL 33037 (305) 451-0164 Melbourne Vet Center 2098 Sarno Road Melbourne, FL 32935 (321) 254-3410 Miami Vet Center 8280 NW 27th St., Suite 511 Miami, FL 33122 (305) 718-3712 Orlando Vet Center 5575 S. Semoran Blvd., #36 Orlando, FL 32822 (407) 857-2800 Palm Beach Vet Center Spectrum Center 2311 10th Ave. N., #13 Lake Worth, FL 33461 (561) 585-0441

STATE	ADDRESS/TELEPHONE
	Pensacola Vet Center 4501 Twin Oaks Drive, Suite 104 Pensacola, FL 32506 (850) 456-5886
	Sarasota Vet Center 4801 Swift Rd., Suite A Sarasota, FL 34231 (941) 927-8285
	St. Petersburg Vet Center 2880 1st Ave. North St. Petersburg, FL 33713 (727) 893-3791
	Tallahassee Vet Center 548 Bradford Road Tallahassee, FL 32303 (850) 942-8810
	Tampa Vet Center 8900 N Armenia Ave., #312 Tampa, FL 33604 (813) 228-2621
Georgia	Atlanta Vet Center 1440 Dutch Valley Place, Suite 1100, Box 55 Atlanta, GA 30324 (404) 347-7264
	Macon Vet Center 750 Riverside Drive Macon, GA 31201 (478) 272-1210
	North Atlanta Vet Center 930 River Centre Place Lawrenceville, GA 30043 (770) 963-1809
	Savannah Vet Center 308A Commercial Dr. Savannah, GA 31406 (912) 652-4097
Guam	Guam Vet Center 222 Chalan Santo Papa Reflection Ctr., Ste 201 Hagatna, GU 96910 (671) 472-7160

STATE	ADDRESS/TELEPHONE
Hawaii	Hilo Vet Center 126 Pu'uhonu Way, Suite 2 Hilo, HI 96720 (808) 969-3833 Honolulu Vet Center 1680 Kapiolani Blvd., Suite F-3 Honolulu, HI 96814 (808) 973-8387 Kailua-Kona Vet Center 73-4976 Kamanu St., Suite 207 Kailua-Kona, HI 96740 (808) 329-0574 Kauai Vet Center 3-3367 Kuhio Hwy., Ste #101 Lihue, HI 96766 (808) 246-1163 Maui Vet Center 35 Lunalilo Street, Suite #101 Wailuku, HI 96793 (808)-2428557
Idaho	Boise Vet Center 5440 Franklin Road, Suite 100 Boise, ID 83705 (208) 342-3612 Pocatello Vet Center 1800 Garrett Way Pocatello, ID 83201 (208) 232-0316
Illinois	Chicago Heights Vet Center 1600 Halsted Street Chicago Heights, IL 60411 (708) 754-0340 Chicago Veterans Resource Center 7731 S. Halsted Street Chicago, IL 60620-2412 (773) 962-3740 East St. Louis Vet Center 1265 N. 89th Street, Suite 5 East St. Louis, IL 62203 (618) 397-6602 Evanston Vet Center 565 Howard St. Evanston, IL 60202 (847) 332-1019

STATE	ADDRESS/TELEPHONE
	Oak Park Vet Center 155 S. Oak Park Avenue Oak Park, IL 60302 (708) 383-3225 Peoria Vet Center 3310 N. Prospect Road Peoria, IL 61603 (309) 688-2170 Quad Cities Vet Center 1529 46th Avenue, #6 Moline, IL 61265 (309) 762-6954 Rockford Vet Center Outstation 4960 E. State St., #3 Rockford, IL 61108 (815) 395-1276 Springfield Vet Center 1227 S. Ninth Street Springfield, IL 62703 (217) 492-4955
Indiana	Evansville Vet Center 311 N. Weinbach Avenue Evansville, IN 47711 (812) 473-5993 Fort Wayne Vet Center 528 W. Berry Street Fort Wayne, IN 46802 (260) 460-1456 Gary Area Vet Center 6505 Broadway Ave. Merrillville, IN 46410 (219) 736-5633 Indianapolis Vet Center 3833 N. Meridian Street, Suite 120 Indianapolis, IN 46208 (317) 988-1600
Iowa	Cedar Rapids Vet Center 1642 42nd Street NE Cedar Rapids, IA 52402 (319) 378-0016 Des Moines Vet Center 2600 Martin Luther King Pkwy Des Moines, IA 50310 (515) 284-4929

STATE	ADDRESS/TELEPHONE
	Sioux City Vet Center 1551 Indian Hills Drive, Suite 214 Sioux City, IA 51104 (712) 255-3808
Kansas	Manhattan Vet Center 205 South 4th Street, Suite B Manhattan, KS 66502 (785) 587-8257 Wichita Vet Center 251 N. Water St. Wichita, KS 67202 (316) 685-2221
Kentucky	Lexington Vet Center 301 E. Vine Street, Suite C Lexington, KY 40507 (859) 253-0717 Louisville Vet Center 1347 S. Third Street Louisville, KY 40208 (502) 634-1916
Louisiana	Baton Rouge Vet Center 5207 Essen Lane, Suite 2 Baton Rouge, LA 70809 (225) 757-0042 New Orleans Veterans Resource Center 2200 Veterans Blvd., Suite 114 Kenner, LA 70062 (504) 464-4743 Shreveport Vet Center 2800 Youree Dr., Bldg. 1, Suite 105 Shreveport, LA 71104 (318) 861-1776
Maine	Bangor Vet Center 352 Harlow St. Bangor, ME 04401 (207) 947-3391 Caribou Vet Center York Street Complex 456 York Street Caribou, ME 04736 (207) 496-3900

STATE	ADDRESS/TELEPHONE
	Lewiston Vet Center 29 Westminster St. Lewiston, ME 04240 (207) 783-0068 Portland Vet Center 475 Stevens Ave. Portland, ME 04103 (207) 780-3584 Sanford Vet Center 628 Main Street Springvale, ME 04083 (207) 490-1513
Maryland	Mid-Atlantic Regional Office 305 W. Chesapeake Ave., Suite 300 Towson, MD 21204 (410) 828-6619 Aberdeen Vet Center Outstation 2223 W. Bel Air Avenue Aberdeen, MD 21001 (410) 272-6771 Baltimore Vet Center 1777 Reisterstown Road, Suite 199 Baltimore, MD 21208 (410) 764-9400 Cambridge Vet Center Outstation 1830 Chesapeake Drive Cambridge, MD 21613 (410) 228-6305 Elkton Vet Center 103 Chesapeake Blvd., Suite A Elkton, MD 21921 (410) 392-4485 Silver Spring Vet Center 1015 Spring Street, Suite 101 Silver Spring, MD 20910 (301) 589-1073
Massachusetts	Boston Vet Center 665 Beacon St., Suite 100 Boston, MA 02215 (617) 424-0665 Brockton Vet Center 1041L Pearl St. Brockton, MA 02301 (508) 580-2730

STATE	ADDRESS/TELEPHONE
	Hyannis Vet Center 474 West Main Street Hyannis, MA 02601 (508) 778-0124 Lowell Vet Center 73 East Merrimack St. Lowell, MA 08152 (978) 453-1151 New Bedford Vet Center 468 North St. New Bedford, MA 02740 (508) 999-6920 Springfield Vet Center 1985 Main St. Northgate Plaza Springfield, MA 01103 (413) 737-5167 Worcester Vet Center 691 Grafton Street Worcester, MA 01604 (508) 753-7902
Michigan	Dearborn Vet Center 2881 Monroe Street, Suite 100 Dearborn, MI 48124 (313) 277-1428 Detroit Vet Center 4161 Cass Avenue Detroit, MI 48201 (313) 831-6509 Escanaba Vet Center 3500 Ludington Street, Suite # 110 Escanaba, MI 49829 (906) 233-0244 Grand Rapids Vet Center 2050 Breton Rd SE Grand Rapids, MI 49546 (616) 285-5795 Saginaw Vet Center 4048 Bay Road Saginaw, MI 48603 (989) 321-4650

STATE	ADDRESS/TELEPHONE
Minnesota	Duluth Vet Center 405 E. Superior Street Duluth, MN 55802 (218) 722-8654 St. Paul Veterans Resource Center 2480 University Avenue St. Paul, MN 55114 (651) 644-4022
Mississippi	TB>Biloxi Vet Center 288 Veterans Ave. Biloxi, MS 39531 (228) 388-9938 Jackson Vet Center 1755 Lelia Dr., Suite 104 Jackson, MS 39216 (601) 965-5727
Missouri	Central Regional Office 2122 Kratky Rd. St. Louis, MO 63114 (314) 426-5864 Kansas City Vet Center 301 East Armour Blvd., Suite 305 Kansas City, MO 64111 (816) 753-1866 St. Louis Vet Center 2901 Olive St. St. Louis, MO 63103 (314) 531-5355
Montana	Billings Vet Center 1234 Ave. C Billings, MT 59102 (406) 657-6071 Missoula Vet Center 500 N. Higgins Avenue Missoula, MT 59802 (406) 721-4918
Nebraska	Omaha Vet Center 2428 Cuming Street Omaha NE 68131-1600 (402) 346-6735

STATE	ADDRESS/TELEPHONE
Nevada	Las Vegas Vet Center 1919 S. Jones Blvd., Suite A Las Vegas, NV 89146 (702) 251-7873 Reno Vet Center 1155 W. 4th Street, Suite 101 Reno, NV 89503 (775) 323-1294
New Hampshire	Northeast Regional Office 15 Dartmouth Drive, Suite 204 Auburn, NH 03032 (603) 623-4204 Berlin Vet Center 515 Main Street Gorham, NH 03581 (603) 752-2571 Manchester Vet Center 103 Liberty St. Manchester, NH 03104 (603) 668-7060
New Jersey	Jersey City Vet Center 110A Meadowlands Parkway, Suite 102 Secaucus, NJ 07094 (201) 223-7787 Newark Vet Center 2 Broad St., Suite 703 Bloomfield, NJ 07003 (973) 748-0980 Trenton Vet Center 934 Parkway Ave., 2nd Fl. Ewing, NJ 08618 (609) 882-5744 Ventnor Vet Center 6601 Ventnor Ave., Suite 105 Ventnor, NJ 08406 (609) 487-8387
New Mexico	Albuquerque Vet Center 1600 Mountain Road NW Albuquerque, NM 87104 (505) 346-6562 Farmington Vet Center Satellite 4251 E. Main, Suite B Farmington, NM 87402 (505) 327-9684

STATE	ADDRESS/TELEPHONE
	Las Cruces Vet Center 230 S. Water Street Las Cruces, NM 88001 (575) 523-9826 Sante Fe Vet Center 2209 Brothers Road, Suite 110 Santa Fe, NM 87505 (505) 988-6562
New York	Albany Vet Center 17 Computer Drive West Albany, NY 12205 (518) 626-5130 Babylon Vet Center 116 West Main St. Babylon, NY 11702 NY (631) 661-3930 Bronx Vet Center 130 W. Kingsbridge Road, Suite 7A-13 Bronx, NY 10468 (718) 367-3500 Brooklyn Veterans Resource Center 25 Chapel St., Suite 604 Brooklyn, NY 11201 (718) 624-2765 Buffalo Vet Center 564 Franklin Street, 2nd Floor Buffalo, NY 14202 (716) 882-0505 Harlem Vet Center 55 West 125th St., 11th Floor New York, NY 10027 (212) 426-2200 Manhattan Vet Center 32 Broadway, Suite 200 New York, NY 10004 (212) 742-9591 Middletown Vet Center 726 East Main Street, Suite 203 Middletown, NY 10940 (845) 342-9917 Queens Vet Center 75-10 91st Ave. Woodhaven, NY 11421 (718) 296-2871

STATE	ADDRESS/TELEPHONE
	Rochester Vet Center 1867 Mount Hope Ave. Rochester, NY 14620 (585) 232-5040 Staten Island Vet Center 150 Richmond Terrace Staten Island, NY 10301 (718) 816-4499 Syracuse Vet Center 716 East Washington St., Suite 101 Syracuse, NY 13210 (315) 478-7127 Watertown Vet Center 210 Court Street Watertown, NY 13601 (866) 610-0358 White Plains Vet Center 300 Hamilton Ave., 1st Floor White Plains, NY 10601 (914) 682-6250
North Carolina	Charlotte Vet Center 223 S. Brevard St., Suite 103 Charlotte, NC 28202 (704) 333-6107 Fayetteville Vet Center 4140 Ramsey St., Suite 110 Fayetteville, NC 28311 (910) 488-6252 Greensboro Vet Center 2009 S. Elm-Eugene St. Greensboro, NC 27406 (336) 333-5366 Greenville Vet Center 150 Arlington Blvd., Suite B Greenville, NC 27858 (252) 355-7920 Raleigh Vet Center 1649 Old Louisburg Rd. Raleigh, NC 27604 (919) 856-4616
North Dakota	Bismarck Vet Center Outstation 1684 Capital Way Bismarck, ND 58501 (701) 224-9751

STATE	ADDRESS/TELEPHONE
	Fargo Vet Center 3310 Fiechtner Drive., Suite 100 Fargo, ND 581038730 (701) 237-0942
	Minot Vet Center 1400 20th Avenue SW Minot, ND 58701 (701) 852-0177
	Lincoln Vet Center 920 L Street Lincoln, NE 68508 (402) 476-9736
Ohio	Cincinnati Vet Center 801B W. 8th St., Suite 126 Cincinnati, OH 45203 (513) 763-3500
	Cleveland Heights Vet Center 2022 Lee Road Cleveland, OH 44118 (216) 932-8471
	Columbus Vet Center 30 Spruce Street Columbus, OH 43215 (614) 257-5550
	Dayton Vet Center 627 Edwin C. Moses Blvd., 6th Floor Dayton, OH 45408 (937) 461-9150
	McCafferty Vet Center Outstation 4242 Lorain Avenue, Suite 201 Cleveland, OH 44113 (216) 939-0784
	Parma Vet Center 5700 Pearl Road, Suite 102 Parma, OH 44129 (440) 845-5023
Oklahoma	Oklahoma City Vet Center 1024 NW 47th St., Suite B Oklahoma City, OK 73118 (405) 270-5184
	Tulsa Vet Center 1408 S. Harvard Ave. Tulsa, OK 74112 (918) 748-5105

STATE	ADDRESS/TELEPHONE
Oregon	Eugene Vet Center 1255 Pearl Street, Suite 200 Eugene, OR 97402 (541) 465-6918 Grants Pass Vet Center 211 S.E. 10th St. Grants Pass, OR 97526 (541) 479-6912 Portland Vet Center 8383 N.E. Sandy Blvd., Suite 110 Portland, OR 97220 (503) 273-5370 Salem Vet Center 617 Chemeketa St., NE, Suite 100 Salem, OR 97301 (503) 362-9911
Pennsylvania	DuBois Vet Center 100 Meadow Lane, Suite 8 DuBois, PA 15801 (814) 372-2095 Erie Vet Center Renaissance Centre 1001 State St., Suite 102 Erie, PA 16501 (814) 453-7955 Harrisburg Vet Center 1500 N. Second Street, Suite 2 Harrisburg, PA 17102 (717) 782-3954 McKeesport Veterans Resource Center 2001 Lincoln Way McKeesport, PA 15131 (412) 678-7704 Philadelphia Vet Center 801 Arch Street, Suite 102 Philadelphia, PA 19107 (215) 627-0238 Philadelphia Vet Center NE 101 E. Olney Avenue Philadelphia, PA 19120 (215) 924-4670 Pittsburgh Vet Center 2500 Baldwick Rd. Pittsburgh, PA 15205 (412) 920-1765

STATE	ADDRESS/TELEPHONE
	Scranton Vet Center 1002 Pittston Ave. Scranton, PA 18505 (570) 344-2676 Williamsport Vet Center 49 E. Fourth Street, Suite 104 Williamsport, PA 17701 (570) 327-5281
Puerto Rico	Arecibo Vet Center 50 Gonzalo Marin St. Arecibo, PR 612 (787) 879-4510 Ponce Vet Center 35 Mayor St., Suite 1 Ponce, PR 730 (787) 841-3260 San Juan Vet Center Medical Center Plaza, Suite LC 8, 9 & 11, Urb. La Riviera Rio Piedras, PR 0921 (787) 749-4409
Rhode Island	Providence Vet Center 2038 Warwick Ave Warwick, RI 02889 (401) 739-0167
South Carolina	Charleston Vet Center 5603-A Rivers Ave. N. Charleston, SC 29406 (843) 747-8387 Columbia Vet Center 1513 Pickens St. Columbia, SC 29201 (803) 765-9944 Greenville Vet Center 14 Lavinia Ave. Greenville, SC 29601 (864) 271-2711
South Dakota	Pine Ridge Vet Center Outstation P.O. Box 910 105 E. Hwy 18 Martin, SD 57747 (605) 685-1300

STATE	ADDRESS/TELEPHONE
	Rapid City Vet Center 621 6th St., Suite 101 Rapid City, SD 57701 (605) 348-0077 Sioux Falls Vet Center 601 S. Cliff Ave., Suite C Sioux Falls, SD 57104 (605) 330-4552
Tennessee	Chattanooga Vet Center 951 Eastgate Loop Road, Suite 300 Chattanooga, TN 37411 (423) 855-6570 Johnson City Vet Center 1615A Market St. Johnson City, TN 37604 (423) 928-8387 Knoxville Vet Center 2817 E. Magnolia Ave. Knoxville, TN 37914 (865) 545-4680 Memphis Vet Center 1835 Union, Suite 100 Memphis, TN 38104 (901) 544-0173 Nashville Vet Center 1420 Donelson Pike, Suite A-5 Nashville, TN 37217 (615) 366-1220
Texas	South Central Regional Office 4500 S. Lancaster Rd., Building 69 Dallas, TX 75216 (214) 857-1254 Amarillo Vet Center 3414 Olsen Blvd., Suite E Amarillo, TX 79109 (806) 354-9779 Austin Vet Center 1110 West William Cannon Dr., Suite 301 Austin, TX 78745 (512) 416-1314 Corpus Christi Vet Center 4646 Corona, Suite 250 Corpus Christi, TX 78411 (361) 854-9961

STATE	ADDRESS/TELEPHONE
	Dallas Vet Center 10501 N. Central, Suite 213 Dallas, TX 75231 (214) 361-5896
	El Paso Vet Center 1155 Westmoreland, Suite 121 El Paso, TX 79925 (915) 772-0013
	Ft. Worth Vet Center 1305 W. Magnolia St., Suite B Ft. Worth, TX 76104 (817) 921-9095
	Houston Vet Center 2990 Richmond, Suite 325 Houston, TX 77098 (713) 523-0884
	Houston Vet Center 701 N. Post Oak Road, Suite 102 Houston, TX 77024 (713) 682-2288
	Killeen Heights Vet Center 302 Millers Crossing, Suite 4 Harker Heights, TX 76548 (254) 953-7100
	Laredo Vet Center 6020 McPherson Road, Suite 1A Laredo, TX 78041 (956) 723-4680
	Lubbock Vet Center 3208 34th St. Lubbock, TX 79410 (806) 792-9782
	McAllen Vet Center 801 Nolana Loop, Suite 140 McAllen, TX 78504 (956) 631-2147
	Midland Vet Center 3404 W. Illinois, Suite 1 Midland, TX 79703 (432) 697-8222
	San Antonio Vet Center 231 W. Cypress St., Suite 100 San Antonio, TX 78212 (210) 472-4025

STATE	ADDRESS/TELEPHONE
Utah	Provo Vet Center 1807 No. 1120 West Provo, UT 84604 (801) 377-1117 Salt Lake Vet Center 1354 East 3300 South Salt Lake, UT 84106 (801) 584-1294
Vermont	South Burlington Vet Center 359 Dorset St. South Burlington, VT 05403 (802) 862-1806 White River Junction Vet Center Gilman Office, Building #2 222 Holiday Inn Drive White River Junction, VT 05009 (802) 295-2908
Virginia	Alexandria Vet Center 6940 South Kings Highway, #208 Alexandria, VA 22310 (703) 360-8633 Norfolk Vet Center 1711 Church Street, Suites A&B Norfolk, VA 23504 (757) 623-7584 Richmond Vet Center 4902 Fitzhugh Avenue Richmond, VA 23230 (804) 353-8958 Roanoke Vet Center 350 Albemarle Ave., SW Roanoke, VA 24016 (540) 342-9726
Virgin Islands	St. Croix Vet Center The Village Mall RR 2 Box 10553 Kingshill St. Croix, VI 0850 (340) 778-5553 St. Thomas Vet Center Buccaneer Mall, Suite #8 St. Thomas, VI 0802 (340) 774-6674

STATE	ADDRESS/TELEPHONE
Washington	Bellingham Vet Center 3800 Byron Ave, Suite 124 Bellingham, WA 98229 (360) 733-9226 Everett Vet Center (Est. opening date: 2008) Everett, WA Seattle Vet Center 2030 9th Ave., Suite 210 Seattle, WA 98121 (206) 553-2706 Spokane Vet Center 100 No. Mullan Rd., Suite 102 Spokane, WA 99206 (509) 444-8387 Tacoma Vet Center 4916 Center St., Suite E Tacoma, WA 98409 (253) 565-7038 Yakima Valley Vet Center 1111 N. 1st Street, Suite #1 Yakima, WA 98901 (509) 457-2736
West Virginia	Beckley Vet Center 1000 Johnstown Road Beckley, WV 25801 (304) 252-8220 Charleston Vet Center 521 Central Avenue Charleston, WV 25302 (304) 343-3825 Huntington Vet Center 3135 16th Street Road, Suite 11 Huntington, WV 25701 (304) 523-8387 Logan Vet Center Outstation 21 Veterans Avenue Henlawson, WV 25624 (304) 752-4453 Martinsburg Vet Center 900 Winchester Avenue Martinburg, WV 25401 (304) 263-6776

STATE	ADDRESS/TELEPHONE
	Morgantown Vet Center 1083 Greenbag Road Morgantown, WV 26508 (304) 291-4303 Parkersburg Vet Center Outstation 2311 Ohio Avenue, Suite D Parkersburg, WV 26101 (304) 485-1599 Princeton Vet Center 905 Mercer Street Princeton, WV 24740 (304) 425-5653 Wheeling Vet Center 1206 Chapline Street Wheeling, WV 26003 (304) 232-0587
Wisconsin	Madison Vet Center 706 Williamson Street Madison, WI 53703 (608) 264-5342 Milwaukee Vet Center 5401 N. 76th St. Milwaukee, WI 53218 (414) 536-1301
Wyoming	Casper Vet Center 1030 North Poplar, Suite B Casper, WY 82601 (307) 261-5355 Cheyenne Vet Center 3219 E Pershing Blvd. Cheyenne, WY 82001 (307) 778-7370

Source: U.S. Veterans Administration.

APPENDIX 9:
VETERAN'S APPLICATION FOR
COMPENSATION AND/OR PENSION
(FORM 21-526)

OMB Approved No. 2900-0001
Respondent Burden: 1 hour 30 minutes

(DO NOT WRITE IN THIS SPACE)

VETERAN'S APPLICATION FOR COMPENSATION AND/OR PENSION,
VA Form 21-526, Part A: General information

Please read the attached "General Instructions" before you fill out this form.

SECTION I	Tell us what you are applying for	1. What are you applying for? If you are unsure please refer to the "General Instructions" page 2

Section 1: Preparing your application

Check the box that says what you are applying for. Be sure to complete the other Parts you need.

☐ Compensation	Fill out Part A of VA Form 21-526 and Parts B and C
☐ Pension	Fill out Part A of VA Form 21-526 and Parts C and D
☐ Compensation and Pension	Fill out Part A of VA Form 21-526 and Parts B, C and D

2a. Have you ever filed a claim with VA

☐ No *(If "No," skip Item 2b and go to Item 3)*
(If "Yes," provide file number below)

☐ Yes _____ *(Go to 2b)*

2b. I filed a claim for

☐ Compensation ☐ Pension

☐ Other

SECTION II	Tell us about you

We need information about you to process your claim faster.

3. What is your name?

| First | Middle | Last | Suffix (If applicable) |

4. What is your Social Security number?

_____

5. What is your sex?

☐ Male ☐ Female

6a. Did you serve under another name?

☐ Yes *(If "Yes," go to Item 6b)*

☐ No *(If "No," go to Item 7)*

6b. Please list the other name(s) you served under

_____
_____

Give us your current mailing address in the space provided. If it will change within the next three months, give us that

7. What is your address?

_____
Street address, Rural Route, or P.O. Box   Apt. number

_____
City   State   ZIP Code   Country

---

new address in block 29 "Remarks." Also in block 29, give us the date you think you will be at the new address.

OWCP used to be called the U.S. Bureau of Employees Compensation

8. What are your telephone numbers?

Daytime _____

Evening _____

9. What is your e-mail address?

_____

10. What is your date of birth?

_____

11. Where were you born? (City, State and Country)

_____

12a. Are you receiving disability benefits from the Office of Workers' Compensation *(OWCP)*?

☐ Yes   ☐ No

(If "Yes," answer 12b and 12c also)

12b. When was the claim filed?

_____

12c. What disability are you receiving benefits for?

_____

13a. What is the name of your nearest relative or other person we could contact if necessary?

13b. What is his/her telephone number?

Daytime _____

Evening _____

13c. What is this person's address?

13d. How is this person related to you?

SUPERSEDES STOCKS OF VA FORM 21-526, APR 2003
WHICH WILL NOT BE USED

21-526, Part A   *page 1*

SECTION III **Tell us about your active duty**	**14a.** I entered active service the **first** time. . . _____ *mo day yr*	**14b.** Place:	**14c.** My service number was . . .

1. Enter complete information for all periods of service. If more space is needed use Item 29 "Remarks."

2. Attach your original DD214 or a certified copy to this form. (We will return original documents to you.)

14d. I left this active service. . . . _____ *mo day yr*	**14e.** Place:	**14f.** Branch of Service	**14g.** Grade, rank, or rating
14h. I entered my **second** period of active service. . . . _____ *mo day yr*	**14i.** Place:	**14j.** My service number was . . .	
14k. I left this active service. . . . _____ *mo day yr*	**14l.** Place:	**14m.** Branch of Service	**14n.** Grade, rank, or rating

The VA has a registry of veterans who served in the Gulf War. This area has also been called the "Persian Gulf." If you served there, we will include your name in the registry. If you want your medical information included, you must check "Yes" in Item 16b. For more information about the registry, see page 4 of the General Instructions for VA Form 21-526.

15a. Did you serve in Vietnam? ☐ Yes ☐ No *(If "Yes," answer Item 15b also)*	**15b.** When were you in Vietnam? *from* _____ *to* _____ _____ _____ *mo day yr* *mo day yr*
16a. Were you stationed in the Gulf after August 1, 1990? ☐ Yes ☐ No *(If "Yes," answer Item 16b also)*	**16b.** Do you want to have medical and other information about you included in the "Gulf War Veterans' Health Registry?" ☐ Yes ☐ No
17a. Have you ever been a prisoner of war? ☐ Yes ☐ No *(If "Yes," answer Items 17b, 17c, and 17d also)*	**17b.** What country or government imprisoned you?
17c. When were you confined? *from* _____ *to* _____ _____ _____ *mo day yr* *mo day yr*	**17d.** What was the name of the camp or sector and what are the names of the city and country near its location?

SECTION IV **Tell us about your reserve duty**	**18a.** Are you currently assigned to an active reserve unit? ☐ Yes ☐ No *(If "Yes," answer Item 18b also)*	**18b.** What is the name, mailing address, and telephone number of your current unit?
	18c. Were you previously assigned to an active reserve unit within the last 2 years? ☐ Yes ☐ No *(If "Yes," answer Item 18d also)*	**18d.** What is the name, mailing address, and telephone number of that unit?

21-526, Part A   page 2

SECTION *(Continued)* **IV** **Tell us about your reserve duty**	**18e.** Do you have an inactive reserve obligation? (You perform no active duty, but you could be activated if there was a national emergency) ☐ Yes ☐ No ☐ Don't Know *(If "Yes," answer Item 18f also)*	**18f.** What is your reserve obligation termination date? _____ *mo day yr*

Instructions 18g-18k *If you are currently or have ever been a full time reservist for operational or support duty.* *1. Complete 18g-18k for that service only.* *2. Attach proof of reserve service.*	**18g.** I entered reserve service. . . . Place: _____ *mo day yr*		**18h.** My service number was . . .
	18i. I left reserve service. . . . Place: _____ *mo day yr*	**18j.** Branch of service	**18k.** Grade, rank, or rating

Instructions 18l-18p *If your disability occurred or was aggravated during any period of reserve duty.* *1. Complete 18l-18p for the period when your disability occurred.* *2. Attach proof that your disability occurred during reserve service.*	**18l.** I entered reserve service. . . . Place: _____ *mo day yr*		**18m.** My service number was . . .
	18n. I left reserve service. . . . Place: _____ *mo day yr*	**18o.** Branch of service	**18p.** Grade, rank, or rating

SECTION V **Tell us about your National Guard duty**	**19a.** Are you currently a member of the National Guard? ☐ Yes ☐ No ☐ Not Assigned *(If "Yes," answer Item 19h also)*	**19b.** What is the name, mailing address, and telephone number of your current unit?
	19c. Were you previously assigned to a guard unit within the last 2 years? ☐ Yes ☐ No *(If "Yes," answer Item 19d also)*	**19d.** What is the name, mailing address, and telephone number of that unit?

Instructions 19e-19i *If you were activated to Federal Active Duty under the Authority of Title 10, United States Code.* *1. Complete 19e-19i for that service only.* *2. Attach proof of this Federal Active Duty.*	**19e.** I entered Federal Active Duty. . . . Place: _____ *mo day yr*		**19f.** My service number was . . . .
	19g. I left Federal Active Duty. . . . Place: _____ *mo day yr*	**19h.** Branch of service	**19i.** Grade, rank, or rating

Instructions 19j-19n *If your disability occurred or was aggravated during any period of guard duty.* *1. Complete 19j-19n for the period when your disability occurred.* *2. Attach proof that your disability occurred during National Guard Service.*	**19j.** I entered National Guard. . . . Place: _____ *mo day yr*		**19k.** My service number was . . . .
	19l. I left National Guard. . . . Place: _____ *mo day yr*	**19m.** Branch of service	**19n.** Grade, rank, or rating

21-526, Part A   *page 3*

SECTION VI	**Tell us about your travel status**	**20a.** Were you injured while traveling to or from your military assignment? *(If "Yes," answer Items 20b thru 20e and Section I of Part B: Compensation)* ☐ Yes ☐ No	**20b.** When did your injury happen? mo day yr	**20c.** Where did your injury happen? *(City, State, Country)*	**20d.** Where were you treated? *(Provide name and address of doctor's office, hospital, etc.)*	**20e.** What agency did you file an accident report with?

SECTION VII	**Tell us about your military benefits**

When you file this application, you are telling us that you want to get VA compensation instead of military retired pay. If you currently receive military retired pay, you should be aware that we will reduce your retired pay by the amount of any compensation that you are awarded. VA will notify the Military Retired Pay Center of all benefit changes.

You must sign 21e if you want to keep getting military retired pay instead of VA compensation.

Please see page 4 of the General Instructions for VA Form 21-526.

If you have gotten both military retired pay and VA compensation, some of the amount you get may be recouped by VA, or in the case of VSI, by the Department of Defense.

21a. Are you receiving or will you receive retired or retainer pay that is based on your military service? ☐ Yes ☐ No *(If "Yes," answer Items 21b thru 21f. If "No," skip to Item 22)*

21b. What branch of service is paying or will pay your retired or retainer pay?

21c. What is the monthly amount? $ _____

21d. What is your retirement based on?

☐ Length of service   ☐ Disability   ☐ TDRL (Temporary Disability Retired List)

21e. Sign here if you want to receive military retired pay *instead of* VA compensation

_____

21f. Have you received or will you receive any of the following military benefits? **(Please check the appropriate boxes and tell us the amount)**

Benefit		**Amount**
(1) ☐	Lump Sum Readjustment Pay	$
(2) ☐	Separation pay under 10 USC 1174	$
(3) ☐	Special Separation Benefit (SSB)	$
(4) ☐	Voluntary Separation Incentive (VSI)	$
(5) ☐	Disability Severance Pay *(name of disability* _____ *)*	$
(6) ☐	Other *(tell us the type of benefit* _____ *)*	$

SECTION VIII	**Give us direct deposit information**

If benefits are awarded we will need more information in order to process any payments to you. Please read the paragraph starting with, *"All federal payments..."* and then either:

1. Attach a voided check, or

2. Answer questions 22-24 to the right.

All federal payments beginning January 2, 1999, must be made by electronic funds transfer (EFT) also called Direct Deposit. Please attach a voided personal check or deposit slip or provide the information requested below in Items 22, 23 and 24 to enroll in Direct Deposit. If you do not have a bank account we will give you a waiver from Direct Deposit, just check the box below in Item 22. The Treasury Department is working on making bank accounts available to you. Once these accounts are available, you will be able to decide whether you wish to sign-up for one of the accounts or continue to receive a paper check. You can also request a waiver if you have other circumstances that you feel would cause you a hardship to be enrolled in Direct Deposit. You can write to: Department of Veterans Affairs, 125 S. Main Street Suite B, Muskogee OK 74401-7004, and give us a brief description of why you do not wish to participate in Direct Deposit.

22. Account number (Please check the appropriate box and provide that account number, if applicable)

☐ Checking   ☐ I certify that I **do not** have an account with a financial institution or certified payment agent
☐ Savings
Account number _____

23. Name of financial institution _____

24. Routing or transit number

_____

21-526, Part A   *page 4*

SECTION IX **Give us your signature**

1. Read the box that starts, "I certify and authorize the release of information:"

2. Sign the box that says, "Your signature."

3. If you sign with an "X", then you must have 2 people you know witness you as you sign. They must then sign the form and print their names and addresses also.

I certify and authorize the release of information:
I certify that the statements in this document are true and complete to the best of my knowledge. I authorize any person or entity, including but not limited to any organization, service provider, employer, or government agency, to give the Department of Veterans Affairs any information about me except protected health information, and I waive any privilege which makes the information confidential.

25. Your signature	26. Today's date

27a. Signature of witness (If claimant signed above using an "X")	27b. Printed name and address of witness

28a. Signature of witness (If claimant signed above using an "X")	28b. Printed name and address of witness

SECTION X

Remarks - Use this space for any additional statements that you would like to make concerning your application for Compensation and/or Pension

IMPORTANT
Penalty: The law provides severe penalties which include fine or imprisonment, or both, for the willful submission of any statement or evidence of a material fact, knowing it to be false, or for the fraudulent acceptance of any payment which you are not entitled to.

29. Remarks *(If you need more space to answer a question or have a comment about a specific item number on this form please identify your answer or statement by the part and item number). (See page 5 "Tips For Filling Out Your VA Form 21-526.")*

VA Form 21-526, Part B: Compensation

Use this form to apply for compensation. Remember that you must also fill out a VA Form 21-526, Part A: General Information, for your application to be processed. Be sure to write your name and Social Security number in the space provided on page 2.

SECTION I	Tell us about your disability	In the table below, tell us more about your disability or disabilities. Be sure to:

- List all disabilities you believe are related to military service.
- List all the treatments you received for your disabilities, including
  - treatments you received in a military facility before and after discharge.
  - treatments you received from civilian and VA sources before, during, and after your service.

1. What disability are you claiming?	2. When did your disability begin?	3. When were you treated?		4a. What medical facility or doctor treated you?	4b. What is the address of that medical facility or doctor?
		from	*to*		
	mo day yr	*mo day yr*	*mo day yr*		
		from	*to*		
	mo day yr	*mo day yr*	*mo day yr*		
		from	*to*		
	mo day yr	*mo day yr*	*mo day yr*		
		from	*to*		
	mo day yr	*mo day yr*	*mo day yr*		
		from	*to*		
	mo day yr	*mo day yr*	*mo day yr*		
		from	*to*		
	mo day yr	*mo day yr*	*mo day yr*		
		from	*to*		
	mo day yr	*mo day yr*	*mo day yr*		
		from	*to*		
	mo day yr	*mo day yr*	*mo day yr*		
		from	*to*		
	mo day yr	*mo day yr*	*mo day yr*		

VA FORM
JAN 2004
21-526

21-526 , Part B   *page 1*

SECTION II Tell us if any of the disabilities you listed on Page 1 were because of exposures	**5a.** Were you exposed to Agent Orange or other herbicides? ☐ Yes ☐ No	**5b.** What is your disability?	**5c.** In what country were you exposed?

6a. Were you exposed to asbestos?

☐ Yes ☐ No

(If "Yes," answer Item 6b and 6c also)

6b. What is your disability?

6c. When and how were you exposed?

7a. Were you exposed to mustard gas?

☐ Yes ☐ No

(If "Yes," answer Item 7b and 7c also)

7b. What is your disability?

7c. When and how were you exposed?

8a. Were you exposed to ionizing radiation?

☐ Yes ☐ No

(If "Yes," answer Items 8b, 8c, and 8d also)

8b. What is your disability?

8c. When was your last exposure?

_____
mo   day   yr

8d. How were you exposed to radiation?

☐ Atmospheric testing

☐ Nagasaki/Hiroshima

☐ Other, describe _____

9a. Were you exposed to an environmental hazard in the Gulf War?

☐ Yes ☐ No

(If "Yes," answer Items 9b and 9c also)

9b. What is your disability?

9c. What was the hazard?

10a. Did you have a separation or retirement physical examination?

☐ Yes ☐ No

(If "Yes," answer Items 10b and 10c also)

10b. When was the exam?

_____
mo   day   yr

10c. Where did the exam occur?

SECTION III Tell us how your disabilities listed on Page 1 are related to your military service	**11. Explanation**

Your Name	Your Social Security Number

VETERAN'S APPLICATION FOR COMPENSATION AND/OR PENSION

VA Form 21-526, Part C: Dependency

Use this form to tell us more about your dependents. Remember that you must also fill out a VA Form 21-526, Part A: General Information, Part B and/or Part D, for your application to be processed. Be sure to write your name and Social Security number in the space provided on page 3.

SECTION I	Tell us about your marriage

NOTE: You should provide a copy of your marriage certificate

1. What is your marital status?

☐ Married ☐ Surviving Spouse ☐ Divorced ☐ Never Married

(If your spouse died, you are "divorced." or "never married" skip to Section III beginning on page 2)

2. When were you married?

_____
month   day   year

3. Where did you get married?
(city/state or country)

_____

4. What is your spouse's name?

First   Middle   Last

5. What is your spouse's birthday?

_____
month   day   year

6. What is your spouse's Social Security number?

_____

7a. Is your spouse also a veteran?

☐ Yes ☐ No

(If "Yes," answer Item 7b also)

7b. What is your spouse's VA file number (If any)?

_____

8. Do you live with your spouse?

☐ Yes *(If "Yes," go to Item 12)*
☐ No *(If "No," go to Item 9)*

9. What is your spouse's address?

_____
Street address, Rural Route, or P.O. Box   Apt. number

_____
City   State   Zip code   Country

10. Tell us why you are not living with your spouse

11. How much do you contribute monthly to your spouse's support?

$ _____

12. How were you married?

a. ☐ Ceremony by a clergyman or other authorized public official
b. ☐ Common-law

c. ☐ Tribal
d. ☐ Proxy
e. ☐ Other *(please describe in the space below)*

_____
_____
_____

VA Form JAN 2004 **21-526**

21-526, Part C   *page 1*

Veterans' Rights and Benefits   **183**

VETERAN'S APPLICATION FOR COMPENSATION AND/OR PENSION

SECTION II	Tell us about any previous marriages	In the table below, tell us about:
NOTE: You should provide copies of divorce decrees or death certificates.		• Your previous marriages, and • Your spouse's previous marriages

Your previous marriages

13a. How many times have you been married before? _____

13b. When were you married?	13c. Where were you married? *(city/state or country)*	13d. Who were you married to? *(first, middle initial, last)*	13e. When did your marriage end?	13f. Why did your marriage end? *(death, divorce)*	13g. Where did your marriage end? *(city/state or country)*
mo day yr			*mo day yr*		
mo day yr			*mo day yr*		

Your spouse's previous marriages

14a. How many times has your current spouse been married before? _____

14b. When was your spouse married?	14c. Where was your spouse married? *(city/state or country)*	14d. Who was your spouse married to? *(first, middle initial, last)*	14e. When did your spouse's marriage end?	14f. Why did your spouse's marriage end? *(death, divorce)*	14g. Where did your spouse's marriage end? *(city/state or country)*
mo day yr			*mo day yr*		
mo day yr			*mo day yr*		

SECTION III	Tell us about your other dependents	In this section we want to know whether your parents are financially dependent on you (Question 15) and more about your **dependent children**. VA may recognize a veteran's biological children, adopted children, and stepchildren as dependent. These children must be unmarried and: • be under the age of 18, **or** • be at least 18 but under 23 and pursuing an approved course of education, **or** • have become permanently unable to support themselves before reaching the age of 18.

	15. Are your parents financially dependent on you? ☐ Yes ☐ No *(If "Yes," we will request additional information from you later)*
You should provide: a copy of the public record of birth for each child or a copy of the court record of adoption for each adopted child.	**16.** Do you have dependent children? ☐ Yes *(If "No," Skip Items 17-21f). Go to the bottom of page 3 and write your name and Social Security number)* ☐ No

17. How many dependent children do you have?

_____

Give us more information about these children in the tables on the next page (Items 18 through 21f)

21-526, Part C   *page 2*

SECTION III Tell us about your dependents (continued)

18a. What is the name of your unmarried child(ren)? *(first, middle initial, last)*	18b. Date and place of birth *(city/state or country)*	18c. Social Security Number	19a. Biological	19b. Adopted	19c. Stepchild	20a. 18-23 yrs. old and in school	20b. Seriously disabled before age 18	20c. Child previously married
	mo day yr Place:		☐	☐	☐	☐	☐	☐
	mo day yr Place:		☐	☐	☐	☐	☐	☐
	mo day yr Place:		☐	☐	☐	☐	☐	☐
	mo day yr Place:		☐	☐	☐	☐	☐	☐

Tell us about your dependents listed above who *don't live with you*

21a. Do all the children listed above live with you?

☐ Yes *(If "Yes," skip Items 21b thru 21f and write your name and Social Security number below*

☐ No *(If "No," complete Item 21b and the table below (Items 21c -21f) and write your name and Social Security number below)*

21b. How many of the children do not live with you?

_____

21c. What is the name of your child? *(first, middle initial, last)*	21d. What is your child's complete address?	21e. What is the name of the person your child lives with (If applicable)? *(first, middle initial, last)*	21f. How much do you contribute each month to the support of your child?
			$
			$
			$
			$

Your name	Your Social Security Number

VA Form 21-526, Part D: Pension

Use this form to apply for pension. Remember that you must also fill out a VA Form 21-526, Part A: General Information, for your application to be processed. Be sure to write your name and Social Security number in the space provided on page 4.

SECTION I Tell us about your disability and background	**1a.** What disability(ies) prevent you from working?

1b. When did the disability(ies) begin?

_____
month day year

Complete this section if you are claiming pension because of permanent and total disability not caused by your military service.

2. Are you claiming a special monthly pension because you need the regular assistance of another person, are blind, nearly blind, or having severe visual problems, or are housebound?

☐ Yes   ☐ No

3a. Are you now, or have you recently been hospitalized or given outpatient or home-based care?

☐ Yes   ☐ No

(If "Yes," answer Items 3b and 3c also)

Attach current medical evidence showing that you are permanently and totally disabled.

3b. Tell us the dates of the recent hospitalization or care.

Began _____
month day year

Ended _____
month day year

3c. What is the name and complete mailing address of the facility or doctor?

Note: If you are a veteran who is age 65 or older, or determined to be disabled by the Social Security Administration, you DO NOT have to submit medical evidence with your application.

4a. Are you now employed?

☐ Yes   ☐ No

(If "No," answer Item 4b also)

4b. When did you last work?

_____
month day year

4c. Were you self-employed before becoming totally disabled?

☐ Yes   ☐ No

(If "Yes," answer Item 4d and 4e also)

4d. What kind of work did you do?

4e. Are you still self-employed?

☐ Yes   ☐ No

(If "Yes," answer Item 4f also)

4f. What kind of work do you do now?

4g. Have you claimed or are you receiving disability benefits from the Social Security Administration (SSA)?

☐ Yes   ☐ No

4h. Circle the highest year of education you completed:

Grade school: ☐ 1 ☐ 2 ☐ 3 ☐ 4
☐ 5 ☐ 6 ☐ 7 ☐ 8
☐ 9 ☐ 10 ☐ 11 ☐ 12

College: ☐ 1 ☐ 2 ☐ 3 ☐ 4 ☐ over 4

4i. List the other training or experience you have and any certificates that you hold.

_____
_____
_____
_____

VA Form
JAN 2004   **21-526**

21-526, Part D   *Page 1*

SECTION II	Tell us your work history	In the table below, tell us about all of your employment, including self-employment, for one year before you became disabled to the present.

5a. What was the name and address of your employer?	5b. What was your job title?	5c. When did your work begin?	5d. When did your work end?	5e. How many days were lost due to disability?	5f. What were your total annual earnings?
		mo day yr	*mo day yr*		$
		mo day yr	*mo day yr*		$
		mo day yr	*mo day yr*		$

SECTION III	Tell us if you are in a nursing home	In this section, tell us if you are in a nursing home. If you are in a nursing home, give us more information about the nursing home.

To get your claim processed faster, provide a statement by an official of the nursing home that tells us that you are a patient in the nursing home because of a physical or mental disability and tells us the daily charge for your care.

6a. Are you now in a nursing home?

☐ Yes ☐ No

(If "Yes," answer Item 6b also)

6b. What is the name and complete mailing address of the facility or doctor?

6c. Does Medicaid cover all or part of your nursing home costs?

☐ Yes ☐ No

(If "No," answer Item 6d also)

6d. Have you applied for Medicaid?

☐ Yes ☐ No

SECTION IV	Tell us the net worth of you and your dependents	In this section, we ask you to give us specific information about your net worth and the net worth of your dependents. You will need to enter this information in the tables on page 3.

VA cannot pay you pension if your net worth is sizeable.

You must include all assets in your net worth except those items you use everyday (See definition of net worth below.)
You should subtract from the market value of your real estate any amounts that you owe on it (such as mortgages, liens, etc.)
You can subtract mortgages on any property, and the value of the house or part of a building that you live in as your primary residence.
You can report farms or buildings that you or a dependent own by reporting its value as "real property."

Definitions:
Net worth is the market value of all interest and rights in any kind of property less any mortgages or other claims against the property. However, net worth does not include the house you live in or a reasonable area of land it sits on. Net worth also does not include the value of personal things you use everyday like your vehicle, clothing, and furniture.

Go to Page 3 and fill out the table.

21-526, Part D   Page 2

VETERAN'S APPLICATION FOR COMPENSATION AND/OR PENSION

SECTION IV (Continued)	Tell us about your net worth and your dependents' net worth.				
	For items 7a-h: provide the amounts. If none, write "0" or "None"				

Source	Veteran	Spouse	Child(ren) I. Name: *(first, middle initial, last)*	II. Name: *(first, middle initial, last)*	III. Name: *(first, middle initial, last)*
7a. Cash, non-interest bearing bank accounts					
7b. Interest bearing bank accounts, certificates of deposit (CDs)					
7c. IRAs, Keogh Plans, etc.					
7d. Stocks and bonds					
7e. Mutual funds					
7f. Value of business assets					
7g. Real property (not your home)					
7h. All other property					

SECTION V Tell us about the income you have received and you expect to receive

In this section, we ask you to give us specific information about the income you have received and the income you expect to receive from all sources. You will need to enter this information in the tables on Page 4. In these tables,

Report the total amounts before you take out deductions for taxes, insurance, etc.
Do not report the same information in both tables.
If you expect to receive a payment, but you don't know how much it will be, write "Unknown" in the space.
If you do not receive any payments from one of the sources that we list, write "0" or "None" in the space.
If you are receiving monthly benefits, give us a copy of your most recent award letter. This will help us determine the amount of benefits you should be paid.

Payments from any source will be counted, unless the law says that they don't need to be counted. VA will determine any amount that does not count.

8. Will you receive any income from rental property or from operation of a business within 12 months of the day you sign this form?

☐ Yes ☐ No

9. Will you receive any income from the operation of a farm within 12 months of the day you sign this form?

☐ Yes ☐ No

10. Do you expect to receive money from a civilian agency, corporation, or individual, because of personal injury or death within 12 months of the day you sign this form?

☐ Yes ☐ No

21-526, Part D   Page 3

SECTION V (Continued)   **Monthly Income - Tell us the income you and your dependents receive every month.**

For Items 11a-12f if none write "0" or "None"

Sources of recurring monthly income	Veteran	Spouse	Child(ren)		
			I. Name: *(first, middle initial, last)*	II. Name: *(first, middle initial, last)*	III. Name: *(first, middle initial, last)*
11a. Social Security					
11b. U.S. Civil Service					
11c. U.S. Railroad Retirement					
11d. Military Retired Pay					
11e. Black Lung Benefits					
11f. Supplemental Security (SSI)/ Public Assistance					
11g. Other income received monthly *(Please write in the source below:)*					

Next 12 months - Tell us about other income for you and your dependents

Sources of income for the next 12 months	Veteran	Spouse	Child(ren)		
			I. Name: *(first, middle initial, last)*	II. Name: *(first, middle initial, last)*	III. Name: *(first, middle initial, last)*
12a. Gross wages and salary					
12b. Total interest and dividends					
12c. Worker's compensation for injury					
12d. Unemployment compensation					
12e. Other military benefit *(Please write in the source below:)*					
12f. Other one-time benefit *(Please write in the source below:)*					

SECTION VI

IMPORTANT - Items 13A through 13E should be completed only if you are applying for nonservice-connected pension.

Tell us any information concerning, Medical, Legal or Other Expenses - Family medical expenses actually paid by you may be deductible from your income. Show the amount of unreimbursed medical expenses you paid for yourself or relatives you are under an obligation to support. Also, show medical, legal or other expenses you paid because of a disability for which civilian disability benefits have been awarded. When determining your income, we may be able to deduct them from the disability benefits for the year in which the expenses are paid. **Do not** include any expenses for which you were reimbursed. Show the Medicare deduction in line 1. If more space is needed attach a separate sheet.

13A. AMOUNT PAID BY YOU	13B. DATE PAID	13C. PURPOSE *(Doctor's fees, hospital charges, Attorney fees, etc.)*	13D. PAID TO *(Name of doctor, hospital, pharmacy, Attorney, etc.)*	13E. DISABILITY OR RELATIONSHIP OF PERSON FOR WHOM EXPENSES PAID

Your Name	Your Social Security Number

VETERAN'S APPLICATION FOR COMPENSATION AND/OR PENSION

OMB Approved No. 2900-0001
Respondent Burden: 5 Mins.

VA Department of Veterans Affairs

AUTHORIZATION AND CONSENT TO RELEASE INFORMATION TO THE DEPARTMENT OF VETERANS AFFAIRS (VA)

Important Notice About Information Collection: We need this information to obtain your treatment records. Title 38, United States Code, allows us to ask for this information. We estimate that you will need an average of 5 minutes to review the instructions, find the information and complete this form. VA cannot conduct or sponsor a collection of information unless a valid OMB control number is displayed. You are not required to respond to a collection of information if this number is not displayed. Valid OMB control numbers can be located on the OMB Internet Page at www.whitehouse.gov/library/omb/OMBINVC.html#VA. If desired, you can call 1-800-827-1000 to get information on where to send comments or suggestions about this form.

IF YOU HAVE ANY QUESTIONS ABOUT THIS FORM, CALL VA TOLL-FREE AT 1-800-827-1000
(TDD 1-800-829-4833 FOR HEARING IMPAIRED).

SECTION I - VETERAN/CLAIMANT IDENTIFICATION

1. LAST NAME - FIRST NAME - MIDDLE NAME OF VETERAN *(Type or print)*	2. VETERAN'S VA FILE NUMBER
3. CLAIMANT'S NAME *(If other than Veteran)* LAST NAME, FIRST, MIDDLE	4. VETERAN'S SOCIAL SECURITY NUMBER
5. RELATIONSHIP OF CLAIMANT TO VETERAN	6. CLAIMANT'S SOCIAL SECURITY NUMBER

SECTION II - SOURCE OF INFORMATION

7A. LIST THE NAME AND ADDRESS OF THE SOURCE SUCH AS A PHYSICIAN, HOSPITAL, ETC.*(Include ZIP Codes, and also a telephone number, if available)*	7B. DATE(S) OF TREATMENT, HOSPITALIZATIONS, OFFICE VISITS, DISCHARGE FROM TREATMENT OR CARE, ETC. *(Include month and year)*	7C. CONDITION(S) *(Illness, injury, etc.)*

8. COMMENTS·

YOU MUST SIGN AND DATE THIS FORM ON PAGE 2 AND CHECK THE APPROPRIATE BLOCK IN ITEM 9C.

VA FORM
MAY 2004   **21-4142**   EXISTING STOCKS OF VA FORM 21-4142, SEP 2003, WILL BE USED.

SECTION III - CONSENT TO RELEASE INFORMATION

READ ALL PARAGRAPHS CAREFULLY BEFORE SIGNING. YOU MUST CHECK THE APPROPRIATE STATEMENT UNDERLINED IN PARENTHESES IN PARAGRAPH 9C.

9A. Privacy Act Notice: The VA will not disclose information collected on this form to any source other than what has been authorized under the Privacy Act of 1974 or Title 38, Code of Federal Regulations 1.576 for routine uses (i.e., civil or criminal law enforcement, congressional communications, epidemiological or research studies, the collection of money owed to the United States, litigation in which the United States is a party or has an interest, the administration of VA programs and delivery of VA benefits, verification of identity and status, and personnel administration) as identified in the VA system of records, 58VA21/22/28 Compensation, Pension, Education, and Rehabilitation Records - VA, and published in the Federal Register. Your obligation to respond is voluntary. However, if the information including your Social Security Number (SSN) is not furnished completely or accurately, the health care provider to which this authorization is addressed may not be able to identify and locate your records, and provided a copy to VA. VA uses your SSN to identify your claim file. Providing your SSN will help ensure that your records are properly associated with your claim file. Giving us your SSN account information is voluntary. Refusal to provide your SSN by itself will not result in the denial of benefits. The VA will not deny an individual benefits for refusing to provide his or her SSN unless the disclosure of the SSN is required by Federal Statute of law in effect prior to January 1, 1975, and still in effect.

9B. I, the undersigned, hereby authorize the hospital, physician or other health care provider or health plan shown in Item 7A to release any information that may have been obtained in connection with a physical, psychological or psychiatric examination or treatment, with the understanding that VA will use this information in determining my eligibility to veterans benefits I have claimed. I understand that the health care provider or health plan identified in Item 7A who is being asked to provide the Veterans Benefits Administration with records under this authorization may not require me to execute this authorization before it will, or will continue to, provide me with treatment, payment for health care, enrollment in a health plan, or eligibility for benefits provided by it. I understand that once my health care provider sends this information to VA under this authorization, the information will no longer be protected by the HIPAA Privacy Rule, but will be protected by the Federal Privacy Act, 5 USC 552a, and VA may disclose this information as authorized by law. I also understand that I may revoke this authorization, at anytime (except to the extent that the health care provider has already released information to VA under this authorization) by notifying the health care provider shown in Item 7A. Please contact the VA Regional Office handling your claim or the Board of Veterans' Appeals, if an appeal is pending, regarding such action. If you do not revoke this authorization, it will automatically end 180 days from the date you sign and date the form (Item 10C).

9C. I ☐ (AUTHORIZE) ☐ (DO NOT AUTHORIZE) the source shown in Item 7A to release or disclose any information or records relating to the diagnosis, treatment or other therapy for the condition(s) of drug abuse, alcoholism or alcohol abuse, infection with the human immunodeficiency virus (HIV), sickle cell anemia or psychotherapy notes. IF MY CONSENT TO THIS INFORMATION IS LIMITED, THE LIMITATION IS WRITTEN HERE:

10A. SIGNATURE OF VETERAN/CLAIMANT OR LEGAL REPRESENTATIVE	10B. RELATIONSHIP TO VETERAN/CLAIMANT *(If other than self, please provide full name, title, organization, city, State and ZIP Code. All court appointments must include docket number, county and State)*	10C. DATE
10D. MAILING ADDRESS *(Number and Street or rural route, city, or P.O. State and ZIP Code)*	10E. TELEPHONE NUMBER *(Include Area Code)*	

The signature and address of a person who either knows the person signing this form or is satisfied as to that person's identity is requested below. This is not required by VA but may be required by the source of the information.

11A. SIGNATURE OF WITNESS	11B. DATE
11C. MAILING ADDRESS OF WITNESS	

PAGE 2

APPENDIX 10:
DIRECTORY OF VA MEDICAL CENTERS

STATE	ADDRESS/TELEPHONE
Alabama	Birmingham VA Medical Center 700 S. 19th Street Birmingham, AL 35233 (205) 933-8101 or (866) 4874243
	Central Alabama Veterans Health Care System East Campus 2400 Hospital Road Tuskegee, AL 36083-5001 (334) 727-0550 or (800) 214-8387
	Central Alabama Veterans Health Care System West Campus 215 Perry Hill Road Montgomery, AL 36109-3798 (334) 272-4670 or (800) 214-8387
	Tuscaloosa VA Medical Center 3701 Loop Road, East Tuscaloosa, AL 35404 (205) 554-2000 or (888) 269-3045
Alaska	Alaska VA Healthcare System and Regional Office 2925 DeBarr Road Anchorage, AK 99508-2989 (888) 353-7574 or (907)-257-4700
Arizona	Northern Arizona VA Health Care System 500 N. Hwy 89 Prescott, AZ 86313 (928) 445-4860 or (800) 949-1005
	Phoenix VA Health Care System 650 E. Indian School Road Phoenix, AZ 85012 (602) 277-5551 or (800) 554-7174

STATE	ADDRESS/TELEPHONE
	Southern Arizona VA Health Care System 3601 South 6th Avenue Tucson, AZ 85723 (520) 792-1450 or (800) 470-8262
Arkansas	Central Arkansas Veterans Healthcare System Eugene J. Towbin Healthcare Center 2200 Fort Roots Drive North Little Rock, AR 72114-1706 (501) 257-1000
	Central Arkansas Veterans Healthcare System John L. McClellan Memorial Veterans Hospital 4300 West 7th Street Little Rock, AR 72205-5484 (501) 257-1000
	Fayetteville VA Medical Center 1100 N. College Avenue Fayetteville, AR 72703 (479) 443-4301 or (800) 691-8387
California	Livermore VA Medical Center 4951 Arroyo Road Livermore, CA 94550 (925) 373-4700
	Menlo Park VA Medical Center 795 Willow Road Menlo Park, CA 94025 (650) 614-9997
	San Francisco VA Medical Center 4150 Clement Street San Francisco, CA 94121-1598 (415) 221-4810
	VA Central California Health Care System 2615 E. Clinton Avenue Fresno, CA 93703 (559) 225-6100 or (888) 826-2838
	VA Greater Los Angeles Healthcare System 11301 Wilshire Boulevard Los Angeles, CA 90073 (310) 478-3711 or (800) 952-4852
	VA Loma Linda Healthcare System 11201 Benton Street Loma Linda, CA 92357 (909) 825-7084 or (800) 741-8387

STATE	ADDRESS/TELEPHONE
	VA Long Beach Healthcare System 5901 E. 7th Street Long Beach, CA 90822 (562) 826-8000 or (888) 769-8387 VA Northern California Health Care System 10535 Hospital Way Mather, CA 95655 (800) 382-8387 or (916) 843-7000 VA Palo Alto Health Care System 3801 Miranda Avenue Palo Alto, CA 94304-1290 (650) 493-5000 or (800) 455-0057 VA San Diego Healthcare System 3350 La Jolla Village Drive San Diego, CA 92161 (858) 552-8585 or (800) 331-8387
Colorado	Grand Junction VA Medical Center 2121 North Avenue Grand Junction, CO 81501 (970) 242-0731 or (866) 206-6415 VA Eastern Colorado Health Care System 1055 Clermont Street Denver, CO 80220 (303) 399-8020 or (888) 336-8262
Connecticut	VA Connecticut Healthcare System Newington Campus 555 Willard Avenue Newington, CT 06111 (860) 666-6951 VA Connecticut Healthcare System West Haven Campus 950 Campbell Avenue West Haven, CT 06516 (203) 932-5711
Delaware	Wilmington VA Medical Center 1601 Kirkwood Highway Wilmington, DE 19805 (302) 994-2511 or (800) 461-8262
District of Columbia	Washington DC VA Medical Center 50 Irving Street, NW Washington, DC 20422 (202) 745-8000 or (888) 553-0242

STATE	ADDRESS/TELEPHONE
Florida	Bay Pines VA Healthcare System 10000 Bay Pines Blvd. Bay Pines, FL 33744 (727) 398-6661 or (888) 8200230
	James A. Haley Veterans' Hospital 13000 Bruce B. Downs Blvd. Tampa, FL 33612 (813) 972-2000 or (888) 716-7787
	Lake City VA Medical Center 619 S. Marion Avenue Lake City, FL 32025-5808 (386) 755-3016 or (800) 308-8387
	Malcom Randall VA Medical Center 1601 S.W. Archer Road Gainesville, FL 32608-1197 (352) 376-1611 or (800) 324-8387
	Miami VA Healthcare System 1201 N.W. 16th Street Miami, FL 33125FL (305) 575-7000 or (888) 276-1785
	Orlando VA Medical Center 5201 Raymond Street Orlando, FL 32803 (407) 629-1599 or (800) 922-7521
	West Palm Beach VA Medical Center 7305 N. Military Trail West Palm Beach, FL 33410-6400 (561) 422-8262 or (800) 972-8262
Georgia	Atlanta VA Medical Center 1670 Clairmont Road Decatur, GA 30033 (404) 321-6111 or (800) 944-9726
	Carl Vinson VA Medical Center 1826 Veterans Blvd. Dublin, GA 31021 (478) 272-1210 or (800) 595-5229
	Charlie Norwood VA Medical Center 1 Freedom Way Augusta, GA 30904-6285 (706) 733-0188 or (800) 836-5561
Hawaii	VA Pacific Islands Health Care System 459 Patterson Road Honolulu, HI 96819-1522 (808) 433-0600 or (800) 214-1306

STATE	ADDRESS/TELEPHONE
Idaho	Boise VA Medical Center 500 West Fort Street Boise, ID 83702 (208) 422-1000
Illinois	Edward Hines Jr. VA Hospital 5th & Roosevelt Rd. P.O. Box 5000 Hines, IL 60141 (708) 202-8387 Jesse Brown VA Medical Center 820 South Damen Avenue Chicago, IL 60612 (312) 569-8387 Marion VA Medical Center 401 West Main Marion, IL 62959 (618) 997-5311 or (866) 289-3300 North Chicago VA Medical Center 3001 Green Bay Road North Chicago, IL 60064 (847) 688-1900 or (800) 393-0865 VA Illiana Health Care System 1900 East Main Street Danville, IL 61832-5198 (217) 554-3000
Indiana	Richard L. Roudebush VA Medical Center 1481 W. 10th Street Indianapolis, IN 46202 (317) 554-0000 or (888) 878-6889 VA Northern Indiana Health Care System Marion Campus 1700 East 38th Street Marion, IN 46953-4589 (765) 674-3321 or (800) 360-8387 VA Northern Indiana Health Care System Fort Wayne Campus 2121 Lake Ave. Fort Wayne, IN 46805 (260) 426-5431 or (800) 360-8387
Iowa	VA Central Iowa Health Care System Des Moines Division 3600 30th Street Des Moines, IA 50310-5774 (515) 699-5999 or 800-294-8387

STATE	ADDRESS/TELEPHONE
	Iowa City VA Medical Center 601 Highway 6 West Iowa City, IA 52246-2208 (319) 338-0581 or (800) 637-0128 VA Central Iowa Health Care System Knoxville Division 1515 W. Pleasant Street Knoxville, IA 50138 (641) 842-3101 or (800) 816-8878
Kansas	Robert J. Dole Department of Veterans Affairs Medical and Regional Office Center 5500 E. Kellogg Wichita, KS 67218 (316) 685-2221 or (888) 878-6881 VA Eastern Kansas Health Care System Colmery-O'Neil VA Medical Center 2200 SW Gage Boulevard Topeka, KS 66622 (785) 350-3111 or (800) 574-8387 VA Eastern Kansas Health Care System Dwight D. Eisenhower VA Medical Center 4101 S. 4th Street Leavenworth, KS 66048-5055 (913) 682-2000 or (800) 952-8387
Kentucky	Lexington VA Medical Center 1101 Veterans Drive Lexington, KY 40502-2236 (859) 233-4511 Lexington VA Medical Center Cooper Drive Division 1101 Veterans Drive Lexington, KY 40502 (859) 233-4511 or (888) 824-3577 Lexington VA Medical Center Leestown Division 2250 Leestown Rd. Lexington, KY 40511 (859) 233-4511 or (888) 824-3577 Louisville VA Medical Center 800 Zorn Avenue Louisville, KY 40206 (502) 287-4000 or (800) 376-8387

STATE	ADDRESS/TELEPHONE
Louisiana	Alexandria VA Medical Center 2495 Shreveport Hwy. 71 North Pineville, LA 71360 (318) 473-0010 or (800) 375-8387 Overton Brooks VA Medical Center 510 E. Stoner Ave. Shreveport, LA 71101-4295 (318) 221-8411 or (800) 863-7441 Southeast Louisiana Veterans Health Care System 1601 Perdido Street New Orleans, LA 70112 (800) 935-8387 or (504) 412-3700
Maine	Togus VA Medical Center 1 VA Center Augusta, ME 04330 (207) 623-8411 or (877) 421-8263
Maryland	Baltimore VA Rehabilitation and Extended Care Center 3900 Loch Raven Boulevard Baltimore, MD 21218 (410) 605-7000 Baltimore VA Medical Center VA Maryland Health Care System 10 North Greene Street Baltimore, MD 21201 (410) 605-7000 or (800) 463-6295 Perry Point VA Medical Center VA Maryland Health Care System Perry Point, MD 21902 (410) 642-2411 or (800) 949-1003
Massachusetts	Edith Nourse Rogers Memorial Veterans Hospital 200 Springs Rd. Bedford, MA 01730 (781) 687-2000 or (800) 422-1617 Northampton VA Medical Center 421 North Main Street Leeds, MA 01053-9764 (413) 584-4040 or (800) 893-1522 VA Boston Healthcare System Brockton Campus 940 Belmont Street Brockton, MA 02301 (508) 583-4500

STATE	ADDRESS/TELEPHONE
	VA Boston Healthcare System Jamaica Plain Campus 150 South Huntington Avenue Jamaica Plain, MA 02130 (617) 232-9500 VA Boston Healthcare System West Roxbury Campus 1400 VFW Parkway West Roxbury, MA 02132 (617) 323-7700
Michigan	Aleda E. Lutz VA Medical Center 1500 Weiss Street Saginaw, MI 48602 (989) 497-2500 or (800) 406-5143 Battle Creek VA Medical Center 5500 Armstrong Road Battle Creek, MI 49037 (269) 966-5600 or (888) 214-1247 Iron Mountain VA Medical Center 325 East H Street Iron Mountain, MI 49801 (906) 774-3300 John D. Dingell VA Medical Center 4646 John Rd. Detroit, MI 48201 (313) 576-1000 or (800) 511-8056 VA Ann Arbor Healthcare System 2215 Fuller Road Ann Arbor, MI 48105 (734) 769-7100 or (800) 361-8387
Minnesota	Minneapolis VA Medical Center One Veterans Drive Minneapolis, MN 55417 (612) 725-2000 or (866) 414-5058 St. Cloud VA Medical Center 4801 Veterans Drive St. Cloud, MN 56303 (320) 252-1670 or (800) 247-1739
Mississippi	G.V. Montgomery VA Medical Center 1500 E. Woodrow Wilson Drive Jackson, MS 39216 (601) 362-4471 or (800) 949-1009

STATE	ADDRESS/TELEPHONE
Missouri	VA Gulf Coast Veterans Health Care System 400 Veterans Avenue Biloxi, MS 39531 (228) 523-5000 or (800) 296-8872
	Harry S. Truman Memorial Hospital 800 Hospital Drive Columbia, MO 65201-5297 (573) 814-6000 or (800) 349-8262
	John J. Pershing VA Medical Center 1500 N. Westwood Blvd. Poplar Bluff, MO 63901 (573) 686-4151
	Kansas City VA Medical Center 4801 Linwood Boulevard Kansas City, MO 64128 (816) 861-4700 or (800) 525-1483
	St. Louis VA Medical Center Jefferson Barracks Division 1 Jefferson Barracks Drive Saint Louis, MO 63125 (314) 652-4100 or (800) 228-5459
	St. Louis VA Medical Center John Cochran Division 915 North Grand Blvd. Saint Louis, MO 63106 (314) 652-4100 or (800) 2285459
Montana	VA Montana Health Care System 3687 Veterans Drive P.O. Box 1500 Fort Harrison, MT 59636 (406) 442-6410
Nebraska	VA Nebraska Western Iowa Health Care System Grand Island Division 2201 No. Broadwell Avenue Grand Island, NE 68803-2196 (308) 382-3660 or (866) 580-1810
	VA Nebraska Western Iowa Health Care System Lincoln Division 600 South 70th Street Lincoln, NE 68510 (402) 4893802 or (866) 8516052

STATE	ADDRESS/TELEPHONE
	VA Nebraska Western Iowa Health Care System Omaha Division 4101 Woolworth Avenue Omaha, NE 68105 (402) 346-8800 or (800) 451-5796
Nevada	VA Sierra Nevada Health Care System 1000 Locust Street Reno, NV 89502 (775) 786-7200 or (888) 838-6256 VA Southern Nevada Healthcare System 901 Rancho Lane Las Vegas, NV 89106 (702) 636-3000 or (888) 633-7554
New Hampshire	Manchester VA Medical Center 718 Smyth Road Manchester, NH 03104 (603) 624-4366 or (800) 892-8384
New Jersey	VA New Jersey Health Care System East Orange Campus 385 Tremont Avenue East Orange, NJ (973) 676-1000 VA New Jersey Health Care System Lyons Campus 151 Knollcroft Road Lyons, NJ 07939 (908) 647-0180
New Mexico	New Mexico VA Health Care System 1501 San Pedro Drive, SE Albuquerque, NM 87108-5153 (505) 265-1711 or (800) 465-8262
New York	Albany VA Medical Center 113 Holland Avenue Albany, NY 12208 (518) 626-5000 Bath VA Medical Center 76 Veterans Avenue Bath, NY 14810 (607) 664-4000 or (877) 845-3247 VA NY Harbor Healthcare System Brooklyn Campus 800 Poly Place Brooklyn, NY 11209 (718) 836-6600

STATE	ADDRESS/TELEPHONE
	Canandaigua VA Medical Center 400 Fort Hill Avenue Canandaigua, NY 14424 (585) 394-2000
	VA Hudson Valley Health Care System Castle Point Campus Route 9D Castle Point, NY 12511 (845) 831-2000 or (800) 269-8749
	VA Hudson Valley Health Care System Franklin Delano Roosevelt Campus 2094 Albany Post Rd. Route 9A, P.O. Box 100 Montrose, NY 10548 (914) 737-4400 or (800) 269-8749
	James J. Peters VA Medical Center 130 West Kingsbridge Road Bronx, NY 10468 (718) 584-9000 or (800) 877-6976
	VA NY Harbor Healthcare System Manhattan Campus 423 East 23rd Street New York, NY 10010 (212) 686-7500
	Northport VA Medical Center 79 Middleville Road Northport, NY 11768 (631) 261-4400 or (800) 551-3996
	Syracuse VA Medical Center 800 Irving Avenue Syracuse, NY 13210 (315) 425-4400 or (800) 792-4334
	VA Western New York Healthcare System at Batavia 222 Richmond Avenue Batavia, NY 14020 (585) 297-1000 or (888) 798-2302
	VA Western New York Healthcare System at Buffalo 3495 Bailey Avenue Buffalo, NY 14215 (716) 834-9200 or (800) 532-8387
North Carolina	Asheville VA Medical Center 1100 Tunnel Road Asheville, NC 28805 (828) 298-7911 or (800) 932-6408

STATE	ADDRESS/TELEPHONE
	Durham VA Medical Center 508 Fulton Street Durham, NC 27705 (919) 286-0411 or (888) 878-6890 Fayetteville VA Medical Center 2300 Ramsey Street Fayetteville, NC 28301 (910) 488-2120 or (800) 771-6106 Salisbury - W.G. Hefner VA Medical Center 1601 Brenner Avenue Salisbury, NC 28144 (704) 638-9000 or (800) 469-8262
North Dakota	Fargo VA Medical Center 2101 Elm Street Fargo, ND 58102 (701) 232-3241 or (800) 410-9723
Ohio	Chalmers P. Wylie Independent Outpatient Clinic 543 Taylor Avenue Columbus, OH 43203-1278 (614) 257-5200 or (888) 615-9448 Chillicothe VA Medical Center 17273 State Route 104 Chillicothe, OH 45601 (740) 773-1141 or (800) 358-8262 Cincinnati VA Medical Center 3200 Vine Street Cincinnati, OH 45220 (513) 861-3100 or (888) 267-7873 Dayton VA Medical Center 4100 W. 3rd Street Dayton, OH 45428 (937) 268-6511 or (800) 368-8262 Louis Stokes VA Medical Center 10701 East Boulevard Cleveland, OH 44106 (216) 791-3800
Oklahoma	Jack C. Montgomery VA Medical Center 1011 Honor Heights Drive Muskogee, OK 74401 (918) 577-3000 or (888) 397-8387 Oklahoma City VA Medical Center 921 N.E. 13th Street Oklahoma City, OK 73104 (405) 270-0501 or (866) 835-5273

STATE	ADDRESS/TELEPHONE
Oregon	Portland VA Medical Center 3710 SW U.S. Veterans Hospital Road Portland, OR 97239 (503) 220-8262 or (800) 949-1004 VA Roseburg Healthcare System 913 NW Garden Valley Blvd. Roseburg, OR 97470-6513 (541) 440-1000 or (800) 549-8387
Pennsylvania	James E. Van Zandt VA Medical Center 2907 Pleasant Valley Boulevard Altoona, PA 16602-4377 (814) 943-8164 Coatesville VA Medical Center 1400 Black Horse Hill Road Coatesville, PA 19320-2096 (610) 384-7711 Erie VA Medical Center 135 East 38 Street Erie, PA 16504 (814) 868-8661 or (800) 274-8387 Lebanon VA Medical Center 1700 South Lincoln Avenue Lebanon, PA 17042 (717) 272-6621 or (800) 409-8771 Philadelphia VA Medical Center University and Woodland Avenues Philadelphia, PA 19104 (800) 949-1001 or (215) 823-5800 VA Butler Healthcare 325 New Castle Road Butler, PA 16001-2480 (724) 287-4781 or (800) 362-8262 VA Pittsburgh Healthcare System H. John Heinz III Progressive Care Center Delafield Road Pittsburgh, PA 15260 (866) 482-7488 or (412) 688-6000 VA Pittsburgh Healthcare System Highland Drive Division 7180 Highland Drive Pittsburgh, PA 15206 (412) 365-4900 or (866) 482-7488

STATE	ADDRESS/TELEPHONE
	VA Pittsburgh Healthcare System University Drive Division University Drive Pittsburgh, PA 15240 (866) 482-7488 Wilkes-Barre VA Medical Center 1111 East End Blvd. Wilkes-Barre, PA 18711 (570) 824-3521 or (877) 928-2621
Puerto Rico	VA Caribbean Healthcare System 10 Casia Street San Juan, PR 00921-3201 (787) 641-7582 or (800) 449-8729
Rhode Island	Providence VA Medical Center 830 Chalkstone Avenue Providence, RI 02908-4799 (401) 273-7100 or (866) 590-2976
South Carolina	Ralph H. Johnson VA Medical Center 109 Bee Street Charleston, SC 294015799 (843) 577-5011 or (888) 878-6884 Wm. Jennings Bryan Dorn VA Medical Center 6439 Garners Ferry Road Columbia, SC 29209-1639 (803) 776-4000
South Dakota	Sioux Falls VA Medical Center 2501 W. 22nd Street PO Box 5046 Sioux Falls, SD 57117-5046 (605) 336-3230 or (800) 316-8387 VA Black Hills Health Care System Hot Springs Campus 500 North 5th Street Hot Springs, SD 57747 (605) 745-2000 or (800) 764-5370 VA Black Hills Health Care System Fort Meade Campus 113 Comanche Road Fort Meade, SD 57741 (605) 347-2511 or (800) 743-1070
Tennessee	Memphis VA Medical Center 1030 Jefferson Avenue Memphis, TN 38104 (901) 523-8990 or (800) 636-8262

STATE	ADDRESS/TELEPHONE
	Mountain Home VA Medical Center Corner of Lamont Street and Veterans Way Mountain Home, TN 37684 (423) 926-1171 or (877) 573-3529
	Tennessee Valley Healthcare System Alvin C. York Campus 3400 Lebanon Pike Murfreesboro, TN 37129 (615) 867-6000 or (800) 876-7093
	Tennessee Valley Healthcare System Nashville Campus 1310 24th Avenue South Nashville, TN 37212-2637 (615) 327-4751 or (800) 228-4973
Texas	Amarillo VA Health Care System 6010 Amarillo Boulevard, West Amarillo, TX 79106 (806) 355-9703 or (800) 687-8262
	Central Texas Veterans Health Care System 1901 Veterans Memorial Drive Temple, TX 76504-7451 (254) 778-4811 or (800) 423-2111
	Central Texas Veterans Health Care System Olin E Teague Veterans' Center 1901 Veterans Memorial Drive Temple, TX 76504 (254) 778-4811 or (800) 423-2111
	Central Texas Veterans Health Care System Waco VA Medical Center 4800 Memorial Drive Waco, TX 76711 (254) 752-6581 or (800) 423-2111
	El Paso VA Health Care System 5001 North Piedras Street El Paso, TX 79930-4211 (915) 564-6100 or (800) 672-3782
	Kerrville VA Medical Center 3600 Memorial Blvd. Kerrville, TX 78028 (830) 896-2020
	Michael E. DeBakey VA Medical Center 2002 Holcombe Blvd. Houston, TX 77030-4298 (713) 791-1414 or (800) 553-2278

STATE	ADDRESS/TELEPHONE
	South Texas Veterans Health Care System 7400 Merton Minter Blvd. San Antonio, TX 78229 (210) 617-5300 or (888) 686-6350 VA North Texas Health Care System Dallas VA Medical Center 4500 South Lancaster Road Dallas, TX 75216 (214) 742-8387 or (800) 849-3597 VA North Texas Health Care System Sam Rayburn Memorial Veterans Center 1201 E. 9th Street Bonham, TX 75418 (903) 583-2111 or (800) 924-8387 West Texas VA Health Care System 300 Veterans Blvd. Big Spring, TX 79720 (432) 263-7361 or (800) 472-1365
Utah	VA Salt Lake City Health Care System 500 Foothill Drive Salt Lake City, UT 84148 (801) 582-1565
Vermont	White River Junction VA Medical Center 215 North Main Street White River Junction, VT 05009 (802) 295-9363 or (866) 687-8387
Virginia	Hampton VA Medical Center 100 Emancipation Drive Hampton, VA 23667 (757) 722-9961 Hunter Holmes McGuire VA Medical Center 1201 Broad Rock Boulevard Richmond, VA 23249 (804) 675-5000 or (800) 784-8381 Salem VA Medical Center 1970 Roanoke Boulevard Salem, VA 24153 (540) 982-2463 or (888) 982-2463
Washington	Jonathan M. Wainwright Memorial VA Medical Center 77 Wainwright Drive Walla Walla, WA 99362 WA (509) 525-5200 or (888) 687-8863

STATE	ADDRESS/TELEPHONE
	Portland VA Medical Center Vancouver Campus 1601 E. 4th Plain Blvd. Vancouver, WA 98661 WA (360) 696-4061 or (800) 949-1004
	Spokane VA Medical Center 4815 N. Assembly Street Spokane, WA 99205-6197 (509) 434-7000 or (800) 325-7940
	VA Puget Sound Health Care System American Lake Division 9600 Veterans Dr. Tacoma, WA 98493 (253) 582-8440 or (800) 329-8387
	VA Puget Sound Health Care System 1660 S. Columbian Way Seattle, WA 98108-1597 (800) 329-8387 or (206) 762-1010
West Virginia	Beckley VA Medical Center 200 Veterans Avenue Beckley, WV 25801 (304) 255-2121 or (877) 902-5142
	Clarksburg - Louis A. Johnson VA Medical Center One Medical Center Drive Clarksburg, WV 26301 (304) 623-3461 or (800) 733-0512
	Huntington VA Medical Center 1540 Spring Valley Drive Huntington, WV 25704 (304) 429-6741 or (800) 827-8244
	Martinsburg VA Medical Center 510 Butler Avenue Martinsburg, WV 25405 (304) 263-0811 or (800) 817-3807
Wisconsin	Clement J. Zablocki Veterans Affairs Medical Center 5000 West National Avenue Milwaukee, WI 53295-1000 (888) 469-6614 or (414) 384-2000
	Tomah VA Medical Center 500 E. Veterans Street Tomah, WI 54660 WI (608) 372-3971 or (800) 872-8662

STATE	ADDRESS/TELEPHONE
	William S. Middleton Memorial Veterans Hospital 2500 Overlook Terrace Madison, WI 53705-2286 (608) 256-1901
Wyoming	Cheyenne VA Medical Center 2360 E. Pershing Blvd. Cheyenne, WY 82001 (307) 778-7550 or (888) 483-9127 Sheridan VA Medical Center 1898 Fort Road Sheridan, WY 82801 (307) 672-3473 or (866) 822-6714

Source: U.S. Veterans Administration.

APPENDIX 11:
APPLICATION FOR HEALTH BENEFITS (FORM 10-10EZ)

OMB Approved No. 2900-0091
Estimated Burden Avg. 45 min.

VA Department of Veterans Affairs	**APPLICATION FOR HEALTH BENEFITS**

SECTION I - GENERAL INFORMATION

Federal law provides criminal penalties, including a fine and/or imprisonment for up to 5 years, for concealing a material fact or making a materially false statement. (See 18 U.S.C. 1001)

1. VETERAN'S NAME *(Last, First, Middle Name)*	2. OTHER NAMES USED	3. MOTHER'S MAIDEN NAME	4. GENDER ☐ MALE ☐ FEMALE

5. ARE YOU SPANISH, HISPANIC, OR LATINO? ☐ YES ☐ NO	6. WHAT IS YOUR RACE? *(You may check more than one.)* *(Information is required for statistical purposes only.)* ☐ AMERICAN INDIAN OR ALASKA NATIVE ☐ BLACK OR AFRICAN AMERICAN ☐ ASIAN ☐ WHITE ☐ NATIVE HAWAIIAN OR OTHER PACIFIC ISLANDER

7. SOCIAL SECURITY NUMBER	9. DATE OF BIRTH *(mm/dd/yyyy)*	10. RELIGION
8. CLAIM NUMBER	9A. PLACE OF BIRTH *(City and State)*	

11. PERMANENT ADDRESS *(Street)*	11A. CITY	11B. STATE	11C. ZIP CODE *(9 digits)*
11D. COUNTY	11E. HOME TELEPHONE NUMBER *(Include area code)*	11F. E-MAIL ADDRESS	
11G. CELLULAR TELEPHONE NUMBER *(Include area code)*	11H. PAGER NUMBER *(Include area code)*		

12. TYPE OF BENEFIT(S) APPLIED FOR *(You may check more than one)* ☐ HEALTH SERVICES ☐ NURSING HOME ☐ DOMICILIARY ☐ DENTAL

13. IF APPLYING FOR HEALTH SERVICES OR ENROLLMENT, WHICH VA MEDICAL CENTER OR OUTPATIENT CLINIC DO YOU PREFER?

14. DO YOU WANT AN APPOINTMENT WITH A VA DOCTOR OR PROVIDER AS SOON AS ONE BECOMES AVAILABLE? ☐ YES ☐ NO I am only enrolling in case I need care in the future.	15. HAVE YOU BEEN SEEN AT A VA HEALTH CARE FACILITY? ☐ YES, **LOCATION:** ☐ NO

16. CURRENT MARITAL STATUS *(Check one)* ☐ MARRIED ☐ NEVER MARRIED ☐ SEPARATED ☐ WIDOWED ☐ DIVORCED ☐ UNKNOWN

17. NAME, ADDRESS AND RELATIONSHIP OF NEXT OF KIN	17A. NEXT OF KIN'S HOME TELEPHONE NUMBER *(Include area code)*
	17B. NEXT OF KIN'S WORK TELEPHONE NUMBER *(Include area code)*
18. NAME, ADDRESS AND RELATIONSHIP OF EMERGENCY CONTACT	18A. EMERGENCY CONTACT'S HOME TELEPHONE NUMBER *(Include area code)*
	18B. EMERGENCY CONTACT'S WORK TELEPHONE NUMBER *(Include area code)*

19. INDIVIDUAL TO RECEIVE POSSESSION OF YOUR PERSONAL PROPERTY LEFT ON PREMISES UNDER VA CONTROL AFTER YOUR DEPARTURE OR AT THE TIME OF DEATH. NOTE: THIS DOES NOT CONSTITUTE A WILL OR TRANSFER OF TITLE *(Check one)*

☐ EMERGENCY CONTACT   ☐ NEXT OF KIN

VA FORM
MAR 2008 **10-10EZ**

PAGE 1

APPLICATION FOR HEALTH BENEFITS, Continued	VETERAN'S NAME *(Last, First, Middle)*	SOCIAL SECURITY NUMBER

SECTION II - INSURANCE INFORMATION *(Use a separate sheet for additional information)*

1. ARE YOU COVERED BY HEALTH INSURANCE? *(Including coverage through a spouse or another person)* ☐ YES ☐ NO	2. HEALTH INSURANCE COMPANY NAME, ADDRESS AND TELEPHONE NUMBER
3. NAME OF POLICY HOLDER	

4. POLICY NUMBER	5. GROUP CODE			
		YES	**NO**	
6. ARE YOU ELIGIBLE FOR MEDICAID?		☐	☐	
7. ARE YOU ENROLLED IN MEDICARE HOSPITAL INSURANCE PART A?		☐	☐	7A. EFFECTIVE DATE *(mm/dd/yyyy)*
8. ARE YOU ENROLLED IN MEDICARE HOSPITAL INSURANCE PART B?		☐	☐	8A. EFFECTIVE DATE *(mm/dd/yyyy)*
9. NAME EXACTLY AS IT APPEARS ON YOUR MEDICARE CARD				10. MEDICARE CLAIM NUMBER

11. IS NEED FOR CARE DUE TO ON THE JOB INJURY? *(Check one)* ☐ YES ☐ NO	12. IS NEED FOR CARE DUE TO ACCIDENT? *(Check One)* ☐ YES ☐ NO

SECTION III - EMPLOYMENT INFORMATION

1. VETERAN'S EMPLOYMENT STATUS *(Check one)* ☐ FULL TIME ☐ NOT EMPLOYED *If employed or retired, complete item 1A* ☐ PART TIME ☐ RETIRED Date of retirement *(mm/dd/yyyy)*	1A. COMPANY NAME, ADDRESS AND TELEPHONE NUMBER
2. SPOUSE'S EMPLOYMENT STATUS *(Check one)* ☐ FULL TIME ☐ NOT EMPLOYED *If employed or retired, complete item 2A* ☐ PART TIME ☐ RETIRED Date of retirement *(mm/dd/yyyy)*	2A. COMPANY NAME, ADDRESS AND TELEPHONE NUMBER

SECTION IV - MILITARY SERVICE INFORMATION

1. LAST BRANCH OF SERVICE	1A. LAST ENTRY DATE	1B. LAST DISCHARGE DATE	1C. DISCHARGE TYPE	1D. MILITARY SERVICE NUMBER

2. CHECK YES OR NO	YES	NO		YES	NO
A. ARE YOU A PURPLE HEART AWARD RECIPIENT?	☐	☐	E1. ARE YOU RECEIVING DISABILITY RETIREMENT PAY INSTEAD OF VA COMPENSATION?	☐	☐
B. ARE YOU A FORMER PRISONER OF WAR?	☐	☐	F. DO YOU NEED CARE OF CONDITIONS POTENTIALLY RELATED TO SERVICE IN SW ASIA DURING THE GULF WAR?	☐	☐
C. DO YOU HAVE A VA SERVICE-CONNECTED RATING?	☐	☐	G. WERE YOU EXPOSED TO AGENT ORANGE WHILE SERVING IN VIETNAM?	☐	☐
C1. IF YES, WHAT IS YOUR RATED PERCENTAGE? %			H. WERE YOU EXPOSED TO RADIATION WHILE IN THE MILITARY?	☐	☐
D. DID YOU SERVE IN COMBAT AFTER 11/11/1998?	☐	☐	I. DID YOU RECEIVE NOSE AND THROAT RADIUM TREATMENTS WHILE IN THE MILITARY?	☐	☐
E. WAS YOUR DISCHARGE FROM MILITARY FOR A DISABILITY INCURRED OR AGGRAVATED IN THE LINE OF DUTY?	☐	☐	J. DO YOU HAVE A SPINAL CORD INJURY?	☐	☐

SECTION V - PAPERWORK REDUCTION ACT AND PRIVACY ACT INFORMATION

The Paperwork Reduction Act of 1995 requires us to notify you that this information collection is in accordance with the clearance requirements of Section 3507 of the Paperwork Reduction Act of 1995. We may not conduct or sponsor, and you are not required to respond to, a collection of information unless it displays a valid OMB number. We anticipate that the time expended by all individuals who must complete this form will average 45 minutes. This includes the time it will take to read instructions, gather the necessary facts and fill out the form.

Privacy Act Information: VA is asking you to provide the information on this form under 38 U.S.C. Sections 1705, 1710, 1712, and 1722 in order for VA to determine your eligibility for medical benefits. Information you supply may be verified through a computer-matching program. VA may disclose the information that you put on the form as permitted by law. VA may make a "routine use" disclosure of the information as outlined in the Privacy Act systems of records notices and in accordance with the VHA Notice of Privacy Practices. You do not have to provide the information to VA, but if you don't, VA may be unable to process your request and serve your medical needs. Failure to furnish the information will not have any affect on any other benefits to which you may be entitled. If you provide VA your Social Security Number, VA will use it to administer your VA benefits. VA may also use this information to identify veterans and persons claiming or receiving VA benefits and their records, and for other purposes authorized or required by law.

VA FORM
MAR 2008 **10-10EZ**   PAGE 2

APPLICATION FOR HEALTH BENEFITS (FORM 10-10EZ)

APPLICATION FOR HEALTH BENEFITS, Continued	VETERAN'S NAME (Last, First, Middle)	SOCIAL SECURITY NUMBER

SECTION VI - FINANCIAL DISCLOSURE

Disclosure allows VA to accurately determine whether certain veterans will be charged copayments for care and medications, their eligibility for other services and enrollment priority. Veterans are not required to disclose their financial information; however, VA is not currently enrolling new applicants who decline to provide their financial information unless they have a special eligibility factor. **Recent combat veterans (e.g., OEF/OIF) who were discharged within the past 5 years or were discharged more than 5 years ago and applying for enrollment by Jan. 27, 2011 are eligible for enrollment without disclosing their financial information** but like other veterans may provide it to establish their eligibility for travel reimbursement, cost-free medication and/or medical care for services unrelated to military experience.

☐ **No, I do not wish to provide financial information in Sections VII through X.** I understand that VA is not enrolling new applicants who do not provide this information and who do not have a special eligibility factor (e.g., recently discharged combat veteran, compensable service connection, receipt of VA pension or Medicaid benefits.) If I am enrolled, I agree to pay applicable VA copayments. *Sign and date the form in Section XII.*

☐ **Yes, I will provide my household financial information for last calendar year.** Complete applicable sections VII through X . *Sign and date the form in Section XII.*

SECTION VII - DEPENDENT INFORMATION *(Use a separate sheet for additional dependents)*

1. SPOUSE'S NAME (Last, Middle Name)	2. CHILD'S NAME (Last, First, Middle Name)	
1A. SPOUSE'S MAIDEN NAME	2A. CHILD'S RELATIONSHIP TO YOU (Check one) ☐ Son ☐ Daughter ☐ Stepson ☐ Stepdaughter	
1B. SPOUSE'S SOCIAL SECURITY NUMBER	2B. CHILD'S SOCIAL SECURITY NUMBER	2C. DATE CHILD BECAME YOUR DEPENDENT (mm/dd/yyyy)
1C. SPOUSE'S DATE OF BIRTH (mm/dd/yyyy) 1D. DATE OF MARRIAGE (mm/dd/yyyy)	2D. CHILD'S DATE OF BIRTH (mm/dd/yyyy)	
1E. SPOUSE'S ADDRESS AND TELEPHONE NUMBER (Street, City, State, ZIP.)	2E. WAS CHILD PERMANENTLY AND TOTALLY DISABLED BEFORE THE AGE OF 18? ☐ YES ☐ NO	
	2F. IF CHILD IS BETWEEN 18 AND 23 YEARS OF AGE, DID CHILD ATTEND SCHOOL LAST CALENDAR YEAR? ☐ YES ☐ NO	
3. IF YOUR SPOUSE OR DEPENDENT CHILD DID NOT LIVE WITH YOU LAST YEAR ENTER THE AMOUNT YOU CONTRIBUTED TO THEIR SUPPORT. SPOUSE $ CHILD $	2G. EXPENSES PAID BY YOUR DEPENDENT CHILD FOR COLLEGE, VOCATIONAL REHABILITATION OR TRAINING (e.g., tuition, books, materials) $	

SECTION VIII - PREVIOUS CALENDAR YEAR GROSS ANNUAL INCOME OF VETERAN, SPOUSE AND DEPENDENT CHILDREN
(Use a separate sheet for additional dependents)

	VETERAN	SPOUSE	CHILD 1
1. GROSS ANNUAL INCOME FROM EMPLOYMENT (wages, bonuses, tips, etc.) EXCLUDING INCOME FROM YOUR FARM, RANCH, PROPERTY OR BUSINESS	$	$	$
2. NET INCOME FROM YOUR FARM, RANCH, PROPERTY OR BUSINESS	$	$	$
3. LIST OTHER INCOME AMOUNTS (e.g., Social Security, compensation, pension interest, dividends) EXCLUDING WELFARE.	$	$	$

SECTION IX - PREVIOUS CALENDAR YEAR DEDUCTIBLE EXPENSES

1. TOTAL NON-REIMBURSED MEDICAL EXPENSES PAID BY YOU OR YOUR SPOUSE (e.g., payments for doctors, dentists, medications, Medicare, health insurance, hospital and nursing home) VA will calculate a deductible and the net medical expenses you may claim.	$
2. AMOUNT YOU PAID LAST CALENDAR YEAR FOR FUNERAL AND BURIAL EXPENSES FOR YOUR DECEASED SPOUSE OR DEPENDENT CHILD (Also enter spouse or child's information in Section VII.)	$
3. AMOUNT YOU PAID LAST CALENDAR YEAR FOR YOUR COLLEGE OR VOCATIONAL EDUCATIONAL EXPENSES (e.g., tuition, books, fees, materials) DO NOT LIST YOUR DEPENDENTS' EDUCATIONAL EXPENSES.	$

SECTION X - PREVIOUS CALENDAR YEAR NET WORTH *(Use a separate sheet for additional dependents)*

	VETERAN	SPOUSE	CHILD 1
1. CASH, AMOUNT IN BANK ACCOUNTS (e.g., checking and savings accounts, certificates of deposit, individual retirement accounts, stocks and bonds)	$	$	$
2. MARKET VALUE OF LAND AND BUILDINGS MINUS MORTGAGES AND LIENS. (e.g., second homes and non-income producing property. Do not count your primary home.)	$	$	$
3. VALUE OF OTHER PROPERTY OR ASSETS (e.g., art, rare coins, collectables). MINUS THE AMOUNT YOU OWE ON THESE ITEMS. INCLUDE VALUE OF FARM, RANCH OR BUSINESS ASSETS. Exclude household effects and family vehicles.	$	$	$

SECTION XI - CONSENT TO COPAYMENTS

If you are a 0% SC veteran and do not receive VA monetary benefits or a NSC veteran (and you are not a Former POW, Purple Heart Recipient or VA pensioner) and your household income (or combined income and net worth) exceeds the established threshold, this application will be considered for enrollment, but only if you agree to pay VA copayments for treatment of your NSC conditions. **If you are such a veteran by signing this application you are agreeing to pay the applicable VA copayments as required by law.**

SECTION XII - ASSIGNMENT OF BENEFITS

I understand that pursuant to 38 U.S.C. Section 1729, VA is authorized to recover or collect from my health plan (HP) for the reasonable charges of nonservice-connected VA medical care or services furnished or provided to me. I hereby authorize payment directly to VA from any HP under which I am covered (including coverage provided under my spouse's HP) that is responsible for payment of the charges for my medical care, including benefits otherwise payable to me or my spouse.

ALL APPLICANTS MUST SIGN AND DATE THIS FORM. REFER TO INSTRUCTIONS WHICH DEFINE WHO CAN SIGN ON BEHALF OF THE VETERAN.

SIGNATURE OF APPLICANT	DATE

APPENDIX 12:
APPLICATION FOR VETERANS' GROUP
LIFE INSURANCE (FORM SGL 8714)

IMPORTANT: No insurance may be granted unless a completed application has been received (38 U.S.C. 1977). See "Follow these easy steps!" before completing this application. Please complete all fields.

1. Service Member Information

For OSGLI Use Only

Action Taken

Last   First   MI

OSGLI Representative

No.   Street

Date

City   State   ZIP

E-mail Address

Telephone Number   Social Security Number   Date of Separation
—   —   /   /

Date of Birth   Gender   Age   Branch of Service
/   /

2. Coverage Amount

I elect the following VGLI coverage amount:

☐ $400,000   ☐ $350,000   ☐ $300,000   ☐ $250,000   ☐ $200,000   ☐ $150,000   ☐ $100,000   ☐ $50,000

☐ Other_____

3. Coverage Election and Payment Method

I agree to make future payments by:

☐ Mail Please select frequency:
  ☐ Monthly   ☐ Quarterly   ☐ Semi-Annually   ☐ Annually
  If you elect Annually, please submit the Annual Premium.

I am enclosing my first premium payment of: $_____

☐ Automatic Monthly Deductions from military retirement pay (or from VA compensation if switched from military retired pay to VA compensation)

☐ Automatic Monthly Deductions from VA compensation. My VA claim file number is _____

Have you been able to work since leaving the service?
☐ Yes   ☐ No

If no, is this due to a disability incurred while in the service?
☐ Yes   ☐ No   Military Disability Rating _____%
(NOT your VA compensation rating)

NOTE: For Those Receiving Military Retirement Pay or VA Disability Compensation—Automatic Monthly Payment option. Your first month's premium must be submitted with this application.

—Detach and Return—

4. Health Statement

(Only complete this section if you are applying more than 120 days after you were discharged from the service.)

Attach separate sheet with complete details for any question answered "Yes.")　　Height _____　　Weight _____

Have you had or been treated for or had known indications of:	Y	N
A. Heart trouble or abnormal pulse?	☐	☐
B. High blood pressure?	☐	☐
C. Mental health conditions?	☐	☐
D. Diabetes or sugar in urine?	☐	☐
E. Cancer or tumors?	☐	☐
F. Lung or respiratory disorders?	☐	☐
G. Disorder of kidney, bladder, or urinary system?	☐	☐
H. Liver or gallbladder disorder?	☐	☐
I. Stomach or intestinal disorders?	☐	☐
J. Arthritis?	☐	☐
K. Have you ever been declined or postponed for any form of life or health insurance or offered a policy with a higher premium because of health reasons only?	☐	☐
L. Have you been absent from work because of sickness or injury during the last six months?	☐	☐

Have you within the past five years:	Y	N
M. Been advised to have a surgical procedure?	☐	☐
N. Been a patient or been advised to enter a hospital or health care facility?	☐	☐
O. Consulted, been attended, or examined by a doctor or other practitioner exclusive of annual or periodic physicals?	☐	☐
P. Used barbiturates, heroin, opiates, or other narcotics, or been treated for alcoholism?	☐	☐
Q. Have you ever been diagnosed as having acquired immunodeficiency syndrome (AIDS) or AIDS-related complex (ARC)?	☐	☐
R. Do you have any known physical impairments, deformities, or ill health not covered above?	☐	☐
S. Do you have a service-connected disability?	☐	☐
If yes, what is the VA claim file number? _____		

(Continued on reverse side)

5. Beneficiary(ies) and Benefit Payment Options

I designate the following beneficiary(ies) to receive my insurance proceeds. I understand that the principal beneficiary(ies) will receive payment upon my death. The share of any principal beneficiary who dies before me will be distributed equally among the remaining principal beneficiaries. If all principal beneficiaries die before me, the insurance will be paid to the contingent beneficiaries. I understand that unless I have named a beneficiary(ies) below, my insurance will be paid under the provisions of the law (38 U.S.C. 1970). The designation below cancels any prior SGLI or VGLI beneficiary designation or payment instruction.

Principal Beneficiary	Relationship To You	Share to Beneficiary* (Use %, $ amount or fractions)	Payment Option (Lump sum or 36 equal monthly installments)
Last First MI Social Security Number (if known)			
No. Street City State ZIP			

Principal Beneficiary	Relationship To You	Share to Beneficiary* (Use %, $ amount or fractions)	Payment Option (Lump sum or 36 equal monthly installments)
Last First MI Social Security Number (if known)			
No. Street City State ZIP			

Contingent Beneficiary	Relationship To You	Share to Beneficiary* (Use %, $ amount or fractions)	Payment Option (Lump sum or 36 equal monthly installments)
Last First MI Social Security Number (if known)			
No. Street City State ZIP			

Contingent Beneficiary	Relationship To You	Share to Beneficiary* (Use %, $ amount or fractions)	Payment Option (Lump sum or 36 equal monthly installments)
Last First MI Social Security Number (if known)			
No. Street City State Zip			

Contingent Beneficiary	Relationship To You	Share to Beneficiary* (Use %, $ amount or fractions)	Payment Option (Lump sum or 36 equal monthly installments)
Last First MI Social Security Number (if known)			
No. Street City State ZIP			

Contingent Beneficiary	Relationship To You	Share to Beneficiary* (Use %, $ amount or fractions)	Payment Option (Lump sum or 36 equal monthly installments)
Last First MI Social Security Number (if known)			
No. Street City State ZIP			

*If more than one principal or contingent beneficiary is designated, the total shares must equal 100% of your death benefit.

Applicant Signature

I understand that I cannot have combined SGLI and VGLI coverage for more than $400,000. I understand that unless I have named a beneficiary(ies) above, my insurance will be paid under provisions of Federal Law.

Print Name of Applicant   Social Security Number of Applicant

Signature of Applicant (Do not print. Sign in ink.)   Date

PENALTY: The law provides that whoever makes any statement of a material fact knowing it to be false shall be punished by fine, imprisonment, or both.

APPENDIX 13:
LIST OF VGLI PARTICIPATING INSURANCE COMPANIES

ALLSTATE LIFE INSURANCE COMPANY

AMALGAMATED LIFE INSURANCE COMPANY

AMERICAN FIDELITY LIFE INSURANCE COMPANY

BANKERS LIFE AND CASUALTY COMPANY

BENEFICIAL LIFE INSURANCE COMPANY

CENTRAL LIFE INSURANCE COMPANY OF FLORIDA

CICALIFE INSURANCE COMPANY OF AMERICA

CONNECTICUT GENERAL LIFE INSURANCE COMPANY

CONTINENTAL GENERAL INSURANCE COMPANY

COTTON STATES LIFE INSURANCE COMPANY

COUNTRY LIFE INSURANCE COMPANY

EMC NATIONAL LIFE COMPANY

EMPIRE STATE LIFE INSURANCE COMPANY

EMPLOYEES LIFE COMPANY

(MUTUAL) FAMILY BENEFIT LIFE INSURANCE COMPANY

FARMERS NEW WORLD LIFE INSURANCE COMPANY

FEDERAL LIFE INSURANCE COMPANY

(MUTUAL) FIRST INVESTORS LIFE INSURANCE COMPANY

GOLDEN STATE MUTUAL LIFE INSURANCE COMPANY

INDIVIDUAL ASSURANCE COMPANY

INVESTORS HERITAGE LIFE INSURANCE COMPANY

JOHN HANCOCK LIFE INSURANCE COMPANY

KANAWHA INSURANCE COMPANY LIFE INSURANCE COMPANY OF ALABAMA

LIFE INSURANCE COMPANY OF NORTH AMERICA

MADISON NATIONAL LIFE INSURANCE COMPANY, INC.

METROPOLITAN LIFE INSURANCE COMPANY

MINNESOTA LIFE INSURANCE COMPANY

MUTUAL SERVICE LIFE INSURANCE COMPANY

NEW YORK LIFE INSURANCE COMPANY

NORTH CAROLINA MUTUAL LIFE INSURANCE COMPANY

NORTH COAST LIFE INSURANCE COMPANY

NORTHWESTERN MUTUAL LIFE INSURANCE COMPANY

OHIO STATE LIFE INSURANCE COMPANY

PENSION LIFE INSURANCE COMPANY OF AMERICA

PRESIDENTIAL LIFE INSURANCE COMPANY

PRUDENTIAL INSURANCE COMPANY OF AMERICA

RELIABLE LIFE INSURANCE COMPANY

RELIASTAR LIFE INSURANCE COMPANY

RELIASTAR OF NEW YORK

SBLI USA MUTUAL LIFE INSURANCE COMPANY, INC.

SECURITY NATIONAL LIFE INSURANCE COMPANY

SOUTHERN SECURITY LIFE INSURANCE COMPANY

TOWER LIFE INSURANCE COMPANY

TRANSAM ASSURANCE COMPANY

TRANS WORLD ASSURANCE COMPANY

UNION LABOR LIFE INSURANCE COMPANY

APPENDIX 14:
APPLICATION FOR VA EDUCATION BENEFITS (FORM 22-1990)

OMB Control No. 2900-0154
Respondent Burden: 1 hour

VA Department of Veterans Affairs	**APPLICATION FOR VA EDUCATION BENEFITS** (See attached Information and Instructions)

INTERNET VERSION AVAILABLE -You can submit this application over the Internet at the following site: www.gibill.va.gov

PART I - APPLICANT AND BENEFIT INFORMATION
(All Applicants Must Complete This Part)

1A. NAME OF APPLICANT *(First, Middle, Last)*

VA DATE STAMP
(Do Not Write In This Space)

1B. SOCIAL SECURITY NUMBER OF APPLICANT | 1C. VA FILE NUMBER *(If previously assigned)*

2A. APPLICANT'S ADDRESS *(Complete street address, city, state, and 9 digit ZIP Code)*

2B. SEX OF APPLICANT | 2C. APPLICANT'S DATE OF BIRTH | 2D. APPLICANT'S E-MAIL ADDRESS

3. APPLICANT'S TELEPHONE NUMBER *(Include Area Code)*

☐ MALE ☐ FEMALE | A. DAY | B. NIGHT

4. DESCRIPTION OF VA EDUCATION PROGRAMS *(Check (✔) the box next to each benefit you wish to apply for)*

A. MONTGOMERY GI BILL EDUCATIONAL ASSISTANCE PROGRAM (title 38, U. S. C., chapter 30). If you served or are currently serving on active duty, you may be eligible to receive this benefit. Check the box to the right if you:

- entered active duty for the first time after June 30, 1985, **OR**

- were eligible to receive Vietnam Era Veterans' Educational Assistance (title 38, U.S.C. chapter 34) benefits on December 31, 1989, **OR**

- were discharged under one of the qualifying separation programs shown in the instructions, **OR**

- were a participant under the Post-Vietnam Era Veterans' Educational Assistance program commonly referred to as VEAP (title 38, U.S.C., chapter 32) and elected this benefit during one of the open window periods shown in the instructions.

☐

B. MONTGOMERY GI BILL - SELECTED RESERVE EDUCATIONAL ASSISTANCE PROGRAM (title 10, U. S. C., chapter 1606). This benefit is based on Selected Reserve service (Reserve or National Guard). Check the box to the right if you had at least a six-year reserve obligation after June 30, 1985.

(NOTE: Department of Defense (DoD) determines eligibility for this program.)

☐

C. RESERVE EDUCATIONAL ASSISTANCE PROGRAM (title 10, U.S.C., chapter 1607). This benefit is for a reservist called to active duty to support contingency operations. Check the box to the right if you were called to active duty to support contingency or other specific operations.

(NOTE: Department of Defense (DoD) determines eligibility for this program)

☐

D. POST-VIETNAM ERA VETERANS' EDUCATIONAL ASSISTANCE PROGRAM commonly referred to as VEAP, (title 38, U.S.C., chapter 32, or section 903 of Public Law 96-342). Check the box to the right if you:

- served on active duty at any time from January 1, 1977 through June 30, 1985, **AND**

- either contributed funds or had your service branch make contributions for you.

☐

E. NATIONAL CALL TO SERVICE PROGRAM (title 10, U.S.C., chapter 31, section 510). Check the box to the right if you:

- entered on or after October 1, 2003, under the National Call to Service program, **AND**

- selected one of the education incentives provided by that program

Check this box to the right only if you've selected one of the two Educational Allowance Incentive options.

(If you checked this box, be sure to complete Part IV)

F. THE "TRANSFER OF ENTITLEMENT" PROGRAM (title 38, U.S.C., chapter 30, section 3020). Check the box to the right if you:

- are a spouse or child of a person who qualified for the Montgomery GI Bill Educational Assistance Program (Chapter 30), **AND**

- believe that your parent or spouse transferred entitlement to you

(If you checked this box, be sure to complete Part V)

VA FORM MAY 2005   **22-1990**   SUPERSEDES VA FORM 22-1990, SEP 2003, WHICH WILL NOT BE USED.   PAGE 1 OF 6

5. DIRECT DEPOSIT INFORMATION
Please send a voided personal check or provide the following information.
Direct Deposit is not available for the Post-Vietnam Era Veterans' Educational Assistance Program (Chapter 32)

A. TYPE OF ACCOUNT

☐ CHECKING   ☐ SAVINGS   ☐ I DO NOT HAVE AN ACCOUNT

B. NAME OF FINANCIAL INSTITUTION	C. 9 DIGIT ROUTING OR TRANSIT NUMBER	D. ACCOUNT NUMBER

6. TYPE OF VA EDUCATION BENEFITS PREVIOUSLY APPLIED FOR? *(Check all applicable boxes)*

☐ A. VETERAN'S EDUCATION BENEFITS (Any of the VA benefits shown in Item 4) (Specify benefit) _____

☐ B. PREVIOUS VETERAN'S EDUCATION BENEFITS (Specify benefit) _____

☐ C. VOCATIONAL REHABILITATION BENEFITS (Chapter 31)

☐ D. DEPENDENTS' EDUCATIONAL ASSISTANCE BENEFITS (Chapter 35) (Complete Items 7A and 7B)

☐ E. OTHER (Specify benefit) _____

☐ F. NONE

NOTE - COMPLETE ITEMS 7A AND 7B ONLY IF YOU CHECKED ITEM 6D

7A. NAME OF PARENT/SPOUSE *(See Instructions)*	7B. FILE NUMBER OF PARENT/SPOUSE *(See Instructions)*

8. HAVE YOU RECEIVED AN INFORMATION PAMPHLET EXPLAINING THE EDUCATION BENEFIT OR BENEFITS YOU ARE APPLYING FOR? *(See Instructions)*
☐ YES   ☐ NO

9. PROGRAM OF EDUCATION OR TRAINING

A. DO YOU KNOW YOUR EDUCATIONAL OR CAREER GOAL? *(If you know this goal, please specify. If you do not know your goal, check "No" then skip to Item 9C.)*

☐ YES   ☐ NO

B. HAVE YOU SELECTED A SPECIFIC PROGRAM OF EDUCATION?
☐ YES   ☐ NO   (If "Yes," list below each diploma, vocational course, job training program, or test you need to reach your educational or career goal that you indicated in Item 9A. If you have not selected a program, leave this item blank.)

C. EDUCATION OR TRAINING WILL BE BY *(Check more than one if necessary)*

☐ COLLEGE OR OTHER SCHOOL   ☐ CORRESPONDENCE COURSE   ☐ TUITION ASSISTANCE TOP-UP

☐ I SEEK REIMBURSEMENT FOR A LICENSING OR CERTIFICATION TEST   ☐ APPRENTICESHIP OR ON-THE-JOB TRAINING

☐ NATIONAL ADMISSIONS EXAMS OR NATIONAL EXAMS FOR CREDIT   ☐ VOCATIONAL FLIGHT TRAINING

D. HAVE YOU SELECTED YOUR SCHOOL OR TRAINING ESTABLISHMENT?	COMPLETE NAME AND ADDRESS OF SCHOOL (Complete street address, city, state and 9 digit ZIP Code)
☐ YES ☐ NO (If you have selected a school, check "Yes," and specify its complete name and mailing address. If you have not selected a school, check "no.") If you are applying for reimbursement of test fees, don't answer this question. Skip to Item 10.) ▶	

E. DO YOU KNOW THE DATE YOU WILL BEGIN YOUR SCHOOLING OR TRAINING?	DATE (Month, Year) OF ANTICIPATED BEGINNING SCHOOL OR TRAINING
☐ YES ☐ NO (If you do know this date, check "Yes." Specify this date. If you do not know this date check "no.") ▶	

F. DO YOU PLAN TO REPEAT ANY COURSE FOR WHICH YOU RECEIVED CREDIT?	G. INFORMATION ABOUT REPEATED COURSE
☐ YES ☐ NO (If "Yes," write in Item 9G the name of the course, when you originally took this course, and why you plan to repeat it.) ▶	

PAGE 2 OF 6

NOTE - COMPLETE ONLY IF YOU ARE A CIVILIAN EMPLOYEE OF THE U.S. GOVERNMENT

If you are on active military duty, skip question 10.

10. DO YOU EXPECT TO RECEIVE FUNDS FROM YOUR AGENCY OR DEPARTMENT FOR THE SAME COURSE(S) FOR WHICH YOU EXPECT TO RECEIVE VA EDUCATIONAL ASSISTANCE?	Source of educational assistance from government employment:
☐ YES ☐ NO *(If "Yes," show the source of these funds)* ▶	

NOTE - COMPLETE ITEM 11 ONLY IF YOU ARE ON ACTIVE DUTY

11. ARE YOU RECEIVING, OR DO YOU ANTICIPATE RECEIVING, ANY MONEY*(Including but not limited to Federal Tuition Assistance)* FROM THE ARMED FORCES OR PUBLIC HEALTH SERVICE FOR THE COURSE FOR WHICH YOU HAVE APPLIED TO VA FOR EDUCATION BENEFITS? IF YOU WILL RECEIVE SUCH BENEFITS, CHECK "YES" AND GIVE COMPLETE DETAILS INCLUDING THE SOURCE OF THE FUNDS. NOTE: IF YOU ARE ONLY APPLYING FOR TUITION ASSISTANCE TOP-UP, CHECK "NO"	Details of educational assistance from the military:
☐ YES ☐ NO ▶	

12. EDUCATION AND EMPLOYMENT INFORMATION

A. DID YOU GRADUATE FROM HIGH SCHOOL? *(If "Yes," write the date you graduated next to "Yes," and skip to Item 12c. If "No," complete Item 12B)*	B. IF YOU DID NOT GRADUATE FROM HIGH SCHOOL, DO YOU HAVE A HIGH SCHOOL EQUIVALENCY CERTIFICATE?*(If "Yes," write the date you completed the requirements for this certificate in the space provided. If "No," go to Item 12c)*
☐ YES Date _____ ☐ NO	☐ YES Date _____ ☐ NO

C. EDUCATION AFTER HIGH SCHOOL (INCLUDE ALL APPRENTICESHIP, ON-THE-JOB TRAINING, AND FLIGHT TRAINING) *(See Instructions)*

NAME AND LOCATION OF COLLEGE OR OTHER TRAINING PROVIDER *(Include City and State)*	DATES OF TRAINING		NUMBER OF SEMESTER, QUARTER OR CLOCK HOURS COMPLETED	DEGREE, DIPLOMA, OR CERTIFICATE RECEIVED	MAJOR FIELD OR COURSE OF STUDY
	FROM	TO			

D. DO YOU HOLD ANY FAA FLIGHT CERTIFICATES? *(If "Yes," list each certificate.)*	
☐ YES ☐ NO ▶	

EMPLOYMENT *(Complete ONLY if you served in the military)*

EMPLOYMENT	PRINCIPAL OCCUPATION	NUMBER OF MONTHS IN THAT OCCUPATION	LICENSE OR RATING
E. Before Entering Military Service			
F. After Leaving Military Service			

PART II - SERVICE INFORMATION *(All applicants must complete this part)*

13. ACTIVE DUTY INFORMATION

A. ARE YOU NOW ON ACTIVE DUTY OR FULL-TIME NATIONAL GUARD DUTY? (Send us a copy of your orders, if authority for full-time National Guard duty is title 32, U.S.C.)

☐ YES ☐ NO

B. ARE YOU NOW ON TERMINAL LEAVE BEFORE DISCHARGE? (If yes, please provide the date you began your terminal leave)

☐ YES ☐ NO

Date leave began: _____

Date of expected discharge: _____

PAGE 3 OF 6

14. INFORMATION ABOUT YOUR PERIODS OF ACTIVE DUTY

Please complete Items 14A through 14f for each period of your active duty. It will help VA process your claim if you send a copy of your DD214 (copy 4) for *each period* of active service. (Don't report any Active Duty for Training)

A. DATE ENTERED ACTIVE DUTY	B. DATE SEPARATED FROM ACTIVE DUTY	C. BRANCH OF SERVICE OR RESERVE OR GUARD COMPONENT	D. CHARACTER OF DISCHARGE	E. WERE YOU INVOLUNTARILY CALLED TO ACTIVE DUTY FOR THIS PERIOD? (If "Yes," send copies of your orders)		F. IF THIS ACTIVE DUTY IS NATIONAL GUARD DUTY, INDICATE IF AUTHORITY IS TITLE 10 (Federal) OR TITLE 32 (State). (Send copies of any orders)
				☐ YES	☐ NO	
				☐ YES	☐ NO	
				☐ YES	☐ NO	
				☐ YES	☐ NO	
				☐ YES	☐ NO	

You should specify in Item 22, Remarks, any periods of active duty which reflect:
- Full time assignment by a service department to a civilian school for a course of education substantially the same as established courses for civilians;
- Attendance at a service academy; or
- Non-creditable time - (Time lost because of industrial or agricultural furlough, arrest without acquittal, being AWOL, desertion, sentence of court-martial, etc.)

15. DO YOU ALSO HAVE ANY PERIODS OF RESERVE OR NATIONAL GUARD SERVICE THAT ARE NOT ACTIVE DUTY?

☐ YES ☐ NO   (If "Yes," complete information about this service in Item 16. If "No," skip to Item 17)

16. PERIODS OF RESERVE OR NATIONAL GUARD SERVICE (NOT ACTIVE DUTY)

A. ARE YOU NOW IN THE RESERVE OR NATIONAL GUARD?

☐ YES ☐ NO

INFORMATION TO COMPLETE ITEM 16E:
- Place "SR" in Item 16E for each period of reserve service if you were in the Selected Reserve (drilling status).
- Place "IRR" in Item 16E for each period of reserve service if you were in the Individual Ready Reserve.
- Place "IMA" in Item 16E for each period of reserve service if your were in the Individual Mobilization Augmentation.

B. DATE ENTERED RESERVE OR GUARD	C. DATE SEPARATED FROM RESERVE OR GUARD (If applicable)	D. RESERVE OR GUARD COMPONENT	E. RESERVE STATUS (See abbreviations above)

F. DO YOU QUALIFY FOR A "KICKER" BASED ON YOUR RESERVE ENLISTMENT? ("Kickers" are amounts contributed by DoD to an education fund on behalf of individuals to encourage enlistment or retention in the Reserve or National Guard forces, usually in specialized areas.) (**IF YOU QUALIFY FOR A RESERVE "KICKER," CHECK "YES," IT MAY HELP IF YOU SEND VA A COPY OF THE "KICKER" CONTRACT)**

☐ YES ☐ NO

G. COMPLETE ONLY IF YOU ARE APPLYING FOR CHAPTER 1606 (you checked Item 4B). IF YOU ARE PARTICIPATING IN A SENIOR ROTC SCHOLARSHIP PROGRAM, DOES THAT PROGRAM PAY FOR YOUR TUITION, FEES, BOOKS AND SUPPLIES UNDER TITLE 10, U.S.C., SECTION 2107? (Do not include monthly subsistence allowance)

☐ YES ☐ NO

PAGE 4 OF 6

PART III - MONTGOMERY GI BILL QUESTIONS
(Complete this part only if you are applying for chapter 30 benefits)

QUESTIONS	YES (✓)	NO (✓)
17A. DID YOU MAKE ADDITIONAL CONTRIBUTIONS WHILE ON ACTIVE DUTY (Sometimes referred to as "Buy-up") TO INCREASE THE AMOUNT OF MONTHLY MGIB BENEFITS PAYABLE? (If you made any additional contributions, check "Yes."	☐	☐
17B. IF YOU SERVED A PERIOD OF ACTIVE DUTY THAT THE DEPARTMENT OF DEFENSE COUNTS FOR PURPOSES OF REPAYING AN EDUCATION LOAN, PLEASE SHOW THE DATES OF THAT PERIOD OF ACTIVE DUTY: From _____ To _____	☐	☐
17C. DO YOU HAVE A DoD CONTRACT TO RECEIVE A "KICKER"? (Some military services call this the "college fund." "Kickers" are amounts contributed by DoD to an education fund on behalf of individuals to encourage enlistment or retention in the Armed forces, usually in specialized areas. If you qualify for a "kicker", check "Yes." It may help to send us a copy of your kicker contract.	☐	☐

COMMISSIONED OFFICER QUESTIONS

	YES	NO
18A. DID YOU GRADUATE FROM A MILITARY SERVICE ACADEMY (e.g., West Point, Naval Academy, etc.)? (If "Yes," specify the month and year you graduated and received your commission) Graduation month and year: _____	☐	☐
18B. WERE YOU COMMISSIONED AS THE RESULT OF PARTICIPATING IN A SENIOR ROTC (Reserve Officers Training Corps) SCHOLARSHIP PROGRAM? (If "Yes," show the date of your commission and the amount of your scholarship for each school year you were in the Senior ROTC program. Don't report your monthly subsistence allowance. If you received your commission through a Senior ROTC (non-scholarship) program, check "No.") Scholarship Amounts: Commission date: _____ Year:_____ Amount:_____ Year:_____ Amount:_____ Year:_____ Amount:_____ Year:_____ Amount:_____ Year:_____ Amount:_____	☐	☐

MARITAL AND DEPENDENCY STATUS

NOTE: COMPLETE THIS ITEM ONLY IF YOU CHECKED ITEM 4A AND HAVE MILITARY SERVICE **BEFORE** JANUARY 1, 1977 (or delayed entry **before** January 2, 1978). See Instructions.

QUESTIONS	YES	NO
19A. ARE YOU CURRENTLY MARRIED?	☐	☐
19B. DO YOU HAVE ANY CHILDREN WHO ARE:		
(1) UNDER AGE 18? **OR**	☐	☐
(2) OVER 18 BUT UNDER AGE 23, NOT MARRIED AND ATTENDING SCHOOL? **OR**	☐	☐
(3) OF ANY AGE AND PERMANENTLY INCAPABLE OF SELF-SUPPORT DUE TO MENTAL OR PHYSICAL DISABILITY?	☐	☐
19C. IS EITHER YOUR FATHER OR MOTHER DEPENDENT UPON YOU FOR FINANCIAL SUPPORT?	☐	☐

PART IV - NATIONAL CALL TO SERVICE QUESTIONS
(Complete this part only if you are applying for this benefit)

20A. DID YOU SIGN AN ENLISTMENT CONTRACT WITH THE DEPARTMENT OF DEFENSE FOR THE NATIONAL CALL TO SERVICE PROGRAM?
☐ YES ☐ NO

20B. DID YOU RECEIVE AN EDUCATION ASSISTANCE INCENTIVE OPTION? (If "Yes," check the block in Item 20C that identifies the option you received)
☐ YES ☐ NO

20C. WHICH VA EDUCATIONAL ALLOWANCE INCENTIVE OPTION DID YOU ELECT? (Check only one block below)

☐ EDUCATIONAL ALLOWANCE OF UP TO 12 MONTHS OF MONTGOMERY GI BILL BENEFITS (3-year rate)   ☐ EDUCATIONAL ALLOWANCE OF UP TO 36 MONTHS OF MONTGOMERY GI BILL BENEFITS (1/2 the 2-year rate)

NOTE: National Call to Service applicants must furnish VA a copy of DD Form 2863 (National Call to Service Election of Options). This form is needed to document your eligibility and to confirm your incentive option.

PART V - TRANSFER OF ENTITLEMENT QUESTIONS
(Complete this part only if you are applying for this benefit)

NOTE: This benefit requires (1) that the veteran's branch of military service authorized the veteran to transfer MGIB entitlement to his or her dependents, and (2) the veteran, in writing, transferred his or her current education benefits to you (specifying you by name).

IMPORTANT: Only a spouse, surviving spouse, or child of a veteran who has transferred entitlement should complete this information.

21A. WHAT IS YOUR RELATIONSHIP TO THE VETERAN OR SERVICE MEMBER WHO TRANSFERRED ENTITLEMENT TO YOU?
☐ SPOUSE ☐ SURVIVING SPOUSE ☐ CHILD

IMPORTANT: If you checked your relationship as a spouse or child, have the veteran complete and send us VA Form 21-686c. See Instructions.

21B. VETERAN OR SERVICE MEMBER'S NAME (First, Middle, Last)	21C. VETERAN OR SERVICE MEMBER'S SEX ☐ MALE ☐ FEMALE

21D. ADDRESS OF VETERAN OR SERVICE MEMBER WHO TRANSFERRED ENTITLEMENT TO YOU

21E. VETERAN OR SERVICE MEMBER'S DATE OF BIRTH	21F. VETERAN OR SERVICE MEMBER'S SOCIAL SECURITY NUMBER

EMPLOYMENT (IF NO MILITARY SERVICE)

EMPLOYMENT	PRINCIPAL OCCUPATION	NUMBER OF MONTHS IN THAT OCCUPATION	LICENSE OR RATING
21G. JOB 1 (Since leaving high school)			
21H. JOB 2 (Since leaving high school)			

22. REMARKS (Use this space to provide information that does not fit elsewhere on this form or that will help VA process your claim. Refer to other item numbers on this form to help us match your answers to the correct questions. If more space is needed, please attach separate sheets of paper. Be sure to place your name and social security number on each additional page.)

PART VI - CERTIFICATION AND SIGNATURE OF APPLICANT
(All applicants must complete this part)

I CERTIFY THAT all statements in my application are true and correct to the best of my knowledge and belief.

PENALTY - Willful false statements as to a material fact in a claim for education benefits is a punishable offense and may result in the forfeiture of these or other benefits and in criminal penalties.

23A. FULL NAME OF APPLICANT (PRINTED)

23B. SIGNATURE OF APPLICANT (Do NOT Print)) (Minor children must also have their parent or guardian sign in this item)	23C. DATE SIGNED
SIGN HERE IN INK ▶	

PART VII - CERTIFICATION FOR APPLICANTS ON ACTIVE DUTY
(Have your Education Officer complete this part only if you are currently on active duty. This signature is not needed if you are on terminal leave)

I CERTIFY THAT this individual is a member of the branch of the Armed Forces shown below and has consulted with me regarding his/her education program.

24A. SIGNATURE, TITLE AND BRANCH OF SERVICE OF ARMED FORCES EDUCATION OFFICER	24B. DATE SIGNED

PAGE 6 OF 6

APPENDIX 15:
APPLICATION FOR WORK-STUDY ALLOWANCE (FORM 22-8691)

OMB Approved No. 2900-0209
Respondent Burden: 15 minutes

Department of Veterans Affairs

APPLICATION FOR WORK-STUDY ALLOWANCE

(Under Chapters 30,31,32, or 35, Title 38, U.S.C.; Chapters 1606 and 1607, Title 10,; and section 903 of Public Law 96-342)

PART I - IDENTIFICATION INFORMATION

1. NAME OF APPLICANT (First, Middle, Last)

2. MAILING ADDRESS OF APPLICANT (Number, and street or rural route, city or P.O., State and 9 digit ZIP Code)

3A. VA FILE NUMBER (For chapter 35, enter the veteran's file number. Be sure to include the suffix indicator. For chapter 30 dependent's transfer cases, enter the file number of the person who transferred entitlement to you)

3B. SOCIAL SECURITY NUMBER (If not shown in Item 3A)

3C. DATE OF BIRTH OF APPLICANT (Month, Day, Year)

3D. SEX OF APPLICANT
☐ MALE   ☐ FEMALE

4A. TELEPHONE NUMBER (Include Area Code)

4B. PLEASE PROVIDE THE HOURS THAT VA CAN REACH YOU

DAYTIME

EVENING

5. EDUCATION BENEFIT RECEIVING

☐ CHAPTER 30 (Montgomery GI Bill - Active Duty)

☐ CHAPTER 31 (Vocational Rehabilitation)

☐ CHAPTER 32 (Veterans Educational Assistance Program)

☐ CHAPTER 35 (Dependents Educational Assistance)

☐ CHAPTER 1606 (Montgomery GI Bill - Selected Reserve)

☐ CHAPTER 1607 (Reserve Educational Assistance Program)

☐ TRANSFER OF ENTITLEMENT PROGRAM (Parent or Spouse Entitled to Chapter 30 Benefits)

PART II - SCHOOL INFORMATION

6A. NAME AND COMPLETE ADDRESS OF SCHOOL

6B. CURRENT ACADEMIC OR TRAINING PROGRAM

7. CURRENT ENROLLMENT INFORMATION

A. BEGINNING DATE (Month, Day, Year)

B. ENDING DATE (Month, Day, Year)

8. NEXT ENROLLMENT PERIOD YOU PLAN TO ATTEND

A. BEGINNING DATE (Month, Day, Year)

B. ENDING DATE (Month, Day, Year)

PART III - WORK STUDY INFORMATION

9. ADVANCE PAYMENT - DO YOU WANT AN ADVANCE PAYMENT? (See instructions for information on advance payment on reverse under "How Much Can I Earn?")

☐ YES   ☐ NO

10. HAVE YOU EVER PARTICIPATED IN THE VA WORK-STUDY PROGRAM BEFORE? (If "YES," please state where you worked)

☐ YES   ☐ NO

11. WORK SITE PREFERENCE (Tell us the school, VA facility or other government facility where you would prefer to do VA related work. Be specific as many facilities have the same name or perform the same services in different locations or cities.)

12. WORK EXPERIENCE (Tell us about the jobs you had before, other than VA work-study jobs. Please be as specific as possible. If you have no work experience, place "NONE" in this space. If needed, attach a separate sheet with your work-history)	13. SPECIFY THE DAYS AND HOURS DURING THE WEEK YOU ARE AVAILABLE TO WORK		
	(X)	DAYS	WHEN AVAILABLE (From & To)
		MONDAY	
		TUESDAY	
		WEDNESDAY	
		THURSDAY	
		FRIDAY	

14. QUALIFICATIONS (Tell us about any special qualifications you have based on your education or work experience. Include any experience in information technology. Also, tell us what kinds of jobs interest you. If needed, attach a separate sheet with this information)

15. SIGNATURE OF APPLICANT (Do not print)	16. DATE SIGNED

PRIVACY ACT INFORMATION: VA will not disclose information collected by this information collection to any source other than what has been authorized by the Privacy Act of 1974 or Title 38 Code of Federal Regulations 1.526 for routine uses as identified in VA's system of records, 58 VA 21/22, Compensation, Pension, Education and Rehabilitation Records - VA as published in the Federal Register at http://www.va.gov/privacy/system of records/58va21.asp. An example of a routine use allows VA to send educational forms or letters with a veteran's identifying information to the veteran's school or training establishment to (1) assist the veteran in the completion of claims forms or (2) for VA to obtain further information as may be necessary from the school for VA to properly process the veteran's education claim or to monitor his or her progress during training. Your obligation to respond is "required to obtain or retain benefits". We cannot pay you any work-study benefits until we receive this information (38 U.S.C. 3485). Your responses are confidential (38 U.S.C. 5701). Any information provided by applicants may be subject to verification through computer matching programs with other agencies.
Respondent Burden: We need this information to determine your eligibility for VA work-study benefits. Title 38 United States Code allows us to ask for this information. We estimate that you will need an average of 15 minutes to review the instructions, find the information, and complete the form. VA cannot conduct or sponsor a collection of information unless a valid OMB control number is displayed. You are not required to respond to a collection of information if this number is not displayed. Valid OMB control numbers can be located on the OMB Internet page at www.whitehouse.gov/omb/library/OMBINV.VA.EPA.htm#VA. If desired, you can call 1-888-GI-BILL-1 (1-888-442-4551) to get information on where to send comments or suggestions about this information collection.

VA FORM
NOV 2005   **22-8691**   EXISTING STOCKS OF VA FORM 22-8691, NOV 2002. WILL BE USED.

APPENDIX 16:
APPLICATION FOR SURVIVORS' AND DEPENDENTS' EDUCATIONAL ASSISTANCE (FORM 22-5490)

OMB Approved No. 2900-0098
Respondent Burden: 45 minutes

VA Department of Veterans Affairs

APPLICATION FOR SURVIVORS' AND DEPENDENTS' EDUCATIONAL ASSISTANCE
(Under Provisions of Chapter 35, Title 38,U.S.C.)
See attached Information and Instructions

INTERNET VERSION AVAILABLE - You may complete and send your application over the Internet at: www.gibill.va.gov

PART I - APPLICANT INFORMATION

1A. NAME OF APPLICANT (FIRST-MIDDLE-LAST)	1B. SOCIAL SECURITY NUMBER OF APPLICANT	1C. DATE OF BIRTH OF APPLICANT

2A. SEX OF APPLICANT	2B. APPLICANT'S E-MAIL ADDRESS	
☐ MALE ☐ FEMALE		

3A. RELATIONSHIP OF APPLICANT TO VETERAN	3B. APPLICANT'S TELEPHONE NUMBER *(Including Area Code)*	
☐ SPOUSE ☐ SURVIVING SPOUSE ☐ CHILD	DAY	EVENING
☐ STEPCHILD ☐ ADOPTED CHILD	( )	( )

3C. MAILING ADDRESS OF APPLICANT (Number and street or rural route, city or P.O., State and ZIP Code)	**VA DATE STAMP** (For VA Use Only)

4. HAVE YOU RECEIVED AN INFORMATION PAMPHLET EXPLAINING SURVIVORS' AND DEPENDENTS EDUCATIONAL ASSISTANCE BENEFITS?

☐ YES ☐ NO

PART II - INFORMATION CONCERNING DISABLED OR DECEASED VETERAN OR INDIVIDUAL ON ACTIVE DUTY

5A. NAME OF VETERAN OR INDIVIDUAL ON ACTIVE DUTY ON WHOSE ACCOUNT BENEFITS ARE CLAIMED (FIRST- MIDDLE -LAST)

5B. SOCIAL SECURITY NUMBER	5C. VA FILE NUMBER *(If known)*	

6. DATE OF BIRTH	7. BRANCH OF SERVICE	8. SERVICE NUMBER	9. DATE OF DEATH OR DATE LISTED AS MISSING IN ACTION OR P.O.W.

PART III - SPECIAL INFORMATION CONCERNING APPLICANT

10. IF YOU ARE THE SPOUSE OF A DISABLED VETERAN, IS A DIVORCE OR ANNULMENT PENDING?

☐ YES ☐ NO

11A. IF YOU ARE THE SURVIVING SPOUSE OF A DECEASED VETERAN, HAVE YOU REMARRIED SINCE HIS OR HER DEATH ? ☐ YES ☐ NO	11B. SURVIVING SPOUSE'S AGE AT TIME OF REMARRIAGE

NOTE - COMPLETE ITEM 12 ONLY IF YOU ARE A CIVILIAN EMPLOYEE OF THE U.S. GOVERNMENT

12A. DO YOU EXPECT TO RECEIVE FUNDS FROM YOUR AGENCY OR DEPARTMENT FOR THE SAME COURSE FOR WHICH YOU EXPECT TO RECEIVE VA EDUCATIONAL ASSISTANCE? (If you check "Yes," show the source of these funds in Item 12B) ☐ YES ☐ NO	12B. SOURCE OF EDUCATIONAL ASSISTANCE FROM GOVERNMENT EMPLOYMENT

13. HAVE YOU EVER APPLIED FOR ANY OF THE FOLLOWING VA BENEFITS? *(Check applicable box(es)*

A. ☐ DISABILITY COMPENSATION OR PENSION

B. ☐ DEPENDENTS' INDEMNITY COMPENSATION (DIC)

C. ☐ VETERANS' EDUCATION ASSISTANCE BASED ON YOUR OWN SERVICE *(Specify benefit)* _____

D. ☐ VOCATIONAL REHABILITATION BENEFITS

E. ☐ SURVIVORS' AND DEPENDENTS EDUCATIONAL ASSISTANCE *(Complete Items 14A and 14B)*

F. ☐ OTHER *(Specify)* _____

G. ☐ NONE

Complete Item 14 only if you check Item 13E

14A. NAME OF VETERAN ON WHOSE ACCOUNT YOU PREVIOUSLY CLAIMED BENEFITS	14B. VETERAN'S FILE NUMBER

VA FORM
NOV 2005 **22-5490**

SUPERSEDES VA FORM 22-5490, JUN 2003,
WHICH WILL NOT BE USED.

PART IV - APPLICANT'S MILITARY SERVICE

15. HAVE YOU EVER SERVED ON ACTIVE DUTY IN THE ARMED FORCES? (Including an initial period of active duty for training for a period of 3 months or more OR subsequent periods of active duty for training of 6 months or more) (If "NO," skip this part and continue to Part V)

☐ YES ☐ NO

16. INFORMATION ABOUT YOUR PERIODS OF ACTIVE DUTY
(Please complete Items 16A through 16D for each period of your active duty)

A. DATE ENTERED ACTIVE DUTY	B. DATE SEPARATED FROM ACTIVE DUTY	C. BRANCH OF SERVICE OR RESERVE OR GUARD COMPONENT	D. CHARACTER OF DISCHARGE

PART V - PREVIOUS EDUCATION, TRAINING, AND EMPLOYMENT

17A. CHECK THE APPROPRIATE BOX AND ENTER THE DATE IN ITEM 17B

☐ GRADUATED FROM HIGH SCHOOL   ☐ DISCONTINUED HIGH SCHOOL

☐ EXPECT TO GRADUATE   ☐ GED

☐ NEVER ATTENDED HIGH SCHOOL

17B. DATE

18. EDUCATION (Include all apprenticeships and on-the-job training)

TYPE OF SCHOOL	NAME AND LOCATION OF SCHOOL (City and State)	DATES OF TRAINING FROM	DATES OF TRAINING TO	NUMBER OF SEMESTER, QUARTER, OR CLOCK HOURS COMPLETED	DEGREE, DIPLOMA, OR CERTIFICATE RECEIVED	MAJOR FIELD OR COURSE OF STUDY
ELEMENTARY SCHOOL						
HIGH SCHOOL						
COLLEGE						
VOCATIONAL OR TRADE						
OTHER						

19. EMPLOYMENT

EMPLOYMENT	PRINCIPAL OCCUPATION	NUMBER OF MONTHS EMPLOYED IN THAT OCCUPATION	LICENSE OR RATING

PART VI - PROGRAM OF EDUCATION OR TRAINING

20A. DO YOU KNOW YOUR EDUCATIONAL OR CAREER GOAL? (If "YES," please specify)

☐ YES ☐ NO

20B. HAVE YOU SELECTED A SPECIFIC PROGRAM OF EDUCATION? (If "YES," list below each diploma, vocational course, job training program, or test you need to reach the goal specified in Item 20A. If "NO," leave blank) ▶   ☐ YES ☐ NO

20C. EDUCATION OR TRAINING WILL BE BY: (Check more than one if necessary)

☐ COLLEGE OR OTHER SCHOOL
☐ APPRENTICESHIP OR OTHER ON-THE-JOB TRAINING
☐ LICENSING OR CERTIFICATION TEST
☐ NATIONAL ADMISSION EXAMS OR NATIONAL EXAMS FOR CREDIT
☐ CORRESPONDENCE COURSE (Spouse or surviving spouse only)
☐ FARM COOPERATIVE

20D. HAVE YOU SELECTED YOUR SCHOOL OR TRAINING ESTABLISHMENT? (If you have selected a school, check "YES," and specify its complete name and mailing address. If you have not selected a school, check "NO." If you are only applying for reimbursement of test fees, skip to Item 21. ☐ YES ☐ NO ►	NAME AND ADDRESS OF SCHOOL OR TRAINING ESTABLISHMENT *(Number and street or rural route, city or P.O., State and ZIP Code)*
20E. DO YOU KNOW THE DATE YOU WILL BEGIN YOUR SCHOOLING OR TRAINING? *(If, "YES," specify the date)* ►	ANTICIPATED BEGINNING DATE (MONTH/YEAR) OF TRAINING
20F. ARE YOU A HANDICAPPED CHILD, 14 YEARS OR OLDER, SPOUSE, OR SURVIVING SPOUSE SEEKING SPECIAL RESTORATIVE TRAINING? *(See Instructions)* ☐ YES ☐ NO	20G. ARE YOU A HANDICAPPED CHILD, SPOUSE, OR SURVIVING SPOUSE SEEKING SPECIALIZED VOCATIONAL TRAINING? *(See Instructions)* ☐ YES ☐ NO

PART VII - ELECTION (CHILD ONLY)

IMPORTANT: You may not receive payments of Dependency and Indemnity Compensation (DIC) or Pension and you may not be claimed as a dependent in a compensation claim while receiving Survivors' and Dependents' educational assistance (DEA). CAREFULLY READ THE INSTRUCTIONS BEFORE COMPLETING THIS ELECTION BLOCK. YOU ARE STRONGLY ENCOURAGED TO DISCUSS YOUR ELECTION WITH A VA COUNSELOR.

21A. I CERTIFY THAT I understand the effects of an election to receive DEA benefits and that I elect to receive such benefits from the following date: ►	21B. DATE OF ELECTION

22. REMARKS *(Use this space to provide information that does not fit elsewhere on this form or that will help VA process your claim. Refer to the item numbers on this form to help us match your answers to the correct questions. If more space is needed, please attach separate sheets of paper. Be sure to place your name and Social Security Number on each additional page)*

PART VIII - CERTIFICATION AND SIGNATURE OF APPLICANT
(All Applicants Must Complete This Part)

I CERTIFY THAT all statements in my application are true and correct to the best of my knowledge and belief.

PENALTY: Willfully false statements as to a material fact in a claim for education benefits is a punishable offense and may result in the forfeiture of these or other benefits and in criminal penalties.

23A. SIGNATURE OF APPLICANT *(Do NOT Print)* SIGN HERE IN INK ►	23B. DATE SIGNED

PART IX - SIGNATURE OF PARENT, GUARDIAN, OR CUSTODIAN
(This section must be completed if you are a minor child)

24A. NAME OF PARENT, GUARDIAN, OR CUSTODIAN *(Type or print)*	24B. TELEPHONE NUMBER AND MAIL ADDRESS OF PARENT, GUARDIAN, OR CUSTODIAN (Include Area Code),
25A. SIGNATURE OF *(Check one)* *(DO NOT PRINT)* ☐ PARENT ☐ GUARDIAN ☐ CUSTODIAN SIGN HERE IN INK ►	25B. DATE SIGNED

APPENDIX 17:
APPLICATION FOR
VOCATIONAL-EDUCATIONAL
COUNSELING (FORM 28-8832)

OMB Approved No. 2900-0265
Respondent Burden: 30 minutes

VA Department of Veterans Affairs	**APPLICATION FOR COUNSELING**

PRIVACY ACT INFORMATION: The VA will not disclose information collected on this form to any source other than what has been authorized under the Privacy Act of 1974 or Title 38, Code of Federal Regulations 1.576 for routine uses identified in the VA system of records, 58VA21/22, Compensation, Pension, Education and Rehabilitation Records - VA, published in the Federal Register. Your obligation to respond is required to obtain or retain benefits. Giving us your SSN account information is mandatory. Applicants are required to provide their SSN under Title 38 USC 5101 (c) (1). The VA will not deny an individual benefits for refusing to provide his or her SSN unless the disclosure of the SSN is required by a Federal Statute of law in effect prior to January 1, 1975, and still in effect. The requested information is considered relevant and necessary to determine maximum benefits under the law. The responses you submit are considered confidential (38 U.S.C. 5701). Any information provided by applicants, recipients, and others may be subject to verification through computer matching programs with other agencies.
RESPONDENT BURDEN: We need this information to determine if the veteran and other beneficiaries are eligible for counseling services that VR&E. services provide. Title 38, United States Code, allows us to ask for this information. We estimate that you will need an average of 30 minutes to review the instructions, find the information, and complete this form. VA cannot conduct or sponsor a collection of information unless a valid OMB control number is displayed. You are not required to respond to a collection of information if this number is not displayed. Valid OMB control numbers can be located on the OMB Internet Page at www.whitehouse.gov./omb/library/OMBINV.VA.EPA.html#VA. If desired, you can call 1-800-827-1000 to get information on where to send comments or suggestions about this form.

INTERNET VERSION AVAILABLE -You may download this application form at www.va.gov/vaforms

PART I - APPLICANT INFORMATION

1A. NAME OF APPLICANT (FIRST-MIDDLE-LAST)	1B. SOCIAL SECURITY NUMBER OF APPLICANT	AC. VA FILE NUMBER *(If known)*

2A. SEX OF APPLICANT ☐ MALE ☐ FEMALE	B. APPLICANT'S E-MAIL ADDRESS	2C. DATE OF BIRTH

3A. RELATIONSHIP OF APPLICANT TO VETERAN ☐ SELF ☐ SURVIVING SPOUSE ☐ CHILD ☐ SPOUSE ☐ STEPCHILD ☐ ADOPTED CHILD	3B. APPLICANT'S TELEPHONE NUMBER *(Including Area Code)*		
	PRIMARY PHONE NUMBER (Where a message can be left) ( )	OTHER PHONE NUMBER ( )

3C. MAILING ADDRESS OF APPLICANT (Number and street or rural route, city or P.O., State and ZIP Code)	**VA DATE STAMP** (For VA Use Only)

a. ARE YOU A HANDICAPPED CHILD, 14 YEARS OR OLDER, SPOUSE, OR SURVIVING SPOUSE SEEKING SPECIAL RESTORATIVE TRAINING? *(See Instructions)* ☐ YES ☐ NO	B. ARE YOU A HANDICAPPED CHILD,SPOUSE, OR SURVIVING SPOUSE SEEKING SPECIAL VOCATIONAL TRAINING? *(See Instructions)* ☐ YES ☐ NO	5. HAVE YOU RECEIVED AN INFORMATION PAMPHLET EXPLAINING SURVIVORS' AND DEPENDENTS' EDUCATIONAL ASSISTANCE BENEFITS? ☐ YES ☐ NO

PART II - INFORMATION CONCERNING DISABLED OR DECEASED VETERAN OR INDIVIDUAL ON ACTIVE DUTY

a. NAME OF VETERAN OR INDIVIDUAL ON ACTIVE DUTY ON WHOSE ACCOUNT BENEFITS ARE CLAIMED (FIRST- MIDDLE -LAST)

B. SOCIAL SECURITY NUMBER		AC. VA FILE NUMBER *(If known)*	
7. DATE OF BIRTH	8. BRANCH OF SERVICE	9. SERVICE NUMBER	10. DATE OF DEATH OR DATE LISTED AS MISSING IN ACTION OR P.O.W.

PART III - SPECIAL INFORMATION CONCERNING APPLICANT

11. IF YOU ARE THE SPOUSE OF A DISABLED VETERAN, IS A DIVORCE OR ANNULMENT PENDING?

☐ YES ☐ NO

12A. IF YOU ARE THE SURVIVING SPOUSE OF A DECEASED VETERAN, HAVE YOU REMARRIED SINCE HIS OR HER DEATH ?   AB. SURVIVING SPOUSE'S AGE AT TIME OF REMARRIAGE

☐ YES ☐ NO

13. HAVE YOU EVER APPLIED FOR ANY OF THE FOLLOWING VA BENEFITS? *(Check applicable box(yes)*

A. ☐ VOCATIONAL REHABILITATION BENEFITS (Chapter 31)

B. ☐ VETERANS' EDUCATION ASSISTANCE BASED ON YOUR OWN SERVICE *(Specify benefit)* _____

C. ☐ DEPENDENTS' EDUCATIONAL ASSISTANCE (Chapter 35)

D. ☐ SURVIVORS' AND DEPENDENTS EDUCATIONAL ASSISTANCE *(Complete Items a and AB) on reverse)*

E. ☐ OTHER *(Specify)* _____

F. ☐ NONE

VA FORM
JAN 2007 **28-8832**   SUPERSEDES VA FORM 28-8832, FEB 2006,
WHICH WILL NOT BE USED.

NOTE: COMPLETE ITEMS 14A AND 14B ONLY IF YOU CHECKED ITEM 13D

14A. NAME OF VETERAN ON WHOSE ACCOUNT YOU PREVIOUSLY CLAIMED BENEFITS	14B. VETERANS FILE NUMBER OR SOCIAL SECURITY NUMBER

PART IV - APPLICANT'S MILITARY SERVICE

15. HAVE YOU EVER SERVED ON ACTIVE DUTY IN THE ARMED FORCES? (Including an initial period of active duty for training for a period of 3 months or more OR subsequent periods of active duty for training of 6 months or more) (If "NO," skip this part and continue to Part V)

☐ YES ☐ NO

16. SERVICE INFORMATION
(Enter the following information for each period of active duty. Attach a copy of your DD214.
If you have already sent VA a DD214, do not send one with this application)

A. DATE ENTERED ACTIVE DUTY	B. DATE SEPARATED FROM ACTIVE DUTY	C. BRANCH OF SERVICE OR RESERVE OR GUARD COMPONENT	D. CHARACTER OF DISCHARGE

17. REMARKS (Use this space to provide information that does not fit elsewhere on this form or that will help VA process your claim. Refer to the item numbers on this form to help us match your answers to the correct questions. If more space is needed, please attach separate sheets of paper. Be sure to place your name and Social Security Number on each additional page)

PART V - CERTIFICATION AND SIGNATURE OF APPLICANT
(All Applicants Must Complete This Part)

I CERTIFY THAT all statements in my application are true and correct to the best of my knowledge and belief.

PENALTY: Willfully false statements as to a material fact in a claim for counseling benefits is a punishable offense and may result in the forfeiture of these or other benefits and in criminal penalties.

18A. SIGNATURE OF APPLICANT (Do NOT Print)	18B. DATE SIGNED
SIGN HERE IN INK ▶	

PART VI - SIGNATURE OF PARENT, GUARDIAN, OR CUSTODIAN
(This section must be completed if you are a minor child)

19A. NAME OF PARENT, GUARDIAN, OR CUSTODIAN (Type or print)	19B. TELEPHONE NUMBER AND MAIL ADDRESS OF PARENT, GUARDIAN, OR CUSTODIAN (Include Area Code),	
	( )	
20A. SIGNATURE OF (Check one) (DO NOT PRINT) ☐ PARENT ☐ GUARDIAN ☐ CUSTODIAN SIGN HERE IN INK ▶	20B. DATE SIGNED	20C. DATE REFERRED TO VR & E

APPENDIX 18:
REQUEST FOR A CERTIFICATE OF
ELIGIBILITY (FORM 26-1880)

OMB Control No. 2900-0086
Respondent Burden: 15 minutes

VA Department of Veterans Affairs **REQUEST FOR A CERTIFICATE OF ELIGIBILITY**	TO	Department of Veterans Affairs Eligibility Center P.O. Box 20729 Winston-Salem, NC 27120

NOTE: Please read information on reverse before completing this form. If additional space is required, attach a separate sheet.

1. FIRST-MIDDLE-LAST NAME OF VETERAN	2. DATE OF BIRTH	3. VETERAN'S DAYTIME TELEPHONE NO.

4. ADDRESS OF VETERAN (No., street or rural route, city or P.O., State and ZIP Code)	5. MAIL CERTIFICATE OF ELIGIBILITY TO: (Complete ONLY if the Certificate is to be mailed to an address different from the one listed in Item 4)

6. MILITARY SERVICE DATA (ATTACH PROOF OF SERVICE - SEE PARAGRAPH "D" ON REVERSE)

A. ITEM	B. PERIODS OF ACTIVE SERVICE		C. NAME (Show your name exactly as it appears on your separation papers or Statement of Service)	D. SOCIAL SECURITY NUMBER	E. SERVICE NUMBER (If different from Social Security No.)	F. BRANCH OF SERVICE
	DATE FROM	DATE TO				
1.						
2.						
3.						
4.						

7A. WERE YOU DISCHARGED, RETIRED OR SEPARATED FROM SERVICE BECAUSE OF DISABILITY OR DO YOU NOW HAVE ANY SERVICE-CONNECTED DISABILITIES? ☐ YES ☐ NO (If "Yes," complete Item 7B)	7B. VA CLAIM FILE NUMBER C-

8. PREVIOUS VA LOANS (Must answer N/A if no previous VA home loan. DO NOT LEAVE BLANK)

A. ITEM	B. TYPE (Home, Refinance, Manufactured Home, or Direct)	C. ADDRESS OF PROPERTY	D. DATE OF LOAN	E. DO YOU STILL OWN THE PROPERTY? (YES/NO)	F. DATE PROPERTY WAS SOLD (Submit a copy of HUD-1, Settlement Statement, if available)	G. VA LOAN NUMBER (If known)
1.						
2.						
3.						
4.						
5.						
6.						

I CERTIFY THAT the statements herein are true to the best of my knowledge and belief.

9. SIGNATURE OF VETERAN (Do NOT print)	10. DATE SIGNED

FEDERAL STATUTES PROVIDE SEVERE PENALTIES FOR FRAUD, INTENTIONAL MISREPRESENTATION, CRIMINAL CONNIVANCE OR CONSPIRACY PURPOSED TO INFLUENCE THE ISSUANCE OF ANY GUARANTY OR INSURANCE BY THE SECRETARY OF VETERANS AFFAIRS.

REQUEST FOR A CERTIFICATE OF ELIGIBILITY (FORM 26-1880)

FOR VA USE ONLY

11A. DATE CERTIFICATE ISSUED	11B. SIGNATURE OF VA AGENT

VA FORM
JAN 2006   **26-1880**

SUPERSEDES VA FORM 26-1880 JAN 2005,
WHICH WILL NOT BE USED.

APPENDIX 19:
APPLICATION FOR DEPENDENCY AND INDEMNITY COMPENSATION, DEATH PENSION AND ACCRUED BENEFITS BY SURVIVING SPOUSE OR CHILD (FORM 21-534)

OMB Approved No. 2900-0004
Respondent Burden: 1 hour 15 minutes

Department of Veterans Affairs

Application for Dependency and Indemnity Compensation, Death Pension and Accrued Benefits by a Surviving Spouse or Child (Including Death Compensation if Applicable)
VA Form 21-534

Please read the attached "General Instructions" before you fill out this form.

VA DATE STAMP
(DO NOT WRITE IN THIS SPACE)

SECTION I		
Tell us what you are applying for and what you and the deceased veteran have applied for	1. Did the veteran ever file a claim with VA? ☐ YES ☐ NO *(If "Yes," answer Item 2)*	2. What is the VA file number?
	3. Has the surviving spouse or child ever filed a claim with VA? ☐ YES ☐ NO *(If "Yes," answer Items 4 through 6)*	4. What is the VA file number?
	5. What is the name of the person on whose service the claim was filed? First　　　　　Middle　　　　　Last	
	6. What is your relationship to that person?	
	7. Are you claiming service connection for cause of death? ☐ YES ☐ NO	

SECTION II	8. What is the veteran's name?

Tell us about you and the deceased veteran

	First	Middle	Last	Suffix (If applicable)

9. What is the veteran's Social Security number?	10a. Did the veteran serve under another name? ☐ YES ☐ NO *(If "Yes," answer Items 10b)*

10b. Please list the other name(s) the veteran served under:	11. What is the veteran's date of birth? mo day yr

Attach a copy of the death certificate unless the veteran died in active service of the Army, Navy, Air Force, Marine Corps, or Coast Guard, or in a U.S. government institution.

12. What is the veteran's date of death? mo day yr	13. Was the veteran a former prisoner of war? ☐ YES ☐ NO

14. What is your name? (First, Middle, Last Name)	15. What is your relationship to the veteran? (check one) ☐ Surviving Spouse ☐ Child

16. What is your address?

Street address, Rural Route, or P.O. Box	Apt. number

City	State	ZIP Code	Country

17. What are your telephone numbers? (Include Area Code)	18. What is your e-mail address?

19. What is your Social Security number?	20. What is your date of birth? mo day yr

VA FORM
JUN 2005   **21-534**

SUPERSEDES VA FORM 21-534, JUN 1998, WHICH WILL NOT BE USED.

21-534   *PAGE 1*

242   **Veterans' Rights and Benefits**

SECTION III	Tell us about the veteran's active duty service	Note: Skip to Section IV if the veteran was receiving VA compensation or pension at the time of his/her death.			
		21a. Entered Active Service (first period) ___ mo ___ day ___ yr	21b. Place	21c. Service Number	
1. Enter complete information for all periods of service. If more space is needed use Item 48 "Remarks."		21d. Left This Active Service ___ mo ___ day ___ yr	21e. Place	21f. Branch of Service	21g. Grade, Rank, or Rating
2. If the veteran never filed a claim with VA, attach the original DD214 or a certified copy for each period of service listed. We will return original documents to you.		21h. Entered Active Service (second period) ___ mo ___ day ___ yr	21i. Place	21j. Service Number	
		21k. Left This Active Service ___ mo ___ day ___ yr	21l. Place	21m. Branch of Service	21n. Grade, Rank, or Rating

SECTION IV	Tell us about your and the veteran's marital history	Note: Skip to Section V if the veteran was receiving additional VA benefits for you as his/her spouse at the time of his/her death *unless* you remarried after the veteran's death.
	Attach a copy of your marriage certificate showing your marriage to the veteran.	You must furnish complete information about **all** marriages of the surviving spouse and the veteran. If you need additional space, please attach a separate sheet of paper providing the requested information about the marriages.

The veteran's marriages

22a. How many times was the veteran married? _____

22b. Date of Marriage	22c. Place (city/state or country)	22d. To whom married (first, middle initial, last name)	22e. Date marriage ended	22f. Place (city/state or country)	22g. How marriage ended (death, divorce)
mo day yr			mo day yr		
mo day yr			mo day yr		

The surviving spouse's marriages. Note: Items 23a through 27 should be completed by the veteran's surviving spouse. If the claimant is not the surviving spouse, skip to Section V.

23a. How many times were you married? _____   23b. Have you remarried since the death of the veteran? ☐ YES ☐ NO

23c. Date of Marriage	23d. Place (city/state or country)	23e. To whom married (first, middle initial, last name)	23f. Date marriage ended	23g. Place (city/state or country)	23h. How marriage ended (death, divorce)
mo day yr			mo day yr		
mo day yr			mo day yr		

SECTION IV Tell us about your and the veteran's marital history (continued)

Answer Item 24 only if you were married to the veteran for less than one year. ▶

24. Was a child born to you and the veteran during your marriage or prior to your marriage?

☐ YES ☐ NO

25. Are you expecting the birth of a child of the veteran?

☐ YES ☐ NO

26. Did you live continuously with the veteran from the date of marriage to the date of his/her death?

☐ YES ☐ NO

(If "No", answer Item 27)

27. What was the cause of the separation? Give the reason, date(s), and duration of the separation. If the separation was by court order, attach a copy of the order.

SECTION V Tell us about the unmarried children of the veteran

Note: You should provide a copy of the public record of birth or a copy of the court record of adoption for each child listed in Item 28a *unless* the veteran was receiving additional VA benefits for the child.

If you need additional space, please attach a separate sheet of paper providing the requested information about each child.

Note: Skip to Section VI if you are not claiming benefits for any children that meet the following criteria.

VA recognizes the veteran's biological children, adopted children, and stepchildren as dependents. These children must be unmarried and:

- under age 18, or
- between 18 and 23 and pursuing an approved course of education, or
- of any age if they became permanently unable to support themselves before reaching age 18.

"Seriously disabled" (Item 29e) means that the child became permanently unable to support himself/herself before reaching age 18. Furnish a statement from an attending physician or other medical evidence which shows the nature and extent of the physical or mental impairment.

Note to surviving spouse: If entitlement to DIC is established, a "seriously disabled" child over age 18 is entitled to receive DIC benefits in his or her own right. A veteran's child who is seriously disabled and over age 18 must submit a separate VA Form 21-534 to apply for benefits.

28a. Name of child (First, middle initial, Last)	28b. Date and place of birth (City/State or Country)	28c. Social Security Number	29a. Biological	29b. Adopted	29c. Stepchild	29d. 18 - 23 yrs old and in school	29e. Seriously disabled	29f. Child previously married
	mo day yr		☐	☐	☐	☐	☐	☐
	mo day yr		☐	☐	☐	☐	☐	☐
	mo day yr		☐	☐	☐	☐	☐	☐

21-534   PAGE 3

SECTION V Tell us about the unmarried children of the veteran (continued)

Tell us about the children listed above that don't live with you.

30a. Name of child (first, middle initial, last)	30b. Child's Complete Address	30c. Name of person the child lives with (if applicable)	30d. Monthly amount you contribute to child's support
			$
			$
			$
			$

SECTION VI Tell us if you are housebound, in a nursing home or require aid and attendance	31. Are you claiming aid and attendance allowance and/or housebound benefits because you need the regular assistance of another person, are having severe visual problems, or are housebound?	32a. Are you now in a nursing home?
If you answered "yes" to Item 31 and are not in a nursing home, submit a statement from your doctor showing the extent of your disabilities. If you are in a nursing home, attach a statement signed by an official of the nursing home showing the date you were admitted to the nursing home, the level of care you receive, the amount you pay out-of-pocket for your care, and whether Medicaid covers all or part of your nursing home costs.	☐ YES ☐ NO *(If "No," skip to section VII)*	☐ YES ☐ NO *(If "Yes," answer Items 32b and 32c also)*
	32b. What is the name and complete mailing address of the facility?	32c. Does Medicaid cover all or part of your nursing home costs? ☐ YES ☐ NO *(If "No," answer Item 32d also)*
	32d. Have you applied for Medicaid? ☐ YES ☐ NO	

21-534   PAGE 4

Veterans' Rights and Benefits

SECTION VII	Tell us the net worth of you and your dependents

Note: If you are filing this application on behalf of a minor or incompetent child of the veteran and you are the child's custodian, you must report your net worth as well as the net worth of the child for whom benefits are claimed.

VA cannot pay you pension if your net worth is sizeable. Net worth is the market value of all interest and rights you have in any kind of property less any mortgages or other claims against the property. However, net worth does not include the house you live in or a reasonable area of land it sits on. Net worth also does not include the value of personal things you use everyday like your vehicle, clothing, and furniture. You must report net worth for yourself and all persons for whom you are claiming benefits.

For Items 33a through 33f, provide the amounts. If none, write "0" or "None."

Source	Surviving spouse or Custodian of children	Child(ren)		
		Name: *(first, middle initial, last)*	Name: *(first, middle initial, last)*	Name: *(first, middle initial, last)*
33a. Cash, bank accounts, certificates of deposit (CDs)				
33b. IRAs, Keogh Plans, etc.				
33c. Stocks, bonds, mutual funds				
33d. Value of business assets				
33e. Real property (not your home)				
33f. All other property				

SECTION VIII	Tell us about the income of you and your dependents

Payments from any source will be counted, unless the law says that they don't need to be counted. Report **all** income, and VA will determine any amount that does not count.

Note: If you are filing this application on behalf of a minor of whom you are the custodian, you must report your income as well as the income of each child for whom benefits are claimed.

Report the total amounts before you take out deductions for taxes, insurance, etc. Do not report the same information in both tables.
If you expect to receive a payment, but you don't know how much it will be, write "Unknown" in the space.
If you do not receive any payments from one of the sources that we list, write "0" or "None" in the space.
If you are receiving monthly benefits, give us a copy of your most recent award letter. This will help us determine the amount of benefits you should be paid.

34a. Have you claimed or are you receiving benefits from the Social Security Administration on your own behalf or on behalf of child(ren) in your custody? ☐ YES ☐ NO *(If "Yes," answer item 34b)*	34b. Is Social Security based on your own employment? ☐ YES ☐ NO
35. Has a surviving spouse or child filed a claim for compensation from the Office of Worker's Compensation Programs based on the death of the veteran? ☐ YES ☐ NO	36. Has a court awarded damages based on the death of the veteran or is a claim or legal action for damages pending? ☐ YES ☐ NO

37. Have you claimed or are you receiving Survivor Benefit Plan (SBP) annuity from a service department based on the death of the veteran?

☐ YES ☐ NO

21-534   PAGE 5

SECTION VIII Tell us about the income of you and your dependents (continued)

Monthly Income - Tell us the income you and your dependents receive every month

Source	Surviving spouse or Custodian of children	Child(ren) Name: (first, middle initial, last)	Name: (first, middle initial, last)	Name: (first, middle initial, last)
38a. Social Security				
38b. U.S. Civil Service				
38c. U.S. Railroad Retirement				
38d. Military Retirement				
38e. Black Lung Benefits				
38f. Supplemental Security Income (SSI)/ Public Assistance				
38g. Other income received monthly (Please write source below:)				

Expected income next 12 months - Tell us about other income for you and your dependents

Report expected income for the 12 month period following the veteran's death. If the claim is filed more than one year after the veteran died, report the expected income for the 12 month period from the date you sign this application.

Sources of income for the next 12 months	Surviving spouse or Custodian of children	Child(ren) Name: (first, middle initial, last)	Name: (first, middle initial, last)	Name: (first, middle initial, last)
39a. Gross wages and salary				
39b. Total dividends and interest				
39c. Other income expected (Please write source below:)				
39d. Other income expected (Please write source below:)				

21-534   PAGE 6

SECTION IX

Tell us about medical, last illness, burial or other unreimbursed expenses

Family medical expenses and certain other expenses actually paid by you may be deductible from your income. Show the amount of any continuing family medical expenses such as the monthly Medicare deduction or nursing home costs you pay. Also, show unreimbursed last illness and burial expenses and educational or vocational rehabilitation expenses you paid. Last illness and burial expenses are unreimbursed amounts paid by you for the veteran's or his/her child's last illness and burial and the veteran's just debts. Educational or vocational rehabilitation expenses are amounts paid for courses of education, including tuition, fees, and materials. **Do not** include any expenses for which you were reimbursed. If you receive reimbursement after you have filed this claim, promptly advise the VA office handling your claim. If more space is needed attach a separate sheet.

40a. Amount paid by you	40b. Date Paid	40c. Purpose (Medicare deduction, nursing home costs, burial expenses, etc.)	40d. Paid to (Name of nursing home, hospital, funeral home, etc.)	40e. Relationship of person for whom expenses paid
$	mo day yr			
$	mo day yr			
$	mo day yr			
$	mo day yr			

SECTION X

Give us direct deposit information

If benefits are awarded we will need more information in order to process any payments to you. Please read the paragraph starting with, ***"All Federal payments..."*** and then either:

1. Attach a voided check, or

2. Answer questions 41-43 to the right.

All Federal payments beginning January 2, 1999, must be made by electronic funds transfer (EFT) also called Direct Deposit. Please attach a voided personal check or deposit slip or provide the information requested below in Items 41, 42, and 43 to enroll in Direct Deposit. If you do not have a bank account we will give you a waiver from Direct Deposit, just check the box below in Item 41. The Treasury Department is working on making bank accounts available to you. Once these accounts are available, you will be able to decide whether you wish to sign-up for one of the accounts or continue to receive a paper check. You can also request a waiver if you have other circumstances that you feel would cause you a hardship to be enrolled in Direct Deposit. You can write to: Department of Veterans Affairs, 125 S. Main Street Suite B, Muskogee OK 74401-7004, and give us a brief description of why you do not wish to participate in Direct Deposit.

41. Account number (Please check the appropriate box and provide that account number, if applicable)

☐ Checking   ☐ I certify that I **do not** have an account with a financial institution or certified payment agent

☐ Savings

Account number _____

42. Name of financial institution

_____

43. Routing or transit number

_____

21-534   PAGE 7

SECTION XI — Give us your signature	I certify and authorize the release of information: I certify that the statements in this document are true and complete to the best of my knowledge. I authorize any person or entity, including but not limited to any organization, service provider, employer, or government agency, to give the Department of Veterans Affairs any information about me except protected health information, and I waive any privilege which makes the information confidential.

44. Your signature	45. Today's date

46a. Signature of witness (If claimant signed above using an "X")	46b. Printed name and address of witness

47a. Signature of witness (If claimant signed above using an "X")	47b. Printed name and address of witness

SECTION XII

Remarks - Use this space for any additional statements that you would like to make concerning your application.

IMPORTANT

Penalty: The law provides severe penalties which include fine or imprisonment, or both, for the willful submission of any statement or evidence of a material fact, knowing it to be false, or for the fraudulent acceptance of any payment which you are not entitled to.

48. Remarks *(If you need more space to answer a question or have a comment about a specific item number on this form please identify your answer or statement by the part and item number)*

21-534   *PAGE 8*

APPENDIX 20:
DIRECTORY OF VA NATIONAL
CEMETERIES

STATE	ADDRESS/TELEPHONE
Alabama	Alabama VA National Cemetery 3133 Highway 119 Montevallo, AL 35115 205-933-8101 Fort Mitchell National Cemetery 553 Highway 165 Seale, AL 36856 334-855-4731 Mobile National Cemetery 1202 Virginia Street Mobile, AL 36604 850-453-4846
Alaska	Fort Richardson National Cemetery P.O. Box 5-498, Bldg 58-512, Davis Hwy Fort Richardson, AK 99505 907-384-7075 Sitka National Cemetery 803 Sawmill Creek Road Sitka, AK 99835 907-384-7075
Arizona	National Memorial Cemetery of Arizona 23029 North Cave Creek Road Phoenix, AZ 85024 480-513-3600

STATE	ADDRESS/TELEPHONE
	Prescott National Cemetery 500 Highway 89 North Prescott, AZ 86313 520-776-6028
Arkansas	Fayetteville National Cemetery 700 Government Avenue Fayetteville, AR 72701 479-444-5051 Fort Smith National Cemetery 522 Garland Avenue and South 6th Street Fort Smith, AR 72901 479-783-5345 Little Rock National Cemetery 2523 Confederate Boulevard Little Rock, AR 72206 501-324-6401
California	Bakersfield VA National Cemetery 30338 East Bear Mountain Road Arvin, CA 93203 661-632-1894 Fort Rosecrans National Cemetery P.O. Box 6237 Point Loma San Diego, CA 92166 619-553-2084 Golden Gate National Cemetery 1300 Sneath Lane San Bruno, CA 94066 650-589-7737 Los Angeles National Cemetery 950 S Sepulveda Blvd. Los Angeles, CA 90049 310-268-4675 Oakland Memorial Service Network 1301 Clay Street, Suite 1230 North Oakland, CA 94612-5209 510-637-6270 Riverside National Cemetery 22495 Van Buren Blvd. Riverside, CA 92518 951-653-8417 Sacramento Valley VA National Cemetery 5810 Midway Road Dixon, CA 95620 707-693-2460

STATE	ADDRESS/TELEPHONE
	San Francisco National Cemetery 1 Lincoln Boulevard Presidio of San Francisco San Francisco, CA 94129 650-761-1646 San Joaquin Valley National Cemetery 32053 W. McCabe Rd. Santa Nella, CA 95332 209-854-1040
Colorado	Denver Memorial Service Network P.O. Box 25126 Denver, CO 80228 303-914-5720 Fort Logan National Cemetery 4400 W. Kenyon Ave. Denver, CO 80236 303-761-0117 Fort Lyon National Cemetery 15700 County Road HH Las Animas, CO 81054 303-761-0117
Connecticut	None
Delaware	None
District of Columbia	None
Florida	Barrancas National Cemetery 80 Hovey Road Pensacola, FL 32508 850-453-4108 Bay Pines National Cemetery 10000 Bay Pines Boulevard North Bay Pines, FL 33708 727-398-9426 Florida National Cemetery 6502 S.W. 102nd Avenue Bushnell, FL 33513 352-793-7740 Jacksonville VA National Cemetery 4083 Lannie Road Jacksonville, FL 32218 904-358-3510

STATE	ADDRESS/TELEPHONE
	Sarasota VA National Cemetery 9810 State Hwy 72 Sarasota, FL 34241 877-861-19840
	South Florida VA National Cemetery 6501 S. State Road 7 Lake Worth, FL 33449 561-649-6489
	St. Augustine National Cemetery 104 Marine Street St. Augustine, FL 32084 352-793-7740
Georgia	Atlanta Memorial Service Network 1700 Clairmont Road, 4th Floor Decatur, GA 30033 404-929-5899
	Georgia National Cemetery 2025 Mount Carmel Church Lane Canton, GA 30114GA 866-236-8159
	Marietta National Cemetery 500 Washington Avenue Marietta, GA 30060 770-428-3258
Hawaii	National Memorial Cemetery of the Pacific 2177 Puowaina Drive Honolulu, HI 96813 808-532-3720
Idaho	None
Illinois	Abraham Lincoln National Cemetery 20953 W. Hoff Road Elwood, IL 60421 815-423-9958
	Alton National Cemetery 600 Pearl Street Alton, IL 62003 314-263-8691
	Camp Butler National Cemetery 5063 Camp Butler Road Springfield, IL 62707-9722 217-492-4070

STATE	ADDRESS/TELEPHONE
	Danville National Cemetery 1900 East Main Street Danville, IL 61832 217-554-4550 Mound City National Cemetery P.O. Box 128 Junction - Highway 37 & 51 Mound City, IL 62963 314-260-8691 Quincy National Cemetery 36th & Maine Street Quincy, IL 62301 309-782-2094 Rock Island National Cemetery Rock Island Arsenal, Bldg. 118 Rock Island, IL 61299 309-782-2094
Indiana	Crown Hill National Cemetery 700 W. 38th Street Indianapolis, IN 46208 765-674-0284 Indianapolis Memorial Service Network 575 North Pennsylvania Street Indianapolis, IN 46204 317-916-3790 Marion National Cemetery 1700 East 38 Street Marion, IN 46952 765-674-0284 New Albany National Cemetery 1943 Ekin Avenue New Albany, IN 47150 812-948-5234
Iowa	Keokuk National Cemetery 1701 J Street Keokuk, IA 52632 319-524-1304
Kansas	Fort Leavenworth National Cemetery Hancock and Biddle Street Fort Leavenworth, KS 66027 913-758-4105

STATE	ADDRESS/TELEPHONE
	Fort Scott National Cemetery 900 East National Avenue Fort Scott, KS 66701 620-223-2840 Leavenworth National Cemetery P.O. Box 1694 4101 South 4th Street Traffic Way Leavenworth, KS 66048 913-758-4105
Kentucky	Camp Nelson National Cemetery 6980 Danville Road Nicholasville, KY 40356 859-885-5727 Cave Hill National Cemetery 701 Baxter Avenue Louisville, KY 40204 502-893-3852 Danville National Cemetery 277 North First Street Danville, KY 40442 859-885-5727 Lebanon National Cemetery 20 Hwy 208 Lebanon, KY 40033 270-692-3390 Lexington National Cemetery 833 West Main Street Lexington, KY 40508 859-885-5727 Mill Springs National Cemetery 9044 West Highway Nancy, KY 42544 859-885-5727 Zachary Taylor National Cemetery 4701 Brownsboro Road Louisville, KY 40207 502-893-3852
Louisiana	Alexandria National Cemetery 209 East Shamrock Avenue Pineville, LA 71360 601-445-4981

STATE	ADDRESS/TELEPHONE
	Baton Rouge National Cemetery 220 North 19th Street Baton Rouge, LA 70806 225-654-3767 Port Hudson National Cemetery 20978 Port Hickey Road Zachary, LA 70791 225-654-3767
Maine	Togus National Cemetery VA Medical & Regional Office Center Togus, ME 04330 508-563-7113
Maryland	Annapolis National Cemetery 800 West Street Annapolis, MD 21401 410-644-9696 Baltimore National Cemetery 5501 Frederick Avenue Baltimore, MD 21228 410-644-9696 Loudon Park National Cemetery 3445 Frederick Avenue Baltimore, MD 21228 410-644-9696
Massachusetts	Massachusetts National Cemetery Connery Avenue Bourne, MA 02532 508-563-7113
Michigan	Fort Custer National Cemetery 15501 Dickman Rd. Augusta, MI 49012 269-731-4164 Great Lakes National Cemetery 4200 Belford Road Holly, MI 48442 866-348-8603
Minnesota	Fort Snelling National Cemetery 7601 34th Avenue South Minneapolis, MN 55450 612-726-1127

STATE	ADDRESS/TELEPHONE
Mississippi	Biloxi National Cemetery 400 Veterans Avenue Biloxi, MS 39535 228-388-6668 Corinth National Cemetery 1551 Horton Street Corinth, MS 38834 901-386-8311 Natchez National Cemetery 41 Cemetery Road Natchez, MS 39120 601-445-4981
Missouri	Jefferson Barracks National Cemetery 2900 Sheridan Road St. Louis, MO 63125 314-260-8691 Jefferson City National Cemetery 1024 E. McCarty Street Jefferson City, MO 65101 314-260-8691 Springfield National Cemetery 1702 East Seminole Street Springfield, MO 65804 417-881-9499
Montana	None
Nebraska	Fort McPherson National Cemetery 12004 South Spur 56A Maxwell, NE 69151 308-582-4433
Nevada	None
New Hampshire	None
New Jersey	Beverly National Cemetery R.D. #1 Bridgeboro Road Beverly, NJ 08010 609-880-0827
	Finn's Point National Cemetery R.F.D. No. 3, Box 542 Fort Mott Road Salem, NJ 08079 609-880-0827

STATE	ADDRESS/TELEPHONE
New Mexico	Fort Bayard National Cemetery P.O. Box 189 Fort Bayard, NM 88036 915-564-0201 Santa Fe National Cemetery 501 North Guadalupe Street Santa Fe, NM 87501 505-988-6400
New York	Bath National Cemetery VA Medical Center San Juan Avenue Bath, NY 14810 607-664-4853 Calverton National Cemetery 210 Princeton Boulevard Calverton, NY 11933 631-727-5410 Cypress Hills National Cemetery 625 Jamaica Avenue Brooklyn, NY 11208 631-454-4949 Gerald B. H. Solomon Saratoga National Cemetery 200 Duell Road Schuylerville, NY 12871-1721 518-581-9128 Long Island National Cemetery 2040 Wellwood Avenue Farmingdale, NY 117351211 631-454-4949 Woodlawn National Cemetery 1825 Davis Street Elmira, NY 14901 607-664-4853
North Carolina	New Bern National Cemetery 1711 National Avenue New Bern, NC 28560 NC 252-637-2912 Raleigh National Cemetery 501 Rock Quarry Road Raleigh, NC 27610 252-637-2912

STATE	ADDRESS/TELEPHONE
	Salisbury National Cemetery 501 Statesville Boulevard Salisbury, NC 28144 704-636-2661 Wilmington National Cemetery 2011 Market Street Wilmington, NC 28403 910-815-4877
North Dakota	None
Ohio	Dayton National Cemetery VA Medical Center 4100 West Third Street Dayton, OH 45428 937-262-2115 Ohio Western Reserve National Cemetery P.O. Box 8 10175 Rawiga Road Rittman, OH 44270 330-335-3069
Oklahoma	Fort Gibson National Cemetery 1423 Cemetery Road Ft. Gibson, OK 74434 918-478-2334 Fort Sill National Cemetery 2648 NE Jake Dunn Road Elgin, OK 73538 580-492-3200
Oregon	Eagle Point National Cemetery 2763 Riley Rd. Eagle Point, OR 97524 541-826-2511 Roseburg National Cemetery 1770 Harvard Blvd. Roseburg, OR 97470 541-826-2511 Willamette National Cemetery 11800 SE Mt. Scott Blvd. Portland, OR 97086-6937 503-273-5250

STATE	ADDRESS/TELEPHONE
Pennsylvania	Indiantown Gap National Cemetery Box 484 Indiantown Gap Rd. Annville, PA 17003-9618 717-865-5254 National Cemetery of the Alleghenies 1158 Morgan Road Bridgeville, PA 15017 724-746-4363 Philadelphia Memorial Service Network 5000 Wissahickon Avenue Philadelphia, PA 19144 215-381-3787 Philadelphia National Cemetery Haines St. and Limekiln Pike Philadelphia, PA 19138 609-877-5460
Puerto Rico	Puerto Rico National Cemetery Avenue Cementerio Nacional #50 Barrio Hato Tejas Bayamon, PR 00960 787-798-8400
Rhode Island	None
South Carolina	Beaufort National Cemetery 1601 Boundary St. Beaufort, SC 29902-3947 843-524-3925 Columbia/Ft. Jackson Area National Cemetery 4170 Percival Road Columbia, SC 29229 866-577-5248 Florence National Cemetery 803 E National Cemetery Rd. Florence, SC 29501 843-669-8783
South Dakota	Black Hills National Cemetery 20901 Pleasant Valley Drive Sturgis, SD 57785 605-347-3830 Fort Meade National Cemetery Old Stone Rd. Sturgis, SD 57785 605-347-3830

STATE	ADDRESS/TELEPHONE
	Hot Springs National Cemetery VA Medical Center Hot Springs, SD 57747 605-347-3830
Tennessee	Chattanooga National Cemetery 1200 Bailey Ave. Chattanooga, TN 37404 423-855-6590
	Knoxville National Cemetery 939 Tyson St. NW Knoxville, TN 37917 423-855-6590
	Memphis National Cemetery 3568 Townes Ave. Memphis, TN 38122 901-386-8311
	Mountain Home National Cemetery P.O. Box 8 VA Medical Center, Bldg. 117 Mountain Home, TN 37684 423-461-7935
	Nashville National Cemetery 1420 Gallatin Rd., S. Madison, TN 37115-4619 615-860-0086
Texas	Dallas-Fort Worth National Cemetery 2000 Mountain Creek Parkway Dallas, TX 75211 214-467-3374
	Fort Bliss National Cemetery P.O. Box 6342 5200 Fred Wilson Rd. El Paso, TX 79906 915-564-0201
	Fort Sam Houston National Cemetery 1520 Harry Wurzbach Rd. San Antonio, TX 78209 210-820-3891
	Houston National Cemetery 10410 Veterans Memorial Dr. Houston, TX 77038 281-447-8686

STATE	ADDRESS/TELEPHONE
	Kerrville National Cemetery VA Medical Center 3600 Memorial Blvd. Kerrville, TX 78028 210-820-3891 San Antonio National Cemetery 517 Paso Hondo Street San Antonio, TX 78202 210-820-3891
Utah	None
Vermont	None
Virginia	Alexandria National Cemetery 1450 Wilkes St. Alexandria, VA 22314 504-825-0027 Ball's Bluff National Cemetery Rt. 7 Leesburg, VA 22075 540-825-0027 City Point National Cemetery 10th Ave. and Davis St. Hopewell, VA 23860 804-795-2031 Cold Harbor National Cemetery 6038 Cold Harbor Road Mechanicsville, VA 23111 804-795-2031 Culpeper National Cemetery 305 U.S. Ave. Culpeper, VA 22701 540-825-0027 Danville National Cemetery 721 Lee St. Danville, VA 24541 704-636-2661 Fort Harrison National Cemetery 8620 Varina Rd. Richmond, VA 23231 804-795-2031 Glendale National Cemetery 8301 Willis Church Rd. Richmond, VA 23231 804-795-2031

STATE	ADDRESS/TELEPHONE
	Hampton National Cemetery Cemetery Rd. at Marshall Ave. Hampton, VA 23667 757-723-7104
	Hampton National Cemetery VA Medical Center Emancipation Drive Hampton, VA 23667 757-723-7104
	Quantico National Cemetery P.O. Box 10 18424 Joplin Rd. Triangle, VA 22172 703-221-2183
	Richmond National Cemetery 1701 Williamsburg Rd. Richmond, VA 23231 804-795-2031
	Seven Pines National Cemetery 400 E Williamsburg Rd. Sandston, VA 23150 804-795-2031
	Staunton National Cemetery 901 Richmond Ave. Staunton, VA 24401 540-825-0027
	Winchester National Cemetery 401 National Ave. Winchester, VA 22601 540-825-0027
Washington	Tahoma National Cemetery 18600 SE 240th Street Kent, WA 98042-4868 425-413-9614
West Virginia	Grafton National Cemetery 431 Walnut St. Grafton, WV 26354 304-265-2044
	West Virginia National Cemetery Rt. 2, Box 127 Grafton, WV 26354 304-265-2044

STATE	ADDRESS/TELEPHONE
Wisconsin	Wood National Cemetery 5000 W National Ave., Bldg. 1301 Milwaukee, WI 53295-4000 414-382-5300
Wyoming	None

Source: Department of Veterans Affairs.

APPENDIX 21:
APPLICATION FOR STANDARD GOVERNMENT HEADSTONE OR MARKER (FORM 40-1330)

Form approved, OMB No. 2900-0222
Respondent Burden: 15 minutes

Department of Veterans Affairs

IMPORTANT: Please read the General Information Sheet before completing this form. Type or print clearly all information except for signatures. Illegible printing could result in an incorrect headstone or marker or delivery. *Blocks outlined in bold are optional inscription items. Unless indicated otherwise* all other blocks **must** be completed. **MILITARY DISCHARGE DOCUMENTS OR RELATED SERVICE INFORMATION IS REQUIRED.**

1. TYPE OF REQUEST

☐ INITIAL *(First time)* REQUEST

☐ SECOND REQUEST

☐ CORRECTED APPLICATION OR REPLACEMENT

2. NAME OF DECEASED TO BE INSCRIBED ON HEADSTONE OR MARKER *(NO NICKNAMES OR TITLES PERMITTED)*

FIRST *(Or Initial)*	MIDDLE *(Or Initial)*	LAST	SUFFIX

3. GRAVE IS:

☐ CURRENTLY MARKED *(with privately purchased marker)*

☐ NOT MARKED

VETERAN'S SERVICE AND IDENTIFYING INFORMATION *(Use numbers only, e.g., 05-15-1941)*

4. VETERAN'S SOCIAL SECURITY NO. OR SERVICE NO. *(Failure to complete will delay processing.)*

SSN: ____ OR SVC. NO.: ____

5A. DATE OF BIRTH			5B. DATE OF DEATH		
MONTH	DAY	YEAR	MONTH	DAY	YEAR

PERIODS OF ACTIVE MILITARY DUTY *(For additional space use Block 27)*

6A. DATE(S) ENTERED			6B. DATE(S) SEPARATED		
MONTH	DAY	YEAR	MONTH	DAY	YEAR

7. HIGHEST RANK ATTAINED (No pay grades)

8. BRANCH OF SERVICE *(Check applicable box(es) - must be consistent with rank in Box 7)*

ARMY	NAVY	MARINE CORPS	COAST GUARD	AIR FORCE	ARMY AIR FORCES	MERCHANT MARINE	OTHER *(Specify)*
☐	☐	☐	☐	☐	☐	☐	☐

9. VALOR OR PURPLE HEART AWARD(S) *(Documentation must be provided)*

MEDAL OF HONOR	DST SVC CROSS	NAVY CROSS	AIR FORCE CROSS	SILVER STAR	BRONZE STAR MEDAL	PURPLE HEART	OTHER *(Specify)*
☐	☐	☐	☐	☐	☐	☐	☐

10. WAR SERVICE *(Check applicable box(es))*

WORLD WAR II	KOREA	VIETNAM	PERSIAN GULF	OTHER *(Specify)*
☐	☐	☐	☐	☐

11. TYPE OF HEADSTONE OR MARKER REQUESTED *(Check one)*

FLAT BRONZE	FLAT GRANITE	UPRIGHT MARBLE	FLAT MARBLE	BRONZE NICHE	UPRIGHT GRANITE
☐ B	☐ G	☐ U	☐ F	☐ Z	☐ V

12. DESIRED EMBLEM OF BELIEF

☐ NONE

EMBLEM NUMBER ____ *(Specify)(See reverse side of this form for authorized emblems)*

13A. NAME AND MAILING ADDRESS *(No., Street, City, State, and ZIP Code)* OF PERSON TO CONTACT FOR ADDITIONAL INFORMATION

13B. DAYTIME PHONE NO. OF PERSON TO CONTACT FOR ADDITIONAL INFORMATION

14. E-MAIL ADDRESS *(Optional)*

15. FAX NO. *(Optional)*

16. ARE YOU:

☐ NEXT OF KIN   ☐ VETERANS SERVICE OFFICER

☐ FUNERAL DIRECTOR   ☐ CEMETERY OFFICIAL

☐ OTHER *(Specify)*

CERTIFICATION: By signing below I certify the headstone or marker will be installed in the cemetery listed in block 21 at no expense to the Government and all information entered on this form is true and correct to the best of my knowledge.

17. SIGNATURE OF PERSON WHOSE NAME APPEARS IN BLOCK 13A		18. DATE *(MM/DD/YYYY)*
19. NAME AND DELIVERY ADDRESS OF BUSINESS (CONSIGNEE) THAT WILL ACCEPT PREPAID DELIVERY *(No., Street, City, State and ZIP Code):* **P.O. BOX IS NOT ACCEPTABLE**	20. DAYTIME PHONE NO. *(Include Area Code)*	21. NAME AND ADDRESS OF CEMETERY WHERE GRAVE IS LOCATED *(No., Street, City, State and ZIP Code)*

CERTIFICATION: By signing below I agree to accept prepaid delivery of the headstone or marker.

22. PRINTED NAME AND SIGNATURE OF PERSON REPRESENTING BUSINESS (CONSIGNEE) NAMED IN BLOCK 19	23. DATE *(MM/DD/YYYY)*

CERTIFICATION: By signing below I certify the type of headstone or marker checked in block 11 is permitted in the cemetery named in block 21.

24. PRINTED NAME AND SIGNATURE OF CEMETERY OR OTHER RESPONSIBLE OFFICIAL	25. DAYTIME PHONE NO. *(Include Area Code)*	26. DATE *(MM/DD/YYYY)*

27. REMARKS *(Optional inscription space will vary in size according to the type of marker)*	28. CHECK BOX BELOW IF REMAINS ARE NOT BURIED AND EXPLAIN IN BLOCK 27 *(e.g., lost at sea, remains scattered, etc.)* ☐ REMAINS NOT BURIED

STATE VETERANS' CEMETERY AND GRAVE LOCATION *(Cemetery Use Only)*

29. ID CODE	30. SECTION	31. GRAVE NO.

VA FORM
MAY 2008 **40-1330**   **APPLICATION FOR STANDARD GOVERNMENT HEADSTONE OR MARKER**

APPENDIX 22:
APPLICATION FOR U.S. FLAG FOR BURIAL
PURPOSES (FORM 21-2008)

OMB APPROVED NO. 2900-0013
RESPONDENT BURDEN: 15 MINUTES

VA Department of Veterans Affairs | **APPLICATION FOR UNITED STATES FLAG FOR BURIAL PURPOSES**

PRIVACY ACT NOTICE: VA will not disclose information collected on this form to any source other than what has been authorized under the Privacy Act of 1974 or Title 38, Code of Federal Regulations 1.576 for routine uses (i.e., civil or criminal law enforcement, congressional communications, epidemiological or research studies, the collection of money owed to the United States, litigation in which the United States is a party or has an interest, the administration of VA programs and delivery of VA benefits, verification of identity and status, and personnel administration) as identified in the VA system of records, 58VA21/22, Compensation, Pension, Education and Rehabilitation Records - VA, published in the Federal Register. Your obligation to respond is required to obtain or retain benefits. Giving us the veteran's SSN account information is voluntary. Refusal to provide the veteran's SSN by itself will not result in the denial of benefits. VA will not deny an individual benefits for refusing to provide his or her SSN unless the disclosure of the SSN is required by a Federal Statute of law in effect prior to January 1, 1975, and still in effect. The requested information is considered relevant and necessary to determine entitlement to benefits under the law. The responses you submit are considered confidential (38 U.S.C. 5701). Information submitted is subject to verification through computer matching programs with other agencies.

RESPONDENT BURDEN: We need this information to determine eligibility for issuance of a burial flag to a family member or friend of a deceased veteran (38 U.S.C. 2301). Title 38, United States Code, allows us to ask for this information. We estimate that you will need an average of 15 minutes to review the instructions, find the information, and complete this form. VA cannot conduct or sponsor a collection of information unless a valid OMB control number is displayed. You are not required to respond to a collection of information if this number is not displayed. Valid OMB control numbers can be located on the OMB Internet Page at www.whitehouse.gov/omb/library/OMBINV.html#VA. If desired, you can call 1-800-827-1000 to get information on where to send comments or suggestions about this form.

IMPORTANT - Postmaster or other issuing official: Submit this form to the nearest VA regional office. Be sure to complete the stub at the bottom.

INFORMATION ABOUT THE DECEASED VETERAN (Complete as much as possible)

1. FIRST, MIDDLE, LAST NAME OF VETERAN *(Print or type)*	2. OTHER NAMES USED BY VETERAN *(Print or type)*

3. VA FILE NUMBER	4 SOCIAL SECURITY NUMBER	5. MILITARY SERVICE NUMBER/SERIAL NUMBER

6. BRANCH OF SERVICE *(Check box)*
☐ ARMY ☐ NAVY ☐ AIR FORCE ☐ MARINE CORPS ☐ COAST GUARD ☐ SELECTED SERVICE ☐ OTHER *(Specify)*

7. DATE ENTERED ACTIVE DUTY *(or Selected Reserve)*	8. DATE RELEASED FROM ACTIVE DUTY *(or Selected Reserve)*	9. DATE OF BIRTH	10. DATE OF DEATH

11. DATE OF BURIAL	12. PLACE OF BURIAL *(Name of cemetery, city, and State)*

13. HAS DOCUMENTATION BEEN PRESENTED OR ATTACHED THAT SHOWS THE VETERAN MEETS THE ELIGIBILITY CRITERIA? (See Paragraphs C, D, and E of the "Instructions")

☐ YES ☐ NO *(If "No," explain in Item 15, "Remarks" (See paragraph E of the "Instructions"))*

INFORMATION ABOUT THE FLAG RECIPIENT AND APPLICANT

14A. NAME OF PERSON ENTITLED TO RECEIVE FLAG	14B. ADDRESS OF PERSON ENTITLED TO RECEIVE FLAG *(Number and street or rural route, city or P.O., State and ZIP Code)*

14C. RELATIONSHIP TO VETERAN (See Paragraph F of the "Instructions")

15. REMARKS

I CERTIFY that the statements made in this document are true and complete to the best of my knowledge. I further certify that the deceased veteran is eligible, in accordance with the attached instructions, for issue of a United States flag for burial purposes, and such flag has not been previously applied for or furnished.

16. SIGNATURE OF APPLICANT *(Sign in INK)*	17. ADDRESS OF APPLICANT *(Number and street or rural route, city or P.O., and ZIP Code)*	18. RELATIONSHIP TO DECEASED	19. DATE SIGNED

PENALTY - The law provides that whoever makes any statement of a material fact knowing it to be false shall be punished by a fine, imprisonment, or both.

APPLICATION FOR U.S. FLAG FOR BURIAL PURPOSES (FORM 21-2008)

ACKNOWLEDGMENT OF RECEIPT OF FLAG		
I CERTIFY that the flag requested by the applicant will be used to drape the casket of the deceased in whose honor it is issued by the Department of Veterans Affairs, and that Item 6 of the "Use Of The Flag" instructions on the attached sheet will be complied with.		
SIGNATURE OF PERSON RECEIVING FLAG *(Sign in INK)*	DATE FLAG RECEIVED	
NAME AND ADDRESS OF POST OFFICE OR OTHER FLAG ISSUE POINT	**FOR VA USE**	
	DATE NOTIFICATION FORWARDED TO SUPPLY	INITIALS OF RESPONSIBLE VA EMPLOYEE

VA FORM 21-2008, SEP 2005   SUPERSEDES VA FORM 21- 2008, MAY 2003, WHICH WILL NOT BE USED.

This stub is to be completed by the POSTMASTER or other issuing official. Upon receipt the VA Regional Office will detach and forward it to the appropriate Supply Officer.

NOTIFICATION OF ISSUANCE OF FLAG		
DATE FLAG ISSUED	SIGNATURE OF POSTMASTER OR OTHER ISSUING OFFICIAL	ADDRESS OF POST OFFICE OR OTHER FLAG ISSUE POINT
FOR VA USE ▶	DATE OF REPLACEMENT	

VA FORM **21-2008** SEP 2005   SUPERSEDES VA FORM 21- 2008, MAY 2003, WHICH WILL NOT BE USED.   SEE REVERSE

APPENDIX 23:
PRESIDENTIAL MEMORIAL CERTIFICATE
REQUEST (FORM 40-0247)

Form Approved, OMB No. 2900-0567
Respondent Burden: 2 Minutes

| **Department of Veterans Affairs** | **PRESIDENTIAL MEMORIAL CERTIFICATE REQUEST FORM** |

RESPONDENT BURDEN: Public reporting burden for this collection of information is estimated to average two minutes per response. Statutory authority for the Presidential Memorial Certificate (PMC) Program is 38 U.S.C. 112. The information requested is approved under OMB Control Number 2900-0567, and is necessary to allow eligible recipients (next of kin, other relatives or friends) to request additional certificates and/or replacement or correct certificates on receipt of the original PMC.

The National Cemetery Administration does not give, sell or transfer any personal information outside of the agency. VA may not conduct or sponsor, and you are not required to respond to this collection of information unless it displays a valid OMB Control Number. Responding to this collection is voluntary. Send comments regarding this burden estimate or any other aspects of this collection of information, including suggestions for reducing this burden, to VA Clearance Officer (005G2), 810 Vermont Avenue NW, Washington, DC 20420. **SEND COMMENTS ONLY.** *Please do not send applications for benefits to this address.*

INSTRUCTIONS: When inserting the veterans name below, **DO NOT** include nickname, military rank, or civilian title. Complete a new VA Form 40-0247 for each additional name and/or mailing address.

NAME OF VETERAN	NAME AND MAILING ADDRESS OF PERSON REQUESTING CERTIFICATE
NUMBER OF CERTIFICATES REQUESTED	
HOME OR WORK TELEPHONE NUMBER *(Include area code and do not insert spaces between numbers)*	SIGNATURE OF REQUESTOR

RETURN COMPLETED FORM ALONG WITH A COPY OF THE DISCHARGE DOCUMENTS TO:

Presidential Memorial Certificates (41A1C)
National Cemetery Administration
5109 Russell Road
Quantico, VA 22134-3903

Or

Fax To: 1 (800) 455-7143

VA FORM
JUN 2007 (R) **40-0247**

Adobe LiveCycle Designer 7.1

APPENDIX 24:
APPLICATION FOR BURIAL BENEFITS
(FORM 21-530)

OMB Approved No. 2900-0003
Respondent Burden: 20 minutes

VA Department of Veterans Affairs

| | (DO NOT WRITE IN THIS SPACE)
(VA DATE STAMP) |

APPLICATION FOR BURIAL BENEFITS
(Under 38 U.S.C. Chapter 23)

IMPORTANT - Read instructions carefully before completing form. YOUR COMPLIANCE WITH ALL INSTRUCTIONS WILL AVOID DELAY. Type or print all information.

1. FIRST, MIDDLE, LAST NAME OF DECEASED VETERAN

2. SOCIAL SECURITY NUMBER OF VETERAN	3. VA FILE NUMBER

4. FIRST, MIDDLE, LAST NAME OF CLAIMANT	5. TELEPHONE NUMBER(S) (Include Area Code)	
	A. DAYTIME	B. EVENING

6. **MAILING ADDRESS OF CLAIMANT** *(Number and street or rural route, city or P.O., State and ZIP Code)*

PART I - INFORMATION REGARDING VETERAN

7A. DATE OF BIRTH	7B. PLACE OF BIRTH	
8A. DATE OF DEATH	8B. PLACE OF DEATH	8C. DATE OF BURIAL

SERVICE INFORMATION *(The following information should be furnished for the periods of the VETERAN'S ACTIVE SERVICE)*

9A. ENTERED SERVICE		9B. SERVICE NUMBER	9C. SEPARATED FROM SERVICE		9D. GRADE, RANK OR RATING, ORGANIZATION AND BRANCH OF SERVICE
DATE	PLACE		DATE	PLACE	

10. IF VETERAN SERVED UNDER NAME OTHER THAN THAT SHOWN IN ITEM 1, GIVE FULL NAME AND SERVICE RENDERED UNDER THAT NAME	11. ARE YOU CLAIMING THAT THE CAUSE OF DEATH WAS DUE TO SERVICE? ☐ YES ☐ NO

PART II - CLAIM FOR BURIAL BENEFITS AND/OR INTERMENT ALLOWANCE IF PAID BY CLAIMANT		

NOTE - If claiming Plot Allowance Only, do not complete Part II, but complete Parts III and IV on reverse.

12. PLACE OF BURIAL OR LOCATION OF CREMAINS	13. WAS BURIAL (WITHOUT CHARGE FOR PLOT OR INTERMENT) IN A STATE OWNED CEMETERY, OR SECTION THEREOF, USED SOLELY FOR PERSONS ELIGIBLE FOR BURIAL IN A NATIONAL CEMETERY? [ ] YES [ ] NO *(IF "No," complete Items 15 and 16)*	14. WAS BURIAL IN A NATIONAL CEMETERY OR CEMETERY OWNED BY THE FEDERAL GOVERNMENT? [ ] YES [ ] NO *(If "No," complete Items 15 and 16)*
15. BURIAL PLOT, MAUSOLEUM VAULT, COLUMBARIUM NICHE, ETC. COST IS: *(CHECK ONE)* [ ] PAID BY ANOTHER PERSON(S) [ ] PAID BY CLAIMANT FOR BURIAL [ ] DUE FUNERAL DIRECTOR [ ] NONE [ ] DUE CEMETERY OWNER	16. IF PLOT/INTERMENT EXPENSES ARE UNPAID, WHO WILL FILE CLAIM FOR EXPENSES? *(Name and Address)*	

17. TOTAL EXPENSE OF BURIAL, FUNERAL, TRANSPORTATION, AND IF CLAIMED, BURIAL PLOT $	18. AMOUNT PAID $	19. WHOSE FUNDS WERE USED?
20A. HAS PERSON WHOSE FUNDS WERE USED BEEN REIMBURSED? [ ] YES [ ] NO *(If "Yes," complete Items 20B and 20C)*	20B. AMOUNT OF REIMBURSEMENT $	20C. SOURCE OF REIMBURSEMENT
21A. HAS ANY AMOUNT BEEN, OR WILL ANY AMOUNT BE ALLOWED ON EXPENSES BY LOCAL, STATE, OR FEDERAL AGENCY? [ ] YES [ ] NO *(If "Yes," complete Items 21B and 21C)*	21B. AMOUNT $	21C. SOURCE(S)

22. WAS THE VETERAN A MEMBER OF A BURIAL ASSOCIATION OR COVERED BY BURIAL INSURANCE? [ ] YES [ ] NO *(Before answering, read and comply with Instruction 8)*		

VA FORM JUN 2002 **21-530**   EXISTING STOCK OF VA FORM 21-530, SEP 1995. WILL BE USED.

PART III - CLAIM FOR PLOT COST ALLOWANCE

IMPORTANT - Complete only if burial was NOT in a national cemetery or cemetery owned by the Federal Government.

23. WAS BURIAL (WITHOUT CHARGE FOR PLOT OR INTERMENT) IN A STATE OWNED CEMETERY, OR SECTION THEREOF, USED SOLELY FOR PERSONS ELIGIBLE FOR BURIAL IN A NATIONAL CEMETERY?	24. PLACE OF BURIAL OR LOCATION OF CREMAINS	
25A. COST OF BURIAL PLOT (Individual Grave Site, Mausoleum Vault, or Columbarium Niche) $	25B. DATE OF PURCHASE	25C. DATE OF PAYMENT

26A. HAVE BILLS BEEN PAID IN FULL? ☐ YES ☐ NO (If "No," complete Items 26B and 27)	26B. AMOUNT PAID $	27. WHOSE FUNDS WERE USED?
28A. HAS PERSON WHOSE FUNDS WERE USED BEEN REIMBURSED? ☐ YES ☐ NO (If "Yes," complete Items 28B and 28C)	28B. AMOUNT OF REIMBURSEMENT $	28C. SOURCE OF REIMBURSEMENT
29A. HAS ANY AMOUNT BEEN, OR WILL ANY AMOUNT BE ALLOWED ON EXPENSES BY STATE OR FEDERAL AGENCY? ☐ YES ☐ NO (If "Yes," complete Items 29B and 29C)	29B. AMOUNT $	29C. SOURCE

PART IV - CERTIFICATION AND SIGNATURE

I CERTIFY THAT the foregoing statements made in connection with this application on account of the named veteran are true and correct to the best of my knowledge and belief.

30A. SIGNATURE OF CLAIMANT (If signed by mark, complete Items 36A and 37B) (If signing for firm, corporation, or State agency, complete Items 30B thru 31)	30B. OFFICIAL POSITION OF PERSON SIGNING ON BEHALF OF FIRM, CORPORATION OR STATE AGENCY
31. FULL NAME AND ADDRESS OF THE FIRM, CORPORATION, OR STATE AGENCY FILING AS CLAIMANT	

NOTE - Where the claimant is a firm or other unpaid creditor, Items 32A thru 35 MUST be completed by the individual who authorized services.

I CERTIFY THAT the foregoing statements made by the claimant are correct to the best of my knowledge and belief.

32A. SIGNATURE OF PERSON WHO AUTHORIZED SERVICES (If signed by mark, complete Items 36A thru 37B)	32B. NAME OF PERSON AUTHORIZING SERVICES (Type or Print)
33. ADDRESS (Number and street or rural route, city or P.O., State and ZIP Code)	

34. DATE	35. RELATIONSHIP TO VETERAN

WITNESS TO SIGNATURE IF MADE BY "X" MARK

NOTE - Signature made by mark must be witnessed by two persons to whom the person making the statement is personally known, and the signatures and addresses of such witnesses must be shown below.

36A. SIGNATURE OF WITNESS	36B. ADDRESS OF WITNESS
37A. SIGNATURE OF WITNESS	37B. ADDRESS OF WITNESS

PENALTY - The law provides severe penalties which include fine or imprisonment, or both, for the willful submission of any statement or evidence of a material fact knowing it to be false.

DEPARTMENT OF VETERANS AFFAIRS HEADSTONES AND MARKERS

The Department of Veterans Affairs will furnish, upon request, a Government headstone or marker at the expense of the United States for the unmarked graves of certain individuals eligible for burial in a national cemetery, but not buried there. These individuals include any veteran with an other than dishonorable discharge who dies after service or any serviceman or servicewoman who dies on active duty. Certain other individuals may also be eligible for the headstone or marker. Headstones or markers for all individuals in a national or post cemetery are furnished automatically without request from the family.

For additional information and an application, contact the nearest VA office.

APPENDIX 25:
SELECTED PROVISIONS OF THE
SERVICEMEMBERS CIVIL RELIEF ACT
[PUB. L. NO. 108-189, 12/19/03]

TITLE II—GENERAL RELIEF

SEC. 201. Protection of servicemembers against default judgments.

(a) APPLICABILITY OF SECTION—This section applies to any civil action or proceeding in which the defendant does not make an appearance.

(b) AFFIDAVIT REQUIREMENT—

(1) PLAINTIFF TO FILE AFFIDAVIT—In any action or proceeding covered by this section, the court, before entering judgment for the plaintiff, shall require the plaintiff to file with the court an affidavit—

(A) stating whether or not the defendant is in military service and showing necessary facts to support the affidavit; or

(B) if the plaintiff is unable to determine whether or not the defendant is in military service, stating that the plaintiff is unable to determine whether or not the defendant is in military service.

(2) APPOINTMENT OF ATTORNEY TO REPRESENT DEFENDANT IN MILITARY SERVICE—If in an action covered by this section it appears that the defendant is in military service, the court may not enter a judgment until after the court appoints an attorney to represent the defendant. If an attorney appointed under this section to represent a servicemember cannot locate the servicemember, actions by the attorney in the case shall not waive any defense of the servicemember or otherwise bind the servicemember.

(3) DEFENDANT'S MILITARY STATUS NOT ASCERTAINED BY AFFIDAVIT—If based upon the affidavits filed in such an action, the court is unable to determine whether the defendant is in military service, the court, before entering judgment, may require the plaintiff to file a bond in an amount approved by the court. If the defendant is later found to be in military service, the bond shall be available to indemnify the defendant against any loss or damage the defendant may suffer by reason of any judgment for the plaintiff against the defendant, should the judgment be set aside in whole or in part. The bond shall remain in effect until expiration of the time for appeal and setting aside of a judgment under applicable Federal or State law or regulation or under any applicable ordinance of a political subdivision of a State. The court may issue such orders or enter such judgments as the court determines necessary to protect the rights of the defendant under this Act.

(4) SATISFACTION OF REQUIREMENT FOR AFFIDAVIT—The requirement for an affidavit under paragraph (1) may be satisfied by a statement, declaration, verification, or certificate, in writing, subscribed and certified or declared to be true under penalty of perjury.

(c) PENALTY FOR MAKING OR USING FALSE AFFIDAVIT—A person who makes or uses an affidavit permitted under subsection (b) (or a statement, declaration, verification, or certificate as authorized under subsection (b)(4)) knowing it to be false, shall be fined as provided in title 18, United States Code, or imprisoned for not more than one year, or both.

(d) STAY OF PROCEEDINGS—In an action covered by this section in which the defendant is in military service, the court shall grant a stay of proceedings for a minimum period of 90 days under this subsection upon application of counsel, or on the court's own motion, if the court determines that—

(1) there may be a defense to the action and a defense cannot be presented without the presence of the defendant; or

(2) after due diligence, counsel has been unable to contact the defendant or otherwise determine if a meritorious defense exists.

(e) INAPPLICABILITY OF SECTION 202 PROCEDURES—A stay of proceedings under subsection (d) shall not be controlled by procedures or requirements under section 202.

(f) SECTION 202 PROTECTION—If a servicemember who is a defendant in an action covered by this section receives actual notice of the action, the servicemember may request a stay of proceeding under section 202.

(g) VACATION OR SETTING ASIDE OF DEFAULT JUDGMENTS—

(1) AUTHORITY FOR COURT TO VACATE OR SET ASIDE JUDGMENT—
If a default judgment is entered in an action covered by this section
against a servicemember during the servicemember's period of military service (or within 60 days after termination of or release from
such military service), the court entering the judgment shall, upon
application by or on behalf of the servicemember, reopen the judgment for the purpose of allowing the servicemember to defend the
action if it appears that—

(A) the servicemember was materially affected by reason of that
military service in making a defense to the action; and

(B) the servicemember has a meritorious or legal defense to the
action or some part of it.

(2) TIME FOR FILING APPLICATION—An application under this subsection must be filed not later than 90 days after the date of the termination of or release from military service.

(h) PROTECTION OF BONA FIDE PURCHASER—If a court vacates, sets
aside, or reverses a default judgment against a servicemember and the
vacating, setting aside, or reversing is because of a provision of this
Act, that action shall not impair a right or title acquired by a bona fide
purchaser for value under the default judgment.

SEC. 202. Stay of proceedings when servicemember has notice.

(a) APPLICABILITY OF SECTION—This section applies to any civil action
or proceeding in which the defendant at the time of filing an application under this section—

(1) is in military service or is within 90 days after termination of or
release from military service; and

(2) has received notice of the action or proceeding.

(b) STAY OF PROCEEDINGS—

(1) AUTHORITY FOR STAY—At any stage before final judgment in a
civil action or proceeding in which a servicemember described in subsection (a) is a party, the court may on its own motion and shall, upon
application by the servicemember, stay the action for a period of not
less than 90 days, if the conditions in paragraph (2) are met.

(2) CONDITIONS FOR STAY—An application for a stay under paragraph (1) shall include the following:

(A) A letter or other communication setting forth facts stat-ing
the manner in which current military duty requirements materially

affect the servicemember's ability to appear and stating a date when the servicemember will be available to appear.

(B) A letter or other communication from the servicemember's commanding officer stating that the servicemember's current military duty prevents appearance and that military leave is not authorized for the servicemember at the time of the letter.

(c) APPLICATION NOT A WAIVER OF DEFENSES—An application for a stay under this section does not constitute an appearance for jurisdictional purposes and does not constitute a waiver of any substantive or procedural defense (including a defense relating to lack of personal jurisdiction).

(d) ADDITIONAL STAY—

(1) APPLICATION—A servicemember who is granted a stay of a civil action or proceeding under subsection (b) may apply for an additional stay based on continuing material affect of military duty on the servicemember's ability to appear. Such an application may be made by the servicemember at the time of the initial application under subsection (b) or when it appears that the servicemember is unavailable to prosecute or defend the action. The same information required under subsection (b)(2) shall be included in an application under this subsection.

(2) APPOINTMENT OF COUNSEL WHEN ADDITIONAL STAY REFUSED—If the court refuses to grant an additional stay of proceedings under paragraph (1), the court shall appoint counsel to represent the servicemember in the action or proceeding.

(e) COORDINATION WITH SECTION 201—A servicemember who applies for a stay under this section and is unsuccessful may not seek the protections afforded by section 201.

(f) INAPPLICABILITY TO SECTION 301—The protections of this section do not apply to section 301.

SEC. 203. Fines and penalties under contracts.

(a) PROHIBITION OF PENALTIES—When an action for compliance with the terms of a contract is stayed pursuant to this Act, a penalty shall not accrue for failure to comply with the terms of the contract during the period of the stay.

(b) REDUCTION OR WAIVER OF FINES OR PENALTIES—If a servicemember fails to perform an obligation arising under a contract and a penalty is incurred arising from that nonperformance, a court may reduce or waive the fine or penalty if—

(1) the servicemember was in military service at the time the fine or penalty was incurred; and

(2) the ability of the servicemember to perform the obligation was materially affected by such military service.

SEC. 204. Stay of vacation of execution of judgments, attachments, and garnishments.

(a) COURT ACTION UPON MATERIAL AFFECT DETERMINATION—If a servicemember, in the opinion of the court, is materially affected by reason of military service in complying with a court judgment or order, the court may on its own motion and shall on application by the servicemember—

(1) stay the execution of any judgment or order entered against the servicemember; and

(2) vacate or stay an attachment or garnishment of property, money, or debts in the possession of the servicemember or a third party, whether before or after judgment.

(b) APPLICABILITY—This section applies to an action or proceeding commenced in a court against a servicemember before or during the period of the servicemember's military service or within 90 days after such service terminates.

SEC. 205. Duration and term of stays; codefendants not in service.

(a) PERIOD OF STAY—A stay of an action, proceeding, attachment, or execution made pursuant to the provisions of this Act by a court may be ordered for the period of military service and 90 days thereafter, or for any part of that period. The court may set the terms and amounts for such installment payments as is considered reasonable by the court.

(b) CODEFENDANTS—If the servicemember is a codefendant with others who are not in military service and who are not entitled to the relief and protections provided under this Act, the plaintiff may proceed against those other defendants with the approval of the court.

(c) INAPPLICABILITY OF SECTION—This section does not apply to sections 202 and 701.

SEC. 206. Statute of limitations.

(a) TOLLING OF STATUTES OF LIMITATION DURING MILITARY SERVICE—The period of a servicemember's military service may not be included in computing any period limited by law, regulation, or order for the bringing of any action or proceeding in a court, or in any board, bureau, commission, department, or other agency of a State (or political subdivision of a State) or the United States by or against the servicemember or the servicemember's heirs, executors, administrators, or assigns.

(b) REDEMPTION OF REAL PROPERTY—A period of military service may not be included in computing any period provided by law for the redemption of real property sold or forfeited to enforce an obligation, tax, or assessment.

(c) INAPPLICABILITY TO INTERNAL REVENUE LAWS—This section does not apply to any period of limitation prescribed by or under the internal revenue laws of the United States.

SEC. 207. Maximum rate of interest on debts incurred before military service.

(a) INTEREST RATE LIMITATION—

(1) LIMITATION TO 6 PERCENT—An obligation or liability bearing interest at a rate in excess of 6 percent per year that is incurred by a servicemember, or the servicemember and the servicemember's spouse jointly, before the servicemember enters military service shall not bear interest at a rate in excess of 6 percent per year during the period of military service.

(2) FORGIVENESS OF INTEREST IN EXCESS OF 6 PERCENT—Interest at a rate in excess of 6 percent per year that would otherwise be incurred but for the prohibition in paragraph (1) is forgiven.

(3) PREVENTION OF ACCELERATION OF PRINCIPAL—The amount of any periodic payment due from a servicemember under the terms of the instrument that created an obligation or liability covered by this section shall be reduced by the amount of the interest forgiven under paragraph (2) that is allocable to the period for which such payment is made.

(b) IMPLEMENTATION OF LIMITATION—

(1) WRITTEN NOTICE TO CREDITOR—In order for an obligation or liability of a servicemember to be subject to the interest rate limitation in subsection (a), the servicemember shall provide to the creditor written notice and a copy of the military orders calling the servicemember to military service and any orders further extending military service, not later than 180 days after the date of the servicemember's termination or release from military service.

(2) LIMITATION EFFECTIVE AS OF DATE OF ORDER TO ACTIVE DUTY—Upon receipt of written notice and a copy of orders calling a servicemember to military service, the creditor shall treat the debt in accordance with subsection (a), effective as of the date on which the servicemember is called to military service.

(c) CREDITOR PROTECTION—A court may grant a creditor relief from the limitations of this section if, in the opinion of the court, the ability of the servicemember to pay interest upon the obligation or liability at a rate in excess of 6 percent per year is not materially affected by reason of the servicemember's military service.

(d) INTEREST—As used in this section, the term `interest' includes service charges, renewal charges, fees, or any other charges (except bona fide insurance) with respect to an obligation or liability.

TITLE III—RENT, INSTALLMENT CONTRACTS, MORTGAGES, LIENS, ASSIGNMENT, LEASES

SEC. 301. Evictions and Distress.

(a) COURT-ORDERED EVICTION—

(1) IN GENERAL—Except by court order, a landlord (or another person with paramount title) may not—

(A) evict a servicemember, or the dependents of a servicemember, during a period of military service of the servicemember, from premises—

(i) that are occupied or intended to be occupied primarily as a residence; and

(ii) for which the monthly rent does not exceed $2,400, as adjusted under paragraph (2) for years after 2003; or

(B) subject such premises to a distress during the period of military service.

(2) HOUSING PRICE INFLATION ADJUSTMENT—

(A) For calendar years beginning with 2004, the amount in effect under paragraph (1)(A)(ii) shall be increased by the housing price inflation adjustment for the calendar year involved.

(B) For purposes of this paragraph—

(i) The housing price inflation adjustment for any calendar year is the percentage change (if any) by which—

(I) the CPI housing component for November of the preceding calendar year, exceeds

(II) the CPI housing component for November of 1984.

(ii) The term `CPI housing component' means the index published by the Bureau of Labor Statistics of the Department of Labor known as the Consumer Price Index, All Urban Consumers, Rent of Primary Residence, U.S. City Average.

(3) PUBLICATION OF HOUSING PRICE INFLATION ADJUSTMENT—The Secretary of Defense shall cause to be published in the Federal Register each year the amount in effect under paragraph (1)(A)(ii) for that year following the housing price inflation adjustment for that year pursuant to paragraph (2). Such publication shall be made for a year not later than 60 days after such adjustment is made for that year.

(b) STAY OF EXECUTION—

(1) COURT AUTHORITY—Upon an application for eviction or distress with respect to premises covered by this section, the court may on its own motion and shall, if a request is made by or on behalf of a servicemember whose ability to pay the agreed rent is materially affected by military service—

(A) stay the proceedings for a period of 90 days, unless in the opinion of the court, justice and equity require a longer or shorter period of time; or

(B) adjust the obligation under the lease to preserve the interests of all parties.

(2) RELIEF TO LANDLORD—If a stay is granted under paragraph (1), the court may grant to the landlord (or other person with paramount title) such relief as equity may require.

(c) PENALTIES—

(1) MISDEMEANOR—Except as provided in subsection (a), a person who knowingly takes part in an eviction or distress described in subsection (a), or who knowingly attempts to do so, shall be fined as provided in title 18, United States Code, or imprisoned for not more than one year, or both.

(2) PRESERVATION OF OTHER REMEDIES AND RIGHTS—The remedies and rights provided under this section are in addition to and do not preclude any remedy for wrongful conversion (or wrongful eviction) otherwise available under the law to the person claiming relief under this section, including any award for consequential and punitive damages.

(d) RENT ALLOTMENT FROM PAY OF SERVICEMEMBER—To the extent required by a court order related to property which is the subject of a court action under this section, the Secretary concerned shall make an allotment from the pay of a servicemember to satisfy the terms of such order, except that any such allotment shall be subject to regulations prescribed by the Secretary concerned establishing the maximum amount of pay of servicemembers that may be allotted under this subsection.

(e) LIMITATION OF APPLICABILITY—Section 202 is not applicable to this section.

SEC. 302. Protection under installment contracts for purchase or lease.

a) PROTECTION UPON BREACH OF CONTRACT—

(1) PROTECTION AFTER ENTERING MILITARY SERVICE—After a servicemember enters military service, a contract by the service-member for—

(A) the purchase of real or personal property (including a motor vehicle); or

(B) the lease or bailment of such property, may not be rescinded or terminated for a breach of terms of the contract occurring before or during that person's military service, nor may the property be repossessed for such breach without a court order.

(2) APPLICABILITY—This section applies only to a contract for which a deposit or installment has been paid by the servicemember before the servicemember enters military service.

(b) PENALTIES—

(1) MISDEMEANOR—A person who knowingly resumes possession of property in violation of subsection (a), or in violation of section 107 of this Act, or who knowingly attempts to do so, shall be fined as provided in title 18, United States Code, or imprisoned for not more than one year, or both.

(2) PRESERVATION OF OTHER REMEDIES AND RIGHTS—The remedies and rights provided under this section are in addition to and do not preclude any remedy for wrongful conversion otherwise available under law to the person claiming relief under this section, including any award for consequential and punitive damages.

(c) AUTHORITY OF COURT—In a hearing based on this section, the court—

(1) may order repayment to the servicemember of all or part of the prior installments or deposits as a condition of terminating the contract and resuming possession of the property;

(2) may, on its own motion, and shall on application by a servicemember when the servicemember's ability to comply with the contract is materially affected by military service, stay the proceedings for a period of time as, in the opinion of the court, justice and equity require; or

(3) may make other disposition as is equitable to preserve the interests of all parties.

SEC. 303. Mortgages and trust deeds.

(a) MORTGAGE AS SECURITY—This section applies only to an obligation on real or personal property owned by a servicemember that—

(1) originated before the period of the servicemember's military service and for which the servicemember is still obligated; and

(2) is secured by a mortgage, trust deed, or other security in the nature of a mortgage.

(b) STAY OF PROCEEDINGS AND ADJUSTMENT OF OBLIGATION—In an action filed during, or within 90 days after, a servicemember's period of military service to enforce an obligation described in subsection (a), the court may after a hearing and on its own motion and shall upon application by a servicemember when the servicemember's ability to comply with the obligation is materially affected by military service—

(1) stay the proceedings for a period of time as justice and equity require, or

(2) adjust the obligation to preserve the interests of all parties.

(c) SALE OR FORECLOSURE—A sale, foreclosure, or seizure of property for a breach of an obligation described in subsection (a) shall not be valid if made during, or within 90 days after, the period of the servicemember's military service except—

(1) upon a court order granted before such sale, foreclosure, or seizure with a return made and approved by the court; or

(2) if made pursuant to an agreement as provided in section 107.

(d) PENALTIES—

(1) MISDEMEANOR—A person who knowingly makes or causes to be made a sale, foreclosure, or seizure of property that is prohibited

by subsection (c), or who knowingly attempts to do so, shall be fined as provided in title 18, United States Code, or imprisoned for not more than one year, or both.

(2) PRESERVATION OF OTHER REMEDIES—The remedies and rights provided under this section are in addition to and do not preclude any remedy for wrongful conversion otherwise available under law to the person claiming relief under this section, including consequential and punitive damages.

SEC. 304. Settlement of staycases relating to personal property.

(a) APPRAISAL OF PROPERTY—When a stay is granted pursuant to this Act in a proceeding to foreclose a mortgage on or to repossess personal property, or to rescind or terminate a contract for the purchase of personal property, the court may appoint three disinterested parties to appraise the property.

(b) EQUITY PAYMENT—Based on the appraisal, and if undue hardship to the servicemember's dependents will not result, the court may order that the amount of the servicemember's equity in the property be paid to the servicemember, or the servicemember's dependents, as a condition of foreclosing the mortgage, repossessing the property, or rescinding or terminating the contract.

SEC. 305. Termination of residential or motor vehicle leases.

(a) TERMINATION BY LESSEE—The lessee on a lease described in subsection (b) may, at the lessee's option, terminate the lease at any time after—

(1) the lessee's entry into military service; or

(2) the date of the lessee's military orders described in paragraph (1)(B) or (2)(B) of subsection (b), as the case may be.

(b) COVERED LEASES—This section applies to the following leases:

(1) LEASES OF PREMISES—A lease of premises occupied, or intended to be occupied, by a servicemember or a servicemember's dependents for a residential, professional, business, agricultural, or similar purpose if—

(A) the lease is executed by or on behalf of a person who thereafter and during the term of the lease enters military service; or

(B) the servicemember, while in military service, executes the lease and thereafter receives military orders for a permanent change of station or to deploy with a military unit for a period of not less than 90 days.

(2) LEASES OF MOTOR VEHICLES—A lease of a motor vehicle used, or intended to be used, by a servicemember or a servicemember's dependents for personal or business transportation if—

(A) the lease is executed by or on behalf of a person who thereafter and during the term of the lease enters military service under a call or order specifying a period of not less than 180 days (or who enters military service under a call or order specifying a period of 180 days or less and who, without a break in service, receives orders extending the period of military service to a period of not less than 180 days); or

(B) the servicemember, while in military service, executes the lease and thereafter receives military orders for a permanent change of station outside of the continental United States or to deploy with a military unit for a period of not less than 180 days.

(c) MANNER OF TERMINATION—

(1) IN GENERAL—Termination of a lease under subsection (a) is made—

(A) by delivery by the lessee of written notice of such termination, and a copy of the servicemember's military orders, to the lessor (or the lessor's grantee), or to the lessor's agent (or the agent's grantee); and

(B) in the case of a lease of a motor vehicle, by return of the motor vehicle by the lessee to the lessor (or the lessor's grantee), or to the lessor's agent (or the agent's grantee), not later than 15 days after the date of the delivery of written notice under subparagraph (A).

(2) DELIVERY OF NOTICE—Delivery of notice under paragraph (1)(A) may be accomplished—

(A) by hand delivery;

(B) by private business carrier; or

(C) by placing the written notice in an envelope with sufficient postage and with return receipt requested, and addressed as designated by the lessor (or the lessor's grantee) or to the lessor's agent (or the agent's grantee), and depositing the written notice in the United States mails.

(d) EFFECTIVE DATE OF LEASE TERMINATION—

(1) LEASE OF PREMISES—In the case of a lease described in subsection (b)(1) that provides for monthly payment of rent, termination of the lease under subsection (a) is effective 30 days after the first date on which the next rental payment is due and payable after the date

on which the notice under subsection (c) is delivered. In the case of any other lease described in subsection (b)(1), termination of the lease under subsection (a) is effective on the last day of the month following the month in which the notice is delivered.

(2) LEASE OF MOTOR VEHICLES—In the case of a lease described in subsection (b)(2), termination of the lease under subsection (a) is effective on the day on which the requirements of subsection (c) are met for such termination.

(e) ARREARAGES AND OTHER OBLIGATIONS AND LIABILITIES—Rents or lease amounts unpaid for the period preceding the effective date of the lease termination shall be paid on a prorated basis. In the case of the lease of a motor vehicle, the lessor may not impose an early termination charge, but any taxes, summonses, and title and registration fees and any other obligation and liability of the lessee in accordance with the terms of the lease, including reasonable charges to the lessee for excess wear, use and mileage, that are due and unpaid at the time of termination of the lease shall be paid by the lessee.

(f) RENT PAID IN ADVANCE—Rents or lease amounts paid in advance for a period after the effective date of the termination of the lease shall be refunded to the lessee by the lessor (or the lessor's assignee or the assignee's agent) within 30 days of the effective date of the termination of the lease.

(g) RELIEF TO LESSOR—Upon application by the lessor to a court before the termination date provided in the written notice, relief granted by this section to a servicemember may be modified as justice and equity require.

(h) PENALTIES—

(1) MISDEMEANOR—Any person who knowingly seizes, holds, or detains the personal effects, security deposit, or other property of a servicemember or a servicemember's dependent who lawfully terminates a lease covered by this section, or who knowingly interferes with the removal of such property from premises covered by such lease, for the purpose of subjecting or attempting to subject any of such property to a claim for rent accruing subsequent to the date of termination of such lease, or attempts to do so, shall be fined as provided in title 18, United States Code, or imprisoned for not more than one year, or both.

(2) PRESERVATION OF OTHER REMEDIES—The remedy and rights provided under this section are in addition to and do not preclude any remedy for wrongful conversion otherwise available under law

to the person claiming relief under this section, including any award for consequential or punitive damages.

SEC. 306. Protection of life insurance policy.

(a) ASSIGNMENT OF POLICY PROTECTED—If a life insurance policy on the life of a servicemember is assigned before military service to secure the payment of an obligation, the assignee of the policy (except the insurer in connection with a policy loan) may not exercise, during a period of military service of the servicemember or within one year thereafter, any right or option obtained under the assignment without a court order.

(b) EXCEPTION—The prohibition in subsection (a) shall not apply—

(1) if the assignee has the written consent of the insured made during the period described in subsection (a);

(2) when the premiums on the policy are due and unpaid; or

(3) upon the death of the insured.

(c) ORDER REFUSED BECAUSE OF MATERIAL AFFECT—A court which receives an application for an order required under subsection (a) may refuse to grant such order if the court determines the ability of the servicemember to comply with the terms of the obligation is materially affected by military service.

(d) TREATMENT OF GUARANTEED PREMIUMS—For purposes of this subsection, premiums guaranteed under the provisions of title IV of this Act shall not be considered due and unpaid.

(e) PENALTIES—

(1) MISDEMEANOR—A person who knowingly takes an action contrary to this section, or attempts to do so, shall be fined as provided in title 18, United States Code, or imprisoned for not more than one year, or both.

(2) PRESERVATION OF OTHER REMEDIES—The remedy and rights provided under this section are in addition to and do not preclude any remedy for wrongful conversion otherwise available under law to the person claiming relief under this section, including any consequential or punitive damages.

SEC. 307. Enforcement of storage liens.

(a) LIENS—

(1) LIMITATION ON FORECLOSURE OR ENFORCEMENT—A person holding a lien on the property or effects of a servicemember may not,

during any period of military service of the servicemember and for 90 days thereafter, foreclose or enforce any lien on such property or effects without a court order granted before foreclosure or enforcement.

(2) LIEN DEFINED—For the purposes of paragraph (1), the term `lien' includes a lien for storage, repair, or cleaning of the property or effects of a servicemember or a lien on such property or effects for any other reason.

(b) STAY OF PROCEEDINGS—In a proceeding to foreclose or enforce a lien subject to this section, the court may on its own motion, and shall if requested by a servicemember whose ability to comply with the obligation resulting in the proceeding is materially affected by military service—

(1) stay the proceeding for a period of time as justice and equity require; or

(2) adjust the obligation to preserve the interests of all parties.

The provisions of this subsection do not affect the scope of section 303.

(c) PENALTIES—

(1) MISDEMEANOR—A person who knowingly takes an action contrary to this section, or attempts to do so, shall be fined as provided in title 18, United States Code, in or imprisoned for not more than one year, or both.

(2) PRESERVATION OF OTHER REMEDIES—The remedy and rights provided under this section are in addition to and do not preclude any remedy for wrongful conversion otherwise available under law to the person claiming relief under this section, including any consequential or punitive damages.

SEC. 308. Extension of protections to dependents.

Upon application to a court, a dependent of a servicemember is entitled to the protections of this title if the dependent's ability to comply with a lease, contract, bailment, or other obligation is materially affected by reason of the servicemember's military service.

GLOSSARY

Access—The veteran's ability to obtain medical care at his or her desired location.

Active Duty—Full-time duty in the active military service of the United States.

Adjunct Condition—For medical treatment purposes, refers to a non service-connected condition that may be associated with and held to be aggravating an adjudicated service-connected condition.

Administrative Appeal—An appeal taken by an official of the Veterans Administration, authorized to resolve conflict of opinion or questions pertaining to a claim involving benefits under laws administered by the Veterans Administration.

Adult Day Health Care—A therapeutic day care program, provides medical and rehabilitation services to disabled veterans in a congregate setting.

Advance on the Docket—A change in the order in which an appeal is reviewed and decided from the date when it would normally occur to an earlier date.

Agency of Original Jurisdiction (AOJ)—The office where a claim originates.

Aid and Attendance (A&A)—A VA compensation or pension benefit awarded to a veteran determined to be in need of the regular aid and attendance of another person to perform basic functions of everyday life.

Allowable Deductions—Payments made by veterans for certain non-reimbursed medical expenses, funeral and burial expenses and educational expenses.

Annualization—Twelve-month projection of income from the date of entitlement to pension, or from the effective date of change in income.

Appeal—A process used to request that the VA reconsider a previous authorization or claim decision.

Appellant—An individual who has appealed an AOJ claim determination.

Applicant—A person who has submitted a formal request for VA health care benefits and/or for enrollment in the VA health care system.

Armed Forces—U.S. Army, Navy, Marine Corps, Air Force, and Coast Guard.

Asset—Property or resources of an individual including cash, stocks and bonds, individual retirement accounts, income producing property, etc.

ASVET—Assistant Secretary for Veterans' Employment and Training.

Bereavement Counseling—Assistance and support provided to people with emotional and psychological stress after the death of a loved one.

Board—The Board of Veterans' Appeals.

Board of Veterans' Appeals (BVA)—The office of the Veterans Administration that reviews benefit claims appeals and issues decisions on those appeals.

Board Member—A law judge appointed by the Secretary of Veterans Affairs and approved by the president, who decides veterans' benefits appeals.

Burial Allowance—A lump sum benefit paid to the party or parties who assume responsibility for the burial expense of the veteran.

Catastrophically Disabled—A veteran who has a permanent, severely disabling injury, disorder, or disease that compromises the ability to carry out the activities of daily living to such a degree that he or she requires personal or mechanical assistance to leave home or bed, or requires constant supervision to avoid physical harm to self or others.

Chronic Care—Long-term care of individuals with long-standing, persistent diseases or conditions. Chronic care includes care specific to the problem, as well as other measures to encourage self-care, promote health, and prevent loss of function.

Claim—A request for veterans' benefits.

Claimant—The veteran who files a claim for veterans' benefits.

Claim Number—A number assigned by the Veterans Administration that identifies a person who has filed a claim.

Claims File—The file containing all documents concerning a veteran's claim or appeal.

Combat Service—A status applied to a veteran who served on active duty in a theater of combat operations during a period of war recognized by the VA.

Community Residential Care—Health care supervision to eligible veterans not in need of hospital or nursing home care but who, because of medical and/or psychosocial health conditions as determined through a statement of needed care, are not able to live independently and have no suitable family or significant others to provide the needed supervision and supportive care.

Compensable Disabilities—A VA rated service-connected disability for which monetary compensation is authorized for payment.

Compensation—Monthly payments made by the Veterans Administration to a veteran because of a service-connected disability.

Congressional Appropriation—The funding allocated by Congress to the VA for providing benefits and medical services to eligible VA beneficiaries.

Consultation—Service provided by a physician whose opinion or advice regarding evaluation and/or management of a specific problem is requested by another physician.

Contract Provider—Any hospital, skilled nursing facility, extended care facility, individual, organization, or agency that has a contractual agreement with the VA for providing medical services to veterans.

Co-pay—A specific monetary charge for either medical services or outpatient medications provided by the VA to veterans whose financial assessment determines they are able to pay.

Court Appeals for Veterans Claims—An independent United States Administrative Court that reviews appeals of BVA decisions.

Covered Benefit—Medically necessary care and services included in the Medical Benefits Package.

Date of Receipt—The date on which a claim was received in the Department of Veterans Affairs.

Death Compensation—Benefits paid to the spouse or dependent children of a deceased veteran based on a period of wartime service by the veteran. Income limitations and net worth are factors in this benefit.

Decision—The final ruling by BVA after considering the appeal.

Department of Veterans Affairs Health Care Programs Enhancement Act of 2001 (Public Law 107-135)—Act that provides for chiropractic care and services for veterans through Department of Veterans Affairs medical centers and clinics.

Dependency and Indemnity Compensation—Benefits paid to a spouse, dependent children, or dependent parents of a veteran who dies of a service-connected disability or who is rated totally disabled because of a service-connected condition for a period of ten years or more.

Diagnosis—The identity of a medical condition, cause or disease.

Deductible—An amount that a veteran must pay for covered services in a specified time period before VA benefits begin.

Dependent—Spouse or unmarried child who: (1) is under the age of 18, or (2) is between the ages of 18 and 23 and attending school; (3) was permanently and totally disabled before the age of 18).

Disabled Veteran—A veteran who is entitled to compensation under laws administered by the Veterans Administration; or an individual who was discharged or released from active duty because of service-connected disability.

Discharge—Separation including retirement from the active military, naval, or air service.

Disenrollment—The discontinuation of a veteran's enrolled status.

Docket—A listing of appeals that have been filed with the BVA.

Docket Number—The number assigned to an appeal.

Domiciliary—A VA facility that provides care on an ambulatory self-care basis for veterans disabled by age or disease who are not in need of acute hospitalization and who do not need the skilled nursing services provided in a nursing home.

Durable Medical Equipment—Equipment intended for frequent use in the treatment of a medical condition or injury, such as a wheelchair, hospital bed, etc.

DVET—Director for Veterans' Employment and Training.

DVOP—Disabled Veterans' Outreach Program specialist.

Effective Date—The date as of which the Veterans Administration calculates its decision to grant, increase, reduce, suspend, or terminate benefits.

Employment Development Plan (EDP)—An individualized written plan or intervention strategy for serving an individual which, as a result of an assessment of the veteran's economic needs, vocational interests, aptitudes, work history, etc., defines a reasonable vocational or employment goal and the developmental services or steps required to reach the goal and which documents the accomplishments made by the individual.

Enrollee—A veteran who has applied for VA medical services, has been accepted for such care, and who has received confirmation of enrollment in the VA health care system.

Enrollment—The process for providing veterans access to VA health care benefits covered by the medical benefits package.

Enrollment Group Threshold (EGT)—The enrollment priority group level, as determined by the Secretary Veterans Affairs, at which veterans will be accepted for enrollment into the VA health care system.

ETA—The Employment and Training Administration.

Evidence—Any probative material introduced to support the veteran's claim for benefits.

Fair Preponderance—Evidence that must be sufficient to prove that the evidence against the veteran's claim outweighs that evidence offered in support of the claim.

Financial Assessment—A means of collecting income and asset information used to determine a veteran's eligibility for health care benefits.

Formulary—A list of medicines approved by a group of highly trained VA physicians and clinical pharmacists from which a VA provider can choose to treat a veteran's medical condition.

FY—Fiscal Year. For federal government purposes, any twelve-month period beginning on October 1 and ending on September 30.

Geriatric Evaluation—The comprehensive assessment of a veteran's ability to care for his or her physical health and social environment, which leads to a plan of care.

Gross Household Income—Generally, refers to the gross income of the veteran, spouse and dependent children that is counted for determining a veteran's eligibility for VA health care benefits, including earned and unearned income and excluding most need-based payments such as welfare, Supplemental Security Income (SSI).

Gross Income—Income before allowable expenses are subtracted.

Health Insurance Portability and Accountability Act (HIPAA)—A federal law enacted in 1996, designated to improve availability and portability of health coverage and the efficiency of the health care system by standardizing the electronic exchange of health information and protecting the security and privacy of member-identifiable health information.

Hearing—A meeting, similar to an interview, between an appellant and an official from The Veterans Administration who will decide an appellant's case, during which testimony and other evidence supporting the case is presented.

Home Health Care—Skilled nursing and other therapeutic services provided by the VA or a home health care agency in a home setting as an alternative to confinement in a hospital or skilled nursing facility.

The Homemaker/Home Health Aide (H/HHA) Program—Program that provides services as an alternative to nursing home care.

Hospice/Palliative Care Program—Program that offers pain management, symptom control, and other medical services to terminally ill veterans or veterans in the late stages of the chronic disease process.

Hostilities—Any armed conflict in which the members of the Armed Forces are subjected to combat conditions comparable to a period of war.

Housebound Benefit—An additional amount available to an eligible veteran who, because of his or her physical limitations, is unable to walk or travel beyond his or her home and it is reasonably certain the disabilities or confinement will continue throughout the veteran's lifetime.

Individual Unemployability—Total disability evaluation assigned to an individual because of any service-connected impairment of mind or body that fails to meet the criteria for a total disability rating under the Schedule for Rating Disabilities but that nonetheless renders it impossible for that person to follow substantial gainful employment.

Inpatient Care—Services received during a patient's hospital stay.

Insurance—Life insurance benefits paid to the beneficiary designated on the policies at the time of a veteran's death.

In the Line of Duty—An injury or disease incurred or aggravated during a period of active military, naval, or air service.

Ionizing Radiation—Atomic veterans may have been exposed to ionizing radiation in a variety of ways at various locations and are thus eligible to receive treatment for conditions related to this exposure.

Labor Force—The sum of all civilians classified as employed and unemployed and members of the Armed Forces stationed in the United States.

LVER—Local Veterans' Employment Representative.

Marriage—A marriage valid under the law of the place where the parties resided at the time of marriage, or the law of the place where the parties resided when the right to benefits accrued.

Maximum Annual Pension Rate—Maximum amount of pension payable to a veteran, reduced by the amount of the veteran's annual income.

Means Test—The formal financial assessment process used by the VA to: (1) measure a veteran's gross household income and assets; (2) determine the veteran's co-pay responsibilities; and (3) determine the veteran's enrollment priority.

Means Test Co-pay Exempt—Veterans not required to make co-pays for medical care provided by the VA.

Means Test Co-pay Required—A co-pay status assigned to a veteran who is required to make medical care co-pays based on their financial status relative to the applicable means test income threshold.

Medicaid—A jointly funded federal and state program that provides hospital expense and medical expense coverage to persons with low-income and certain aged and disabled individuals.

Medical Benefits Package—A group of health care services that are provided to all enrolled veterans.

Medical Need—The determination that care or services are required to promote, preserve, or restore a veteran's health.

Medicare—A federal program that provides health care coverage for people aged 65 and older, as well as some younger individuals with specific health problems.

Medicare Part A—Medicare coverage for hospitalization, extended care and nursing home care.

Medicare Part B—Medicare coverage for outpatient services, subject to a monthly premium.

Minority Veterans—Veterans who are members of the following ethnic categories: African American, Hispanic, American Indian or Alaskan Native, Asian or Pacific Islander.

Net Worth—The market value of everything an individual owns, minus what he or she owes.

Noncompensable—Awards of service-connection that the VA determines do not warrant the award of monetary compensation.

Non-Service-Connected Disability or Death—A disability that was not incurred or aggravated, or a death that did not result from a disability incurred or aggravated, in the line of duty while the veteran was in the active military, naval, or air service.

Nonservice-Connected Pension—A monetary support benefit awarded to permanently and totally disabled, low-income veterans with 90 days or more of active military service, of which at least one day was during wartime.

Nonservice-Connected Veteran—An eligible veteran who has been discharged from active military duty, and does not have a VA adjudicated illness or injury incurred in or aggravated by military service.

Nursing Home Care—The accommodation of convalescents or other persons who are not acutely ill and not in need of hospital care, but who require nursing care and related medical services, if such nursing care and medical services are prescribed by, or are performed under the general direction of, persons duly licensed to provide such care.

OASVET—Office of the Assistant Secretary for Veterans' Employment and Training.

Open Enrollment—The process of accepting applications for enrollment at any time during the year.

Outpatient Care—Health care a patient receives without being admitted to a hospital. Examples include office visits, x-rays, lab tests and some surgical procedures.

Palliative Care—Care provided primarily to relieve symptoms of a disease or condition rather than for curative purposes.

Pension—Monthly payments to a veteran who meets certain minimum wartime service requirements, who became permanently and totally disabled from disability or disabilities not related to military service, and who meets certain income and net worth limits.

Pension Benefit—A monetary award paid on a monthly basis to eligible veterans with low income who are permanently and totally disabled, or are age 65 and older.

Permanent and Total Disability—For pension purposes, all veterans who are basically unable to secure and follow a substantially gainful occupation by reason of disabilities which are likely to be permanent.

Preferred Facility—The veteran identified VA health care location where the veteran prefers to receive care.

Presumptive Service Connection—The presumption that certain enumerated diseases have been incurred in service, even though there is no evidence of such disease during the period of service.

Preventive Care—Health Care that emphasizes prevention, early detection, and treatment.

Primary Care Provider—The clinician who is responsible for the supervision, coordination, and provision of the veteran's medical care.

Probative Evidence—Evidence that has a tendency to prove or actually prove an alleged entitlement.

Prosthetic Devices—A device, which replaces all, or a portion of a part of the human body. A prosthetic device can be used when a part of the body is permanently damaged, is absent, or is malfunctioning.

Proximate Cause—An event that caused an injury or disease and without such injury or exposure the disability would not have occurred.

Purple Heart—A medal given by the military to a service member injured as a direct result of combat.

Radiation Risk Activity—On site participation in a test involving the atmospheric detonation of a nuclear device, including: (1) Participation in the occupation of Hiroshima or Nagasaki from August 6, 1945 through July 1, 1946; (2) Internment as a Prisoner of War in Japan (or service or active duty in Japan immediately following such internment; (3) Service at Department of Energy plants at Paducah, KY, Portsmouth, OH, or the K25 area at Oak Ridge, TN for at least 250 days before February 1, 1992; and (4) Service at Longshot, Milrow, or Cannikin underground nuclear tests at Amchitka Island, AK prior to January 1, 1974.

Recently Separated Veteran—Refers to any veteran who applies for participation in a funded activity within 48 months after separation from military service.

Referral—The process of referring a veteran from one practitioner to another for health care services.

Representative—Someone familiar with the benefit claim process that assists claimants in the preparation and presentation of an appeal.

Respite Care—Respite care gives the caregiver of a veteran a planned period of relief from the physical and emotional demands associated with providing care.

Restore Health—The process of improving a veteran's quality of life or daily function level that has been lost due to illness or injury.

Schedule for Rating Disabilities—A list of criteria for evaluation of all types of diseases and injuries encountered as a result of or incident to military service.

Secondary Condition—A secondary condition, for medical treatment purposes, may be the result of an adjudicated service-connected condition.

Secondary Service Connection—A disability that is proximately due to or the result of a service-connected disease or injury such that it is considered part of the original condition and thus also warrants service connection.

Service-Connected Disability—Generally a service-connected disability is a disability that the VA determines was incurred or aggravated while on active duty in the military and in the service member's line of duty.

Service-Connected Rating—An official ruling by the VA that the veteran's illness or medical condition is directly related to his or her active military service. Service-connected ratings are established by VA Regional Offices located throughout the country.

Service-Connected Veteran—A veteran who has an illness or injury incurred in or aggravated by military service as determined by the VA.

Simultaneously Contested Claim—A claim where more than one person is trying to obtain a Veterans Administration benefit or status that only one of them is entitled to receive.

Temporary Disability Retirement List—Status of military personnel that are determined to suffer from a physical or psychological disability, not yet determined to be permanent in nature, but that nonetheless disqualifies them from active military duty.

United States Court of Veterans Appeals—An independent court that reviews appeals of BVA decisions.

Urgent Care—Services received for an unexpected illness or injury that is not life threatening but requires immediate outpatient medical care that cannot be postponed. An urgent situation requires prompt medical attention to avoid complications and unnecessary suffering or severe pain, such as a high fever.

USDOL—United States Department of Labor.

USDVA—United States Department of Veterans Affairs, formerly known as the Veterans Administration.

VA—U.S. Department of Veterans Affairs.

Veteran—A person who served in the active military, naval, or air service and who was discharged or released from his or her service under conditions other than dishonorable.

Veterans Health Care Eligibility Reform Act of 1996 (Public Law 104-262)—Act that established national standards of access and equitable health care services to veterans and required that most veterans be enrolled to receive care.

Veteran Service Organization (VSO)—An organization that represents the interests of veterans.

Vocational Rehabilitation—Services and assistance provided to eligible veterans with compensable service-connected disabilities to enable them to achieve maximum independence in daily living and to obtain suitable employment to the greatest extent possible.

War Time Service—Designated periods of time during which a veteran's service in the armed forces will have been considered as serving during a wartime period.